RETHINKING
TEACHING
IN HIGHER
EDUCATION

From a Course Design Workshop
to a Faculty Development Framework

Edited by
Alenoush Saroyan
Cheryl Amundsen

STERLING, VIRGINIA

Published in 2004 by

Stylus Publishing, LLC
22883 Quicksilver Drive
Sterling, Virginia 20166

**Library of Congress
Cataloging-in-Publication Data**
Rethinking teaching in higher education:
from a course design workshop to a
faculty development framework/edited by
Alenoush Saroyan and Cheryl
Amundsen—1st ed.
p. cm.
Includes bibliographical references and index.
ISBN 1-57922-046-0 (alk. paper)—
ISBN 1-57922-047-9 (pbk.:alk. paper)
1. College teachers—In service training.
2. College teaching. 3. Brain. I. Saroyan,
Alenoush, 1949– II. Amundsen, Cheryl.
LB1738.R46 2004
378.1'2—dc22   2003019717.

First edition, 2004
ISBN: hardcover 1-57922-046-0
ISBN: paperback 1-57922-047-9

Printed in the United States of America
All first editions printed on acid free paper

CONTENTS

TABLES

FIGURES

We have written this book for faculty and staff developers, as well as for deans, chairs, and directors charged with the responsibility to assume an active role in promoting university teaching and learning. The language used is intentionally simple and nontechnical so all readers will be able to understand and appreciate both the process and the preparation required to engage in reflective teaching practice.

Writing this book has given us the opportunity to work together to examine our individual and shared perspectives about the development of teaching and learning in higher education. We greeted this occasion as an opportune time to engage in formal discussions about the theories and assumptions that underlie our individual thinking and practice. The reader might be interested to know that in all the years we worked together, we had never had these in-depth conversations. Like many others, we were always more preoccupied with "doing" things than with "thinking" together. This book has provided us the chance to reflect on and write about our own practice of faculty development.

It was clear from the very beginning that the primary vehicle for analyzing and describing our thinking and philosophy about teaching development would be the Course Design and Teaching Workshop, which we have offered together for more than ten years. This Workshop, more than any other activity we do, has prompted us to examine the process by which professors change and develop their thinking about teaching and learning, and subsequently link their thinking to practice.

We decided to write the book's first two chapters (Part I) together—all seven of us! Needless to say, this was a novel experience for us. Nevertheless, we viewed the exercise as critical to providing us, as well as our readers, with a thorough grounding in our joint thinking. We also felt the exercise was necessary before we could go on to write subsequent chapters. Hence came the need for lengthy and enthusiastic discussions, various iterations of drafts, innumerable edits, rewrites, and revisions. The process was time-consuming and sometimes frustrating for its seeming lack of tangible progress. More than a year of discussions ensued before we arrived at a point of convergence where we could write with a single voice. Our task was further complicated by the geographic distance of one editor who had been involved in conceptualizing the Course Design and Teaching Workshop. Here, we turned to existing new technologies, not always with success, to conduct virtual meetings. We now can say, in retrospect, that our perseverance paid off in both the writing of the rest of the book and in the continued cohesion of our team.

The five chapters of Part II present and discuss in detail the Course Design and Teaching Workshop in the five-day format. (The five-day format is how the Workshop has most often been conducted; other formats have been experimented with and tried in recent years.) Each of the chapters is devoted to one of the five days. These chapters may give the impression that the Workshop is a finely tuned and well orchestrated event. Yet every time the Workshop is offered, we introduce new elements, relying on our past experiences and feedback from participants to make changes. We hope the reader will experience differences in the tone and writing of each chapter as a reflection of the flexibility and spontaneity that characterizes the Workshop. Year after year, each group of participants creates a unique dynamic that pushes us to try ideas and approaches outside any seemingly well-articulated and rigid routine. We encourage the reader to view the Workshop format and activities described in the book as not prescriptive and not in need of being adopted in their entirety. We know that every context may be different and may require a different approach.

In Part III, the reader will have the opportunity to hear the voices of four past participants in the Course Design and Teaching Workshop, three of whom have also been co-instructors in the Workshop. These individuals have taken even larger steps toward advancing teaching and learning in their respective faculties; each is also an Affiliate Member of the Centre for University Teaching and Learning (CUTL) and frequently called on for assistance in advancing our mission. The task in the chapters by these four individuals was to talk about ways in which participation in the Workshop has influenced the individual's thinking and actions concerning teaching and learning. The different ways in which these individuals have interpreted this task speak to the relevance of the Workshop to individuals from different disciplines with divergent views of teaching and learning.

In Part IV, we move beyond the Course Design and Teaching Workshop to describe the broader context of faculty development as we see it. We do this both conceptually and by anchoring discussions in two CUTL collaboration case examples with two of our faculties[1]: one with the Faculty of Engineering;

---

[1]In the Canadian context, the term *Faculty,* with a capital *F* is used instead of college or school.

one with the Faculty of Management. These final two chapters, in particular, underscore the notion of this book, in general, that faculty development is about more than only improving teaching. We subscribe to what we characterize as a "distributed" model of faculty development, in the sense that we work toward both the concept and the task of faculty development being understood and practiced by many individuals across the university. We very much wish this book to further discussions about faculty development in higher education in as broad a context as possible.

—*The Editors*

ACKNOWLEDGMENTS

This book is the result of our collective experience working with Faculty to improve teaching and learning at our university. We wish to express our particular gratitude to all the professors who have participated in our annual teaching and course design workshop since its inception over thirteen years ago. The enthusiasm and dedication they devote to their own learning process during the workshop has always been contagious. It has challenged us year after year to make this experience worth their while as we make it a learning experience for ourselves. We are thrilled every time we learn how individuals have applied what they have taken from this workshop to other courses and to teaching and learning-related activities in their departments and Faculties, and in the University. In this book, we have been able to include the perspectives of only four such individuals. There are many more.

Our annual workshop would not be what it is without generous contributions from past participants who come back as co-instructors to help us plan and deliver the workshop to a new group of colleagues. Many of these individuals have taken the next step by taking charge of teaching and learning innovations in their respective units. Through their continued affiliation with our Centre for University Teaching and Learning and related faculty development activities, they have been the main force to help us forge stronger links across the University.

Our word of deep appreciation also goes to all our graduate students who have contributed to the success of our workshop. Through responsible and thoughtful actions, they have made their presence an asset and a resource that we greatly depend on for the successful implementation of the workshop. With their active participation and feedback, we have been able to provide our graduate students with valuable practical experience in faculty development. We are grateful also for the continued support of the Social Sciences and Humanities Research Council of Canada for funding our research into teaching and learning in higher education.

Finally, we are thankful to the Royal Bank of Canada which provided a ten-year grant to CUTL eleven years ago toward the improvement of teaching and learning. This grant has supported many of our teaching development activities in the past decade, including the course design and teaching workshop. Without it, we may not have been able to continue our activities with such intensity and effectiveness.

PART I
INTRODUCTION TO THE WORKSHOP

The two chapters of Part I serve as an overview of the Course Design and Teaching Workshop. Chapter 1 addresses the questions "Why?" and "What?"; it includes the thinking that went into the Workshop's original conceptualization and has gone on in its evolution over the past decade. In Chapter 2, we present the results of analysis of our individual and collective assumptions about faculty development in general, and the Workshop in particular, followed by a description of the working model of teaching development inspired and validated by our research and practice.

I

THE COURSE DESIGN AND TEACHING WORKSHOP

WHY AND WHAT?

Alenoush Saroyan, Cheryl Amundsen, Cynthia Weston,
Lynn McAlpine, Laura Winer, Susan Cowan, and Terry Gandell[1]

The five-day format Course Design and Teaching Workshop has been offered to professors for the past ten years. The intensive Workshop provides professors with an opportunity to discuss and reflect on their teaching and initiate changes to enhance the quality of student learning. Year after year, we are delighted to see what a profound impact the Workshop has on participants.

Here, we explain why we developed the Workshop, including the thinking behind its original conceptualization and evolution over the years. We also discuss exactly what the Workshop is about, explaining each element in detail as we have come to understand it. The reason for our focus on the Workshop is because it represents our thinking and philosophy about teaching development in general, and influences the way we engage in all aspects of our work as faculty developers. We were challenged to find a way to convey our experiences in developing the Workshop because our thinking has evolved over time and has been influenced by a number of factors—including the experiences of working with professors and with each other, the theoretical and empirical literature that informs our scholarship and practice, and our individual and joint research programs that focus on teaching and learning at the postsecondary level. To help in our retrospection, we began by thinking back to where we started and how we built the Workshop to be what it is now.

---

[1]The authors gratefully acknowledge the editorial contributions of Janet Donald who was on sabbatical leave at the time this chapter was prepared.

By recalling the questions that concerned us initially as faculty developers, we were able to "deconstruct" our thinking and experiences. We realized that the activities we have introduced to the Workshop over the past decade were created and designed to address questions such as the following:

- Why do short topical workshops on teaching methods not seem to lead to the changes in teaching—specifically learning-centered teaching—that we seek to promote?

- How does understanding of knowledge development within a subject area influence teaching practice?

- Why is it that some professors can articulate appropriate ideas about teaching but do not put into practice what they seem to understand?

- How can we help professors focus more on student learning than on presenting subject matter content?

- How can we encourage professors to reflect more on their teaching and, therefore, learn from their own teaching practice?

We chose specific activities for the Workshop with these questions in mind, fine-tuning the activities year after year. Now, more than a decade later, we have an effective workshop model on course design and teaching, even though we continually make changes and experiment with various formats.

The Workshop

The Workshop involves 30 hours of group-interaction day activities, plus individual evening activities such as readings and other preparations for the following day. Participant professors from different disciplines work in groups and individually for the five days to design or redesign a course of their choice—the course may be one that has not or has already been taught. By the end of the Workshop, participants have worked through the various course design elements needed to produce a detailed outline or syllabus, including not only content and learning outcomes but also assignments and assessment scheme. We call this event a "workshop" because it is hands-on: Participants come together for five days, six hours per day, to design a course with the benefit of input and feedback from facilitators and other participants. During the process, participants examine and develop their thinking about and practice of teaching. With respect to time and work required, the Workshop is equivalent to a three-credit graduate course by North American standards.

The Workshop usually takes place over a five-day period; we have, however, experimented with other formats, some of which are described in Chapter 12 and Chapter 13. In the typical five-day format, approximately 24 participant professors meet from 8:30 A.M. to 4:30 P.M. Monday through Friday to work on a specific course of their choice. At the start of each day, participants meet as a large group for an introduction to the topic of the day. Then, participants meet in designated small groups led by Centre for University Teaching and Learning (CUTL) facilitators to accomplish design work of their course and practice teaching portions of their course to other participants assigned to their small group. On their own time in the evening, participants complete assigned readings that reinforce the day's activities and prepare them for the activities of the following day. A range of assignments encourages participants to reflect on both the design and the teaching of their chosen course. Participants can expect to gain increased insight into what they hope students will learn from their course, an expanded repertoire of teaching strategies, and greater familiarity with meaningful ways to assess student learning. Many past participants report increased confidence in making teaching-related decisions and most important, a sense of belonging to a community of individuals interested in talking about teaching and learning.

Primary Focus

The primary focus of the Workshop is to encourage participant professors to link their teaching directly to student learning. The Workshop also aims to develop a shared discourse on pedagogical issues and a language to express individual conceptions about teaching and learning to others. We support participants in moving toward the perception that student *learning* is the focus for teaching decisions, and we encourage the development of their teaching practices in a way that is consistent with this perception. Some participant professors in the Workshop already hold this perspective. Others may experience a shift in perspective from a teaching paradigm to a learning paradigm (Barr & Tagg, 1995) as a sudden insight or inspiration. Still others may build gradually on the premise that student learning can serve as the basis for teaching decisions and actions and that every effort in the teaching process should be directed at making intended learning happen.

Workshop facilitators work consciously (and carefully) toward developing this focus on student learning. Participants are probed in ways that help them to articulate their own evolving ideas about what meaningful learning is in their disciplinary context, what a reasoned approach to teaching might be. This process often leads participants to question past teaching habits and disciplinary teaching norms, and it creates opportunities for productive and clarifying discussions. We mean to foster a reasoned and intentional approach to teaching, informed by reflective practice and peer feedback. We strive to provide a safe, supportive environment in which individuals can experiment with new teaching approaches and exchange ideas and experiences about teaching and learning with colleagues across disciplines as a legitimate aspect of their profession (Shulman, 1993). For many participants, the Workshop is the first time they have had the occasion to discuss their ideas openly and to experiment with new approaches and strategies to teaching and learning relevant to their discipline.

Overview of the Process

Individuals affiliated with the Centre for University Teaching and Learning (CUTL) contribute to the Workshop in various ways. Four CUTL staff members are the lead facilitators, or lead instructors. They are joined by four co-instructors selected from among past participants of the Workshop who have shown a particular interest in becoming more involved in activities that promote teaching and learning. The co-instructors contribute to every aspect of the Workshop, including planning, selecting materials, making logistical decisions, instructing the small groups, and providing debriefings. Recent experience as participants themselves in the Workshop makes the co-instructors especially adept at translating pedagogical concepts into a language readily understood and related to by new participants. The facilitator team of lead instructors and co-instructors is complemented by four graduate student assistants, who volunteer to gain practical experience in faculty development. The role of the student assistants is primarily to help with technical aspects of the Workshop, but their valuable input as "learners" is often sought by the course-developing participants. The student assistants are well prepared for their task, having taken a graduate course similar to the Workshop in advance. Being part of the delivery team of the Workshop helps the student assistants further their knowledge of and experience in the faculty development process and offers them the opportunity to apprentice in a "real" milieu.

There are two integrated components to the Workshop: One involves the design of a chosen course, a guided activity that builds toward a detailed course outline. The other involves the opportunity to practice teaching using content from the course being developed. The course design component follows a four-step process drawn from instructional design: articulating course content, defining learning outcomes, selecting and developing instructional strategies, and determining approaches and methods for evaluating student learning. Each participant is provided a binder organized by daily topics on course design that includes examples of materials developed by past participants and selected readings supporting each step of the course design and teaching process (see Appendix B for the list of readings from a recent Workshop). The readings highlight the scholarly dimension of teaching and also provide practical and procedural explanations of Workshop activities; they are updated each year to include the latest research and thinking in the field of higher education.

We use microteaching activities to develop the delivery capacity of participant professors. This process involves videotaping short teaching presentations, followed by analysis and discussion with input from facilitators and other small-group participants. The purpose here is to provide a context for practicing various teaching strategies and to prompt self-evaluation and reflection. Microteaching was initially used in the preservice training of K–12 teachers, and over time it has been used with some adaptation in a range of other programs and higher education settings (Allen & Eve, 1968). How we have adapted the original concept of microteaching is discussed later in this chapter and in subsequent chapters.

The Five Days

On Monday, we provide an overall perspective on the course design process. We ask participant professors to focus on the first step in our course design model: mapping course content. The process of developing a course "concept map" obliges participants to be explicit about why they choose particular content, what are the important concepts, and how concepts are related to one another. For many participants, focusing on a conceptual rather than topical representation of their course is a new way of thinking about course content. A microteaching activity centers on a five-minute presentation of the first draft of a concept map by each participant followed by feedback on clarity and structure from the small-group participants. A videotape of the presentation and feedback is taken home by the participant to review in making revisions to the concept map. Presentation skills are not ordinarily critiqued on this first day, primarily because this is the first opportunity many participants have had to see themselves "teaching" on videotape. We have found that after viewing themselves once on videotape, participants are able to use feedback from others more comfortably and effectively as they can consider it from within their own visual frame of reference.

On Tuesday, participants focus on learning outcomes, the second step of the course design process. Drawing from their concept maps, participants articulate as clearly as possible what they want students to learn about course concepts and the relationships among them. This is possibly their first challenge regarding the need to connect student learning with their subject matter since they are required to frame their course content from the perspective of the learner. The five-minute microteaching session focuses on presentation of learning outcomes, usually delivered in a lecture format. Each participant receives feedback on how clear and meaningful learning outcomes might be for students and how coherent they are in light of the corresponding concept map, as well as on the general effectiveness of the presentation. Again, feedback becomes the basis for revision of the learning outcomes before the next day.

On Wednesday, we concentrate on the teaching methods or strategies participants will use to enable students to accomplish the desired learning outcomes for their course. During this session, participants consider an array of methods and strategies, choosing those most appropriate for the type and level of learning desired. An important additional consideration for participants is that the methods or strategies promote the kind of learning they would want to be evaluated. During the microteaching session, participants teach a ten-minute segment of their course using a method or strategy they have used before and with which they are comfortable. When reviewing the videotape of the session and subsequent feedback in the evening, they are asked to reflect on the effectiveness of their chosen method or strategy for achieving the stated learning outcomes of the session.

Thursday is devoted to the evaluation of student learning, the fourth step of the course design process. By this stage, participants often can appreciate the extent to which teaching and learning are intertwined; they begin to recognize that evaluation with ongoing feedback to students is an excellent tool for formatively guiding and enhancing learning, as well as in assessing each student's progress. On this day, participants teach a second ten-minute segment of the course being designed using a method or strategy with which they are less familiar. By now most participants feel that their small group provides a safe and supportive environment for trying new techniques and approaches.

Friday begins with a brief discussion on the evaluation of teaching. The goal is to review university policies on teaching and relate them to what has occurred during the week, and to inform participants of other CUTL workshops on this topic. Following this discussion, participants share the draft of the course outline that they have assembled throughout the week. Each course outline is distributed and discussed within the small group. Feedback is provided on the coherence of the course plan and how well it serves as a learning tool for students.

While each day of the Workshop focuses on a different topic, the schedule for each day's activities is similar throughout the five days and is described in the following paragraphs. The schedule, however, should not be taken as fixed. Each small-group leader takes advantage of every opportunity to address specific concerns of participants during the sessions. Workshop facilitators meet at the conclusion of each day to debrief and consider participant feedback, and to adjust plans for the following day accordingly.

Large Group (9:00 A.M. to 10:30 A.M.)

Each day begins with an overview session in which participant professors and facilitators meet as a large group. During this Workshop session, an instructor and a co-instructor provide a general introduction to the course design concept that will be the focus of the day (i.e., mapping course content, defining learning outcomes, selecting instructional strategies, or evaluating learning). In providing this introduction, facilitators intentionally model good design and a variety of large-group teaching techniques that participants might use in the future.

Small Groups (10:30 A.M. to 12:30 P.M.)

The large group breaks into designated small groups that meet in separate classrooms for the rest of the morning. During the remainder of the morning session, facilitators use small-group teaching techniques to help participants further explore the course design concept of the day. Lively discussion usually characterizes this part of the morning. Participants spend time working individually to apply the course design concept to the design of their own course with assistance from the facilitators. At the end of the morning, participants are given the chance to discuss their work with one another to get peer feedback.

    As noted, each small group is led by a CUTL instructor and a co-instructor, with the support of a student assistant. Usually there are four small groups of six participants, grouped to provide a mix of disciplines, years of teaching experience, and genders. The rationale for this grouping is that in a multidisciplinary setting, professors are respected as subject matter experts and a focus on student learning is not diverted by contrasting views of a particular content area or department politics. Working in multidisciplinary groups has the added advantage that individuals are able to assume the role of both instructor and student. When they teach concepts from the course they are developing to their small-group participants, their role is as instructor. When they experience the teaching sessions of their peers, their role is that of a student with limited knowledge of the content being taught. This aspect of the Workshop is critical since the participant is put through a personal experience of trying to attain a level of understanding intended by the "instructor" that is perhaps not always made explicit. Many insights can result, perhaps one of the most important being the realization that content-related learning is not the entire scope of what participants want their students to attain. The opportunity to discuss the intricacies of teaching and learning with members of the community in which they have a significant personal and professional investment is another kind of insight. Many realize that they enjoy this immensely and can learn as much from observing others as they can from their own active participation.

Lunch (12:30 P.M. to 1:30 P.M.)

Lunchtime provides an opportunity for participant professors to meet informally. On Monday, CUTL hosts a lunch for participants to get to know each other better and establish a sense of community. Tuesday through Thursday, optional brown-bag sessions are arranged on topics of interest, such as graduate student supervision, integration of technology in teaching and learning, and students with disabilities. On Friday, CUTL again hosts a lunch, this time to celebrate the week's accomplishments and provide a debriefing on the week's activities.

Small Groups (1:30 P.M. to 4:30 P.M.)

In the afternoon, participants return to their small-group classrooms. The focus of the afternoon is microteaching, which we conduct in the following manner. Prior to the initial microteaching session, we discuss how to give and receive constructive feedback to ensure that group participants function as a support group. Participants give brief presentations (5 to 20 minutes depending on day and topic). Each participant is videotaped as he or she teaches. The facilitator invites the presenter to first make comments, then request specific feedback. The small-group participants are invited to provide feedback, focusing first on areas requested by the presenter. The feedback is also videotaped for later review. Participants in interdisciplinary small groups often are initially concerned that it will not be possible for colleagues from different fields to understand their course content. Thus, they are sometimes reluctant or dubious about the value of the activity. However, they usually come to realize that the other participants are adept learners, even though, like the students in their classes, they may be unfamiliar with the concepts and thus require guidance. Participants take home the videotape of their teaching to view and to listen to the feedback. They are provided with a list of suggested criteria they may use to critique themselves as they watch their own videotape. When they view the videotape of their teaching, they often see ways in which they can vary their approach to better facilitate student learning. Reactions to microteaching and viewing of the videos are discussed the following day in the small groups. During the Workshop, as participants present different aspects of their evolving course design, they can return to previous videotaped segments to evaluate their progress.

Debriefing by Facilitators (Post-Day Session)

When participants leave at the end of the day, Workshop facilitators get together to debrief. During these debriefings, each small-group team reports on progress and the extent to which their small group was able to stay on course. Sometimes a particular issue is especially important to a small group and requires a slight digression from the specified schedule. Or, a given small-group might need more time for a particular activity. Small-group facilitators are always at liberty to manage their time in a way that best serves the small group. The debriefing is also the time to share exciting and sometimes stressful experiences, and to get and give advice from or to the others of the team.

Participant Homework (Evening)

The daytime schedule requires that participants spend a good deal of time outside of Workshop hours on preparation for the next day and follow-up. Selected readings on each topic covered in the Workshop are included in the binder given to each participant. Some are directly pertinent to presentations or activities planned for the following day and some are included as supplementary reading. In addition to the designated readings, participants are asked to review their videotaped microteaching segments, noting their own reactions and ideas for follow-up and reflecting on the feedback provided by fellow small-group participants and facilitators. Finally, participants prepare relevant materials, such as revisions and additions to their course outline, and presentations for the next day.

Advance Preparation

Switching from one course design activity to the next may appear seamless, but there is a complex infrastructure underlying the Workshop. Months in advance of a scheduled Workshop, a CUTL member is designated as coordinator. The coordinator takes on the responsibility to convene planning meetings, advertise, communicate with participants, invite other contributors, prepare materials and the course pack, and coordinate each day's activities.

Advertising to the university community at large begins four months in advance. In the first few years that we held the Workshop, an invitation was sent from the office of the Vice Principal, Academic (now Provost and Vice Principal), to the Deans asking for the nomination of three faculty members with an expressed interest in further developing their teaching. The idea was to ensure a fair distribution of participants across disciplines and to reinforce the message that the Workshop is not remedial, but rather an opportunity for potential leaders to become more involved in the promotion of their own scholarship of teaching. For several years now, we have sent an announcement to administrative assistants of each department for distribution to their respective academic staff. We also send the announcement to all CUTL activity participants and new professors. The information circulated emphasizes that the Workshop does not address teaching "problems" but is rather an opportunity for all professors to work on further developing their courses and teaching. The date of the Workshop is intentionally set in the spring, after professors have had sufficient time to submit grades for winter courses and before they begin research commitments and summer teaching. For many, this coincides with the time that they have set aside to plan their courses for the next academic year.

Planning meetings for the Workshop begin weeks in advance. It is during these meetings that the activities of the facilitators and other members of the team contributing to the Workshop are coordinated. One of the first considerations is who among the past participants of the Workshop might be effective as co-instructors. Our primary criterion in selecting these individuals is the extent to which, in our estimation, they will be willing and able to promote teaching and faculty development in their own academic units. Subsequent meetings involve both co-instructors and student assistants in resolving issues of scheduling, assigning facilitators and participants to small groups, selecting presenters for large-group presentations, selecting topics and presenters for the lunch sessions, and finalizing the reading material for the course pack.

Once we have a full complement of professors who have made a commitment to take part in the professional development Workshop, we send them a needs assessment (see Appendix A). The needs assessment elicits a description of the course that is to be designed during the Workshop; general teaching goals, concerns, and experiences; and personal perspectives on teaching and learning. The demographic information gleaned from the needs assessment is used to create the small groups, taking into account disciplinary affiliation, years of teaching experience, and gender. In any given year, we could have senior professors with more than 25 years of experience as well as mid-career and new faculty. We also administer a post-Workshop assessment that includes some of the same questions posed in the needs assessment. This allows us to see how the Workshop activities have influenced the way participants think about teaching and learning and what the experience has meant to participants in terms of planning their course and the confidence with which they make teaching-related decisions. Following is a sampling of comments from past participants of the Workshop that highlight what the experience has meant to these individuals:

DEPARTMENT OF ENGLISH, 1995

The concept map is stuck in my head. . . . I keep asking myself: What do I actually expect them [students] to leave this course knowing or being able to do? How can that be evaluated? It gives me a clear point of focus.

DEPARTMENT OF AGRICULTURAL ECONOMICS, 1995

[I learned] the importance of linking learning outcomes with both the instructional approach and the evaluation/grading systems that might be appropriate—in other words, to NOT forget the students.

CENTRE FOR INDIGENOUS PEOPLES' NUTRITION AND ENVIRONMENT, 1998

I have always used active learning and also formative evaluation, but never as methodically as we learned how to do [them] here. What never occurred to me [before] is how beneficial it is to both teacher and learners to explicitly state learning outcomes and objectives at the outset and throughout.

SCHOOL OF COMPUTER SCIENCE, 2000

I am [now] thinking in a structured manner about course preparation, and have learned a number of teaching strategies and their (dis)advantages. I will use more student-active strategies in class and spend more time in ADVANCE for preparation. I will also look my students in the eyes.

DEPARTMENT OF NATURAL RESOURCE SCIENCES, 2000

Strong impact on my thinking: I will think more of the difference between learning and teaching. The workshop opened some new avenues for me, and started a new way of thinking about teaching.

At two points during the Workshop, we also collect formative feedback. We query participants as to their reactions and elicit suggestions for improvement. This feedback is reviewed and discussed at the debriefing meetings with facilitators at the end of the day and often results in making changes or adjustments to planned activities. As is the case with almost everything else we do during the Workshop, we model the way in which input from class can be acknowledged and applied. We summarize and present participants' formative feedback and talk about incorporated changes the following day.

The single word that best characterizes the five days of the Workshop is "intense." The experience for all—even those of us who have been doing the Workshop for many years—is energizing as well as exhausting. Individual accomplishments are what make the Workshop most worthwhile for both participants and facilitators. The camaraderie and bond of the Workshop is so strong that participants often linger long after lunch on the last day. Some years we have invited past participants to join the current cohort for the last lunch of the Workshop. These guests use this opportunity to talk about what they have done following their Workshop experience. In the past year, each small-group leader has organized informal lunch meetings during the academic year. The goal is to maintain ongoing discussion about teaching and learning in our institution. We hope to be able to assign one day every month when anyone interested in keeping in touch and talking about teaching can join an informal designated "teaching" table at our faculty club. All of these efforts are made in the interests of strengthening a network of individuals seeking to promote the scholarship of teaching in our institution.

References

Allen, D., & Eve, A. (1968). Microteaching. *Theory into practice, 7*(5), 181–185.

Barr, R. B., & Tagg, J. (1995). From teaching to learning: A new paradigm for undergraduate education. *Change, 27*(6), 13–25.

Shulman, L. (1993, November/December). Teaching as community property: Putting an end to pedagogical solitude. *Change,* 6–7.

2

ASSUMPTIONS UNDERLYING WORKSHOP ACTIVITIES

Alenoush Saroyan, Cheryl Amundsen, Lynn McAlpine,
Cynthia Weston, Laura Winer, and Terry Gandell[1]

We come to our work as faculty developers with individual and shared perspectives formed through our experiences as professors, researchers, and faculty developers. In this chapter, we first present the results of analysis of our individual and collective assumptions about faculty development in general, and the Course Design and Teaching Workshop in particular. We then present and describe our working model of teaching development, inspired and validated by our research and practice.

Our assumptions can be broadly described as having to do with the knowledge, skills, and perspectives professors bring to their role as teachers, the nature of the teaching and learning process in higher education, and the institutional context in which professors work and develop as teachers. Each of these areas is discussed respectively in the following sections.

Assumptions About Teaching and Faculty Development

Knowledge, Skills, and Perspectives of Professors

The Subject-Matter Expert and the Pedagogue

We have sought to understand the ways in which individuals manage their responsibility of teaching at the university, often without being directly prepared for this role. Most of our faculty are, after all, the product of North American graduate programs. These programs typically aim at developing highly specialized subject-matter expertise and place little, if any, emphasis

---

[1]The authors gratefully acknowledge the editorial contributions of Janet Donald who was on sabbatic leave when this chapter was prepared.

on developing the ability to teach the subject effectively (Boyer, 1990). It is not surprising, then, that many professors consider themselves subject experts and scholars rather than teachers or even teacher-scholars within their discipline. We take this reality very seriously and readily acknowledge that one's area of expertise is a matter of professional self-identity, often expressed in terms of the disciplinary affiliation—such as "geographer" or "linguist" or "physicist." We think that a more balanced role between subject-matter expert and teacher might be obtained if the attributes of scholarship were also extended to teaching.

However, incorporating teaching as a central component of the professorial role and as a form of scholarship (Boyer, 1990) is far from common. The reality we encounter every day reflects this, and, as a result, remains one of our primary challenges as faculty developers (Kreber, 2000). We often observe professors, particularly those newly appointed, overwhelmed by their teaching responsibilities, especially the array of courses they are assigned to teach. This is not at all surprising. The most recent experience for many young professors will be a narrow literature related to their doctoral research. This particular content, however, is not what they are most likely assigned to teach. Often, their teaching assignments include all sorts of courses, from introductory to specialized. This variety in itself poses a challenge since teaching well in different contexts requires at the least a broader, more general knowledge of the subject matter. When this knowledge is not readily retrievable, the task becomes overwhelming. Planning for and organizing the course content or "what should be covered" takes priority over thinking about *how* to teach the course so that students learn well.

Inadequate grounding in pedagogy disadvantages the professor in creating learning-centered teaching within reasonable time. Without such grounding, professors often rely on models of teaching that they have encountered during their own student years or have seen colleagues apply in their respective classes (Boice, 1991, 1992). Since the lecture is the predominant approach in university teaching today, it is likely to be the only source of inspiration for many as they struggle to prepare themselves for their teaching assignments. The earlier in their career that professors realize different learning outcomes are best attained with the use of different instructional strategies (Gandell, Weston, Finkelstein, & Winer, 2000; Weston & Cranton, 1986), the more likely they are to adopt a learning-centered teaching approach. Part of this realization can come from the recognition that the complex thinking skills expected of students are better developed through a variety of teaching and learning strategies. Moreover, to address the needs of today's diverse student population and help all students succeed, teacher-centered approaches must be replaced by learning- and learner-centered approaches (Biggs, 1999; Dunlap & Grabinger, 1996).

Professors' Perspectives on Roles

One of our main challenges as faculty developers is finding ways to engage professors in a process whereby they examine their views and assumptions about teaching. Such occasions are likely to be met by a superficial understanding of the role of the teacher and the learner, and the teaching and learning process—views often not explicitly articulated and difficult to change. Indeed, if left unexamined, such views may interfere with a professor's inclination and ability to consider other teaching practices that may better encourage and support different types or levels of student learning (Cranton, 1996; Mezirow, 1991). For example, the view that the professor's role is to be a subject expert and disseminate related knowledge may lead to the adopting of a didactic approach to teaching. This frame of reference is likely to be accompanied by the need for strict control over what is learned in class and what particular perspectives students should develop about a content area. Holding this frame of reference can have greater implications than on only the manner of teaching delivery. Professors may shy away from eliciting questions from students, discussing contrasting views and theories, and even engaging in informal conversations with students because they perceive these actions as possibly threatening to their sense of control.

The Nature of University Teaching and Learning

Learning-Centered Teaching

We think about teaching from a learning-centered perspective: Whenever we are involved in instruction, we try to think about the way each of our decisions and actions will influence students and their learning. What we mean by learning-centered teaching is manifest in what we do (and will become more apparent in following chapters), and is to be distinguished from a student-centered approach. This latter term is most often used to indicate that students are the center focus of instruction, as they are engaged in "active" learning strategies (Bonwell & Eison, 1991; Johnson, Johnson, & Smith, 1991; Kember, 1997). A learning-centered approach, in contrast, does not necessarily mean that student activity is the focus of the teaching strategy. Rather, learning-centered teaching means that decisions are made with specific reference to the kind of learning that is desired, and strategies are chosen because they are the most likely to support that kind of learning. For instance, even though a lecture is teacher-centered, the strategy may be a very good choice if the learning goal is an overview or a model for subsequent activities.

We have come to understand that for professors to hold a learning-centered perspective and be able to act on it, they need to have developed a complex and integrated understanding of the nature of teaching and learning (Saroyan, Amundsen, & Cao, 1997). The complex and multilayered nature of the teaching process at the primary and secondary school levels (K–12) has been well described in the literature (see review by Wideen, Mayer-Smith, & Moon, 1998). In higher education, this is not the case. Teaching in this context is usually described in terms of having a solid grasp of the subject matter and knowing how to skillfully present it—in other words, the emphasis is usually on content knowledge and presentation. Items that appear on commonly used student course evaluation forms reflect this orientation to teaching. For example, items about a professor's degree of preparation, organization, clarity of presentation, and ability to demonstrate knowledge of the content and stimulate student interest refer to overt actions typically associated with effective lecturing. We concur that these can be important attributes of effective teaching, but we disagree with the implication that these overt actions effectively describe teaching. In our view, generic skills cannot be considered as unrelated to or independent of subject matter (Saroyan & Amundsen, 2001). Moreover, a good part of teaching involves thinking, problem-solving, and decision making, all of which are unobservable processes. Any discussion about teaching necessitates taking into account multiple dimensions—both observable actions and unobservable processes.

Schwab (1970) notes that in any situation in which teaching and learning is presumed to be occurring, events can be examined by considering the interaction among four commonplaces—students, teacher, subject matter, and context—each of which incorporates a range of factors:

1. What students bring to the educational experience—for example, prior knowledge of the subject matter, conception of learning, expectations about responsibility for learning, extent to which success in learning has been experienced.

2. What the teacher brings to the educational experience—for example, perspective on teaching and learning, prior experience of teaching in general and the course being taught, perspective on the role of the instructor.

3. How the subject matter or discipline affects the educational experience—for example, how the knowledge structures of the discipline influence the nature of the tasks that are engaged in by those in the discipline

(Donald, 1986), the type of learning that is required (often related to the level of the course).

4. How the context or external factors influence the nature of the instruction—for example, whether the course is required or not, size of the class, other responsibilities of the professor and students, institutional factors.

Effective teaching decisions are those made on the basis of the common-places outlined by Schwab rather than out of habit or because of what others do. We argue that professors develop into competent instructional decision makers through an intellectual process. Subject-matter expertise is used to clarify and articulate the student learning that is desired, becoming the reference point for all subsequent decisions. Competency is thus developed through the practice and close examination of decision sequences and teaching actions. Self- and peer analyses assist this process because they enable an individual to explore alternative possibilities and potential outcomes; moreover, they foster an openness to different ways of approaching the teaching task.

Our views have led us to adopt a different strategy for teaching development than the traditional format of short, skill-based faculty development workshops (Weimer & Lenze, 1991). We believe that knowledge of generic teaching approaches gained through skill-based workshops is often not put into practice because most professors are unable to see the relevance of general pedagogies to their particular discipline. Moreover, these workshops often do not provide professors with the opportunity to "practice" in a meaningful way the teaching and learning strategies introduced in the workshop. Consequently, the professors have little opportunity to develop their comfort with the strategy and to determine the relevance of the strategy to student learning in their course or discipline. Without this opportunity, the commitment to incorporate what is learned into teaching practice may never develop. We have even observed professors who "try out" strategies learned in such workshops without understanding the connection between the teaching strategy and student learning. In our experience, without this understanding, a strategy is likely to be quickly abandoned in the face of any challenge—for example, if the strategy is not greeted positively by students or not implemented as easily as planned.

The intellectual exercise of understanding the rationale for a teaching method and how it relates to learning as well as testing out the teaching method is akin to what professors do as scholars. A teaching method that is so presented is more likely to be internalized. Moreover, given the importance of subject matter for faculty and the passion with which it is accompanied, we believe subject matter must be made the focus and underlying thinking of the development of teaching. Shulman (1986) has also suggested that subject matter must be the point of departure for developing teaching. For this reason, the Workshop is consciously aimed at merging generic knowledge of teaching with subject-matter knowledge and rarely deals with development of teaching knowledge separately.

Context in Which Faculty Teach and Develop as Teachers

It is a given that faculty are expected to develop as researchers during their university careers. Accomplishment in this area is determined over time by the number and size of obtained research grants, the number and quality of publications, the number of graduate students supervised, and the recognition of work by prominent researchers in the discipline or field. Research universities, in particular, tend to place greatest weight on this type of accomplishment when evaluating academic performance. In contrast, achievements related to teaching and its development are often accorded less weight. We believe that this is partially because development as a teacher is often less understood and considered difficult to evaluate. Consequently, development as a teacher is less recognized and ultimately under-rewarded. Some professors worry that even if they wish to be innovative in their teaching, their investment in doing so may harm other aspects of their academic life (Houseman, 1997). Others are concerned that any deviation from teaching norms will be met with resistance and negative reactions from students and colleagues, and thus affect their chances of promotion and tenure (Entwistle, Entwistle, & Tait, 1993).

Environments Conducive to Teaching Development

Many professors begin and continue to teach in environments that do not appreciate teaching development as a complex and time-demanding process. More important, these environments provide little support and no incentive for efforts invested, and faculty often feel isolated in terms of this part of their work (Boice, 1992). In our experience, most faculty who engage in the process of teaching development continue to do so because of intrinsic motivation. They find themselves rewarded when they get to know students better as learners, share in the excitement of students' learning accomplishments, observe growing student interest in the subject area, and discuss teaching-related issues with like-minded colleagues (Amundsen, Saroyan, & Frankman, 1996).

The point here is the influence that context has on teaching practice and its development. Although we interpret context in its broadest sense—classroom context (e.g., physical space, level of course, diversity of students) as well as disciplinary and institutional contexts—we will focus on institutional context and how it may orient itself as a favourable catalyst. If the institutional context were to promote teaching as a public activity open to scrutiny and peer review as with research, this would be a large step toward creating an environment more conducive to changing faculty attitudes about teaching. Needless to say, this would necessitate the availability of proper resources to support teaching. The entire enterprise of teaching development, in our view, needs to be both top-down and bottom-up. Institutional policies, practices, and resources are required. Also necessary is interest in and desire for change at the grass roots. To this end, we see a role for units such as the Centre for University Teaching and Learning (CUTL) to actively promote teaching-related policies that would help create a more favorable context for teaching development to occur.

In summary, we consciously strive in the Workshop to pay attention to the issues and concerns raised in the preceding paragraphs. We create a comfortable environment where faculty can begin to understand teaching as a scholarly activity and are given the opportunity to engage in intellectual discussions on teaching with colleagues. We have discovered that cross-disciplinary groupings of instructors create a particularly effective dynamic for these discussions because everyone is placed on a level playing field. The change process—from teaching- to learning-centered—is further facilitated through peer group interaction and with sufficient time to turn thoughts into actions (Elrick, 1990; Kozma, 1985). The Workshop activities themselves are deemed by participants to be meaningful, relevant, and valuable, and our credibility as facilitators is recognized. There is both intrinsic and extrinsic motivation for change: intrinsic because of personal gain; extrinsic because of the potential to meet university expectations for teaching performance. Moreover, there is the opportunity to have meaningful discussions with members of a community in which the participants have a significant professional and personal investment. All these conditions correspond with those outlined by Centra (1993) and others as fundamental in helping faculty embrace teaching development and curricular innovation in higher education.

We now move on to describe the working model that explains how we believe teaching expertise develops.

A Model of Teaching Expertise

We have explained that we see teaching as multidimensional, comprising unobservable constructs (e.g., knowledge, perspectives, reflection) and observable actions. These components exist within a context in which the teaching and learning process takes place. The dynamic relationship among these components

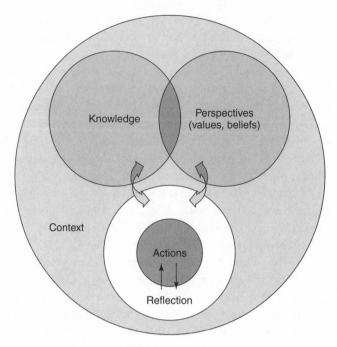

Figure 2.1   Model of teaching expertise.

explains how professors make instructional decisions, implement actions, evaluate the impact of these actions, and develop new knowledge about teaching. Expertise in teaching occurs when there is alignment between unobservable and observable components. In other words, we think of an expert teacher as someone who has highly developed reflective thinking skills, applies those skills continuously, and as a result achieves considerable convergence in thought and action. The components of our model and their relationships are depicted in Figure 2.1 and described in the following paragraphs.

Knowledge

Teaching expertise requires the integration of four kinds of knowledge relevant to teaching (Sherman, Armistead, Fowler, Barksdale, & Reif, 1987; Shulman, 1986). This knowledge of teaching is made up primarily of subject-matter knowledge, pedagogical content knowledge, knowledge of the learner, and knowledge of the context. Each type of knowledge opens a different window on teaching and learning. Subject-matter knowledge refers to the content of the discipline or field in which a professor teaches, and is especially prominent in teaching in higher education. Pedagogical content knowledge is discipline specific, referring to knowledge of teaching a particular subject matter (Sherman et al., 1987; Shulman, 1986). Knowledge of the learner refers to understanding of the range of prior knowledge and experiences of students, in general, and knowledge of the particular students one is teaching (McAlpine, Weston, Beauchamp, Wiseman, & Beauchamp, 1999; Rahilly & Saroyan, 1997). Knowledge of context refers to cognizance of factors influencing both students and professor that may have an impact on teaching and learning (McAlphine & Weston, 2002).

Virtually all participants come to the Workshop recognizing the importance of subject-matter knowledge to university teaching, but only a few recognize the importance of developing and drawing on a broader knowledge base. In the Workshop, we discuss the four kinds of knowledge described above, separately and in concert, as participants engage in the course design process. We want participants to appreciate that the essence of a learning-centered approach is the integration of these four kinds of knowledge.

Perspective

We define perspective as conceptions or beliefs about higher education teaching and learning in general and as they pertain to a particular discipline. A professor may hold a particular belief because of prior experience as a student, disciplinary teaching norms, or a variety of other factors. He or she may be well aware of holding this belief and be able to easily articulate and explain its origin. Conversely, there may be little or no consciousness of this perspective; therefore, identifying or explicating it may be more difficult. The perspectives a professor holds about teaching and learning, conscious or unconscious, are of interest to us because we have found that these perspectives often seem to act as facilitators or barriers to adopting and implementing a learning-centered approach. We agree with Kane, Sandretto, and Heath (2002) that the link between beliefs and teaching practice in higher education is neither simple nor straightforward and has to date not been well explained or documented.

Perspectives may be held about such broad aspects as the nature of learning in a particular discipline or what "types" (e.g., gender, personality) of individuals are best suited to a particular discipline. More specific to the instructional setting are aspects such as a professor's role in the classroom and appropriate modes of interaction with students. A professor may, for instance, believe that his or her task as a subject-matter expert is to disseminate information to students and that it is the sole responsibility of students to develop an understanding of the subject matter based on the information provided by him or her. This perspective, if left unchallenged, would act as a barrier to adopting a learning-centered approach because the professor's expertise is considered the primary determinant of how a course should be designed and taught.

It is also our experience that a professor may simultaneously hold competing or contradictory perspectives. For example, a professor may embrace the image of the ideal professor as one who delivers a flawless lecture, answers all questions adroitly, and, in general, keeps the students in silent awe of him or her. At the same time, the professor may highly value students' active participation in the classroom. There is an obvious conflict in this case because the ideal professorial role does not encourage the learner behavior that is valued. The image of the ideal professor, if acted on in the classroom, will block efforts to increase students' active involvement, leaving the professor at a loss to explain why (Amundsen, Saroyan, & Gryspeerdt, 1999).

We consider the perspectives a professor holds to be critical to the process of making decisions about teaching and learning. These perspectives determine the kind of knowledge a professor draws on in carrying out the teaching task. For example, a professor who believes teaching is simply the transmission of knowledge will draw on only subject-matter knowledge to teach. Similarly, a professor who has come to believe that the main task of teaching is to keep students active will likely try to use as many different teaching and learning strategies as possible (Ramsden, 1992). In this case, the professor may draw on only generic pedagogical knowledge that has an unclear and weak connection to subject-matter learning. Perspectives and knowledge partially overlap, as depicted in our model (Figure 2.1).

Some perspectives, because of this overlap, can potentially overshadow knowledge, creating a situation where newly gained knowledge is not integrated because of previous and closely held perspectives about teaching and learning. In the Workshop, we try to uncover perspectives about teaching and learning by continually engaging professors in discussions about why they think as they do and what their reasons are for developing each aspect of the course they are designing. Inconsistencies between explanations and course elements are pointed out by facilitators and other Workshop participants in ways that encourage professors to reexamine links between what they know and believe (Cranton, 1994; Mezirow, 1981).

Actions

Action refers to the enactment of teaching, and this includes planning, classroom and online teaching, interactions with students outside of class time, and evaluation of student learning. As such, this component of our model represents both process (e.g., planning) as well as product (e.g., overt actions). Here again, the important element is the relationship of knowledge, perspective, and action. Knowledge about teaching, learning and the learner, and perspectives held about teaching and learning lead to actions. We believe that the most competent professors conscientiously and continually try to align their actions with their knowledge and their perspectives. In this case, teaching practice is based on reason and clearly articulated values. Alignment is not easily achieved and requires constant monitoring and reflection by even the most expert teacher.

In the Workshop, participants have an opportunity during the microteaching sessions to begin to "practice" alignment of their knowledge, perspectives, and actions. Sometimes this proves to be straightforward. Sometimes elaborating on why there is not a tighter connection among these elements is difficult. The reason may be attributable to strength of a certain habit or lack of comfort with a particular teaching method. It may also be that teaching practice is not supported by the fourth element of our model: instructional context.

Instructional Context

The context of instruction includes all the external factors that influence or are perceived to influence the teaching task. These could be as broad as the culture of the university, the Faculty,[2] or department (e.g., reward structures, teaching norms) or as specific as factors pertaining to the instructor's teaching assignment (e.g., new course, unexpected changes in curriculum, higher enrollment than expected). For instance, a department may impose certain expectations on the individual in delivering instruction, or the individual may perceive that the department's priority is for a certain amount of content to be covered regardless of impact on student learning. In either case, this context can disturb the existing alignment among the individual's knowledge, perspectives, and actions. Thus, a professor may hold quite sophisticated knowledge relevant to teaching and corresponding perspectives but may not be able to draw on these in actions because of real or perceived contextual constraints.

Reflection

We consider the process of reflection as the glue that holds together knowledge, perspectives, and actions. Reflection supports and encourages the continual realignment of these components and is the mechanism for instructional decision making. In Figure 2.1, reflection is depicted as a process that both influences

---

[2]In the Canadian context, this unit is referred to as *Faculty.* The uppercase use of the letter *F* distinguishes the word from *faculty,* used to denote professors.

and is influenced by actions. The arrows that connect actions to perspectives and knowledge show that reflection also extends to these components and mediates change in thinking. The absence of reflection would be manifest in "the mindless following of unexamined practices" (Sparks-Langer & Colton, 1991).

In the 1980s, Schön (1983, 1987) reawakened interest in the construct of reflection, and coined the terms reflection *in action* and *on action*. He asserted that reflection plays a significant role in helping us understand and improve practice in any professional discipline. The goal of reflection is twofold: to develop new knowledge by considering past experiences about teaching and learning; to improve teaching effectiveness by applying the knowledge gained from reflection to future practice. We believe that as individuals gain expertise in teaching, their ability to reflect both retrospectively (on action) as well as simultaneously (in action) becomes automatic and routine. A highly developed capacity to reflect enables an individual to keep goals in mind while "in action" so as to evaluate the impact of actions and modify them, often on the spot.

Our experience and research lead us to assert that reflection on teaching is particularly important in a university environment where individuals are not necessarily taught how to teach or provided with access to knowledge about teaching. Professors are expected to build their knowledge of teaching and learning largely from their own teaching experiences. Hence, developing a reflective capacity will go a long way in helping individuals take charge of their own learning about teaching. Similar views about reflection and its significance in the practice of teaching in higher education have been expressed by others. For instance, Fox (1983), Ramsden (1992), and Shulman (1987) use reflection in models or theories that describe how the understanding of teaching develops.

In the above descriptions of the major components of our model, brief mention was made of some of the ways in which we initiate Workshop participants into a culture of reflection. Questioning about why a specific action is taken or why a particular perspective is held provides opportunities to practice linking knowledge with action. Peer critique and self-critique further extol the importance of reflection.

Conclusion

In summary, our working model of teaching depicts both the elements that we consider as prominent in teaching and the processes invoked to develop competence in teaching. We firmly believe that any discussion about teaching or activities to develop teaching must take into account both observable actions and underlying unobservable thoughts and processes. Furthermore, since teaching always happens in a context, that context—whether internal or external, perceived or real—interacts with perspectives, knowledge, and actions. The process of developing teaching is facilitated in two ways: first, by the process of reflection both in and on action; second, by examining and making explicit personal perspectives and views about teaching and learning in general, and about student, professor, subject matter, and context in particular. Change, however, happens slowly, is incremental, and is better sustained if ideas can be put into practice and learning occurs from this experiential process.

Workshop activities aim to develop every aspect of teaching as depicted in this model. Explicit learning outcomes of the Workshop are explicating perspectives; developing pedagogical knowledge and grounding it in subject matter; incorporating understanding about students and student learning into course design; understanding the importance of aligning thoughts with appropriate teaching actions; and developing reflective capacity. In Part II, Chapters 3 through 7 describe in detail the progression of the course design process and how Workshop activities support this process.

References

Amundsen, C., Saroyan, A., & Frankman, M. (1996). Changing methods and metaphors: A case study of growth in university teaching. *Journal of Excellence in College Teaching, 7*(3), 3–42.

Amundsen, C., Saroyan, A., & Gryspeerdt, D. (1999, April). *Learning to teach in higher education: A situation of missing models.* Paper presented at the American Educational Research Association, Montréal, Canada.

Biggs, J. (1999). What the student does: Teaching for enhanced learning. *Higher Education Research and Development, 18*(1), 57–75.

Bonwell, C., & Eison, J. (1991). *Active learning: Creating excitement in the classroom.* San Francisco: Jossey-Bass.

Boice, R. (1991). New faculty as teachers. *Journal of Higher Education, 62*(2), 150–173.

Boice, R. (1992). *The new faculty member: Supporting and fostering professional development.* San Francisco: Jossey-Bass.

Boyer, E. L. (1990). *Scholarship reconsidered: Priorities of the professoriate.* Princeton, NJ: Carnegie Foundation for the Advancement of Teaching.

Centra, J. (1993). *Reflective faculty evaluation.* San Francisco: Jossey-Bass.

Cranton, P. (1994). *Understanding and promoting transformative learning.* San Francisco: Jossey-Bass.

Cranton, P. (1996). *Professional development as transformative learning: New perspectives for teachers of adults.* San Francisco: Jossey-Bass.

Donald, J. G. (1986). Knowledge and the university curriculum. *Higher Education, 15*(3-4), 267–282.

Dunlap, J., & Grabinger, S. (1996). Rich environments for active learning in the higher education classroom. In B. Wilson (Ed.), *Constructivist learning environments: Case studies in instructional design* (pp. 65–82). Englewood Cliffs, NJ: Educational Technology.

Elrick, M. F. (1990). Improving instruction in universities: A case study of the Ontario universities' program for instructional development. *Canadian Journal of Higher Education, 20*(2), 61–79.

Entwistle, N., Entwistle, A., & Tait, H. (1993). Academic understanding and contexts to enhance it: A perspective from research on student learning. In T. M. Duffy, J. Lowyck & D. Jonassen (Eds.), *Designing environments for constructive learning* (pp. 331–357). Berlin: Springer-Verlag.

Fox, D. (1983). Personal theories of teaching. *Studies in Higher Education, 8,* 151–163.

Gandell, T., Weston, C., Finkelstein, A., & Winer, L. (2000). Appropriate use of the web in teaching higher education. In B. Mann (Ed.), *Perspectives in web course management* (pp. 61–68). Toronto, Canada: Canadian Scholars' Press.

Houseman, J. (1997). Infusion, not diffusion: A strategy for incorporating information technology into higher education. *Journal of Distance Education, 12*(1/2), 1–28.

Johnson, D., Johnson, R., & Smith, K. (1991). *Active learning: Cooperation in the college classroom.* Edina, MN: Interaction Book Company.

Kane, R., Sandretto, S., & Heath, C. (2002). Telling half the story: A critical review of research on teaching beliefs and practices of university academics. *Review of Educational Research, 72*(2), 177–228.

Kember, D. (1997). A reconceptualization of the research into university academics' conceptions of teaching. *Learning and Instruction, 7*(3), 255–275.

Kozma, R. (1985). A grounded theory of instructional innovation in higher education. *Journal of Higher Education, 56*(3), 300–319.

Kreber, C. (2000). How university teaching award winners conceptualize academic work: Some further thought on the meaning of scholarship. *Teaching in Higher Education, 5*(1), 61–78.

McAlpine, L., & Weston, C. (2002, July). *Reflection on teaching. Using an empirical model to analyze, improve and learn about your own practice.* Paper presented at the Higher Education Research and Development Society of Australia, Perth.

McAlpine, L., Weston, C., Beauchamp, J., Wiseman, C., & Beauchamp, C. (1999). Building a metacognitive model of reflection. *Higher Education, 37,* 105–131.

Mezirow, J. (1981). A critical theory of adult learning and education. *Adult Education, 32*(1), 3–27.

Mezirow, J. (1991). *Transformative dimensions of adult learning.* San Francisco: Jossey-Bass.

Rahilly, T., & Saroyan, A. (1997, March). *Knowledge influencing teaching.* Paper presented at the American Educational Research Association, Chicago, IL.

Ramsden, P. (1992). *Learning to teach in higher education.* London: Routledge.

Saroyan, A., & Amundsen, C. (2001). Evaluating university teaching: Time to take stock. *Assessment and Evaluation in Higher Education, 26*(4), 337–349.

Saroyan, A., Amundsen, C., & Cao, L. (1997). Incorporating theories of teacher growth and adult education in a faculty development program. *To Improve the Academy, 16,* 93–115.

Schön, D. A. (1983). *The reflective practitioner: How professionals think in action.* San Francisco: Jossey-Bass.

Schön, D. A. (1987). *Educating the reflective practitioner: Toward a new design for teaching and learning in the professions.* San Francisco: Jossey-Bass.

Schwab, J. J. (1970). *The practical: A language for curriculum.* Washington, DC: National Education Association.

Sherman, T. M., Armistead, L. P., Fowler, F., Barksdale, M. A., & Reif, G. (1987). The quest for excellence in university teaching. *Journal of Higher Education, 58,* 66–84.

Shulman, L. S. (1986). Those who understand: Knowledge growth in teaching. *Educational Researcher, 15*(2), 4–14.

Shulman, L. S. (1987). Knowledge of teaching: Foundations of the new reform. *Harvard Educational Review, 57*(1), 1–22.

Sparks-Langer, G. M., & Colton, B. (1991). Synthesis of research on teachers' reflective thinking. *Educational Leadership, 48*(6), 37–44.

Weimer, M., & Lenze, L. F. (1991). Instructional interventions: A review of the literature on efforts to improve instruction. In J. Smart (Ed.), *Higher education: Handbook of theory and research* (Vol. 7, pp. 294–333). New York: Agathon.

Weston, C., & Cranton, P. (1986). Selecting instructional strategies. *Journal of Higher Education, 57*(3), 260–288.

Wideen, M., Mayer-Smith, J., & Moon, B. (1998). A critical analysis of the research on learning to teach: Making the case for an ecological perspective on inquiry. *Review of Educational Research, 68*(2), 130–178.

PART II

PLANNING
AND IMPLEMENTING
THE WORKSHOP

The five chapters of Part II provide details on the Course Design and Teaching Workshop. We discuss our rationale for each aspect of the Workshop, often citing the literature that has informed our understanding. We chose to describe a five-day format since this is the format we have used most often for the Workshop; other formats have also been tried and can be equally effective. The integrity of the Workshop, regardless of format, revolves around the five elements of the course design process as we conceive of it. Each chapter in this section addresses one of these elements; each chapter builds on the understanding of the design element considered in the previous chapter. These design elements could certainly be differently sequenced. The sequence we present here simply reflects our usual approach to teaching course design. Our reason for doing so is that subject-matter content is the one aspect of teaching with which most faculty feel confident, and we want to begin this journey using the equipment with which our travelers feel most comfortable.

Throughout these chapters, we describe fully the specific activities of each day of the Workshop as it unfolds. Our goal is for the reader to have enough detail about how we conduct the Workshop to replicate the same activities easily or to adapt it to another context. There is, however, nothing scripted about the Workshop. Over the years, all sorts of changes have been made based on feedback, individual preferences, group dynamics, participant needs, and so on. The progression of activities and the activities described represent a selection of what actually has been done. One thing, however, has not changed: providing an exciting learning experience for faculty that is personally meaningful and relevant to their role as scholar and teacher in their discipline.

Chapter 3 concentrates on the content of the course being developed by each participant in the Workshop. We lead participants to think of their course as a coherent whole and to frame their view of the content from the perspective of learning about it. The groundwork is thus prepared for participants to begin clarifying for themselves the exact nature of the learning they want their students to accomplish. This is the focus of Chapter 4, which describes the process we use to guide participants in developing learning outcomes for their course. Implicit in this activity is participant consideration of the teaching responsibility of professors and the learning responsibility of students. In Chapter 5, we describe the difficult task of combining the perspectives of subject-matter expert and role of instructor as a facilitator of learning. We explain how we support participants in coming to understand that various teaching and learning strategies enable, to a greater or lesser degree, different types and levels of learning. Chapter 6 takes up the often thorny issue of assessment of learning. We take the view that assessment is the mechanism for guiding learning, and as such its formative aspect is very important. We explain ways in which we coach participants to make assessment meaningful not only to the learner but to the integrity of the design process. Chapter 7 closes our consideration of the design process by taking up discussion on the quality and evaluation of teaching. The orientation is about how the teaching experience itself can be used formatively to improve teaching and student learning.

In these five chapters, we attempt to provide the basics of the Workshop and the reasons we conduct it as we do. We also try to communicate the tremendous energy and enthusiasm that this Workshop generates year-in and year-out. This is what sustains our own interest in the Workshop despite our having done it repeatedly. For us and for the many past participants, the experience is a source of growth.

These chapters may give the impression that the Workshop is a finely tuned and well orchestrated event. Yet every time we offer one, we introduce new elements, relying on our past experience and feedback from participants to make these changes. We hope that the reader will connect any difference in tone and writing of the chapters with the flexibility and spontaneity that also characterize the Workshop. Year after year, each group of participants creates a dynamic that is unique, and this leads us to try ideas and approaches outside of a seemingly well-articulated and rigid routine. Our hope is that the reader will take this as a sign that the format of the Workshop presented and the activities described are not prescriptive and need not be adopted in their entirety. We know that every context may be different and as such will require a different approach.

3

ANALYSIS OF COURSE CONTENT

Cheryl Amundsen, Alenoush Saroyan, and Janet Donald

Monday brings the participants of the Course Design and Teaching Workshop together for the first time. A sense of anticipation can be felt as those in the room chat with one another over coffee and muffins. The professors who have come to participate in the Workshop have committed a full workweek of their time and have high expectations about what they will learn and its usefulness to them. We, the instructors and the co-instructors, are keenly aware of this.

An ice-breaker activity starts the morning as a way for participants to get to know one another. We will, after all, be spending the next five days together! We use different techniques for this purpose. For instance, we ask individuals to pair up and learn a little bit about each other, then take turns introducing partners to the group. Or, we ask each person to recall a memorable instance about teaching and describe it to the next person. We then move to the day's first task: introducing the idea of course design. By course design, we mean taking a reasoned approach to teaching so that the multiple aspects of teaching (e.g., planning course content, classroom, or online activities; giving assignments and exams) are directly and clearly linked to student learning. We share with participants a simple representation of the course design process that we have developed (Figure 3.1). The large circle relates content (top) by means of arrows to learning outcome (right), instructional strategy (bottom), and evaluation (left). Student learning is prominently placed at the center of the circle and is thereby directly linked to all aspects of the course design process. The context of instruction surrounds the circle since it, too, directly influences the course design process represented inside the circle. This simple representation allows participants to understand the pathway we will follow for the five days of the Workshop.

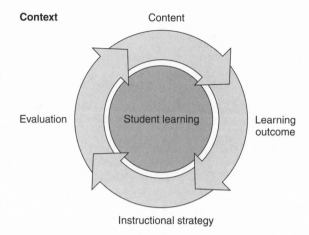

Figure 3.1 Concept map of course design and teaching process.

We begin with the perspective of each participant, concentrating on the content of the course chosen to be developed during the Workshop. We want participants to see the course as a coherent whole and think about the subject matter from the perspective of learning about it. Our goals for this first day are threefold—to support participants in the following:

1. To examine the content of their course by identifying and describing the important course concepts and the relationships among them

2. To become explicit about the content of their course

3. To elucidate to the extent possible the role or position of the course in the academic program

We start with analysis and clarification of course content for two reasons. First, we think it important to begin with an aspect that is most familiar to the majority of the participants, where most feel they have a good deal of expertise. Subject-matter expertise for most participants is a source of passion, enthusiasm, and confidence, and a matter of professional self-identity. This is evident in the way we typically refer to ourselves as, for example, an "economist" or an "educational psychologist" or a "physicist." Deciding on content is the part of course planning with which participants can most readily relate. Taking comfort in their subject-matter expertise from the beginning of the Workshop places the participants in a secure position to start. From this point, they can extend their pedagogical knowledge to plan and implement instruction that will support student learning. The second reason we begin with analysis and clarification of course content is that it prepares the ground for consideration of student learning. Once the content of the course is sorted out in the mind of the participant and can be clearly explained to others, learning outcomes (and often other aspects of course design) become more evident and can be more easily articulated than they would have been earlier. When we address learning outcomes in day two of the Workshop (see Chapter 4), participants are encouraged to ensure congruency between the concept map they create on Monday and the learning outcomes they develop on Tuesday. They are prompted to ask themselves the following questions: "Given this content, what do I want my students to take away?" "What kind of learning do I expect students to achieve now that the content is clear to me?"

The process we use in the Workshop for the analysis of course content is concept mapping. In the next several paragraphs, we discuss some of the literature pertaining to concept mapping, and we identify the reasons we believe it to be a powerful activity that supports professors in the analysis of their thinking about course content and ultimately student learning. The remainder of the chapter describes specifically how we go about teaching participants the utility of concept mapping and the steps we suggest they follow in constructing their maps. There has been a handful of participants who have not found concept mapping to be a meaningful way to think about their course. We support these individuals in accomplishing the goal of content analysis through other means that better match their thinking (e.g., standard outlining techniques, image mapping, and the like).

Concept Mapping: A Tool for Representing Course Content

The idea of a "concept map" brings to mind, for many, a set of boxes or circles connected by lines, typically in one of two arrangements. One is a spiderweblike arrangement with the focal concept in the center, connected by lines to a number of nodes, or groupings. Each node, in turn, displays a "more" major concept surrounded by "less" major concepts. A second common format is more hierarchical and sequential. Here, the more inclusive concepts or terms are placed at the top of the map and the more specific, less inclusive concepts are placed below. The resulting image looks like an upside down tree (Novak & Gowin, 1984). The concept maps produced by participants in the Workshop may resemble one of these formats—or they may not. We use an unstructured form of concept mapping to allow the utmost freedom for participants to represent their thinking. The purpose is to uncover the participant's thinking about the overall concepts in the course, the nature of the relationships among these concepts and the course as a whole. Thus, we pay attention to both the internal integrity (representation of concepts and links among them) and the external integrity (overall structure and shape) of the concept map. The true test of the comprehensiveness of a concept map is that a participant can see every key element of his or her course in the map and can use it to effectively describe the course to someone else. Each example provided in the figures that appear later in the chapter reflects the unique perspective of the individual who created the concept map.

Our understanding of the significance of the nature of course concepts and the relationships among them has been most influenced by the research of Janet Donald, a member of the Centre for University Teaching and Learning (CUTL) and one of the authors featured in this book. In her work with McGill University professors from a variety of disciplines, she has employed a form of concept mapping as well as other methods to examine the structure of knowledge in specific disciplines and courses. Her premise is that the terms or concepts used to describe phenomena in a discipline constitute the most basic level of understanding of that discipline (Donald, 2002).

In an early publication investigating course knowledge structures, Donald (1983) defined a concept as a unit of thought or element of knowledge that allows experiences to be organized. Concepts can exist at various levels of generality and abstraction; they may be simple or complex. Novak (1998) suggests that concept maps are "a good way to help a teacher organize knowledge for instruction, and a good way for students to find the key concepts and principles in lectures, readings, or other instructional material (p. 27)." We would add that concepts are not discrete elements but are related to other concepts and reflect an element of knowledge development.

In the courses examined by Donald, the purpose was to uncover the overall structure of knowledge in each course. She relied on the identified major concepts and relationships among them to achieve her goal. One interesting finding of this study is that there were disciplinary differences in the format of the course concept maps. The physical sciences tended to be hierarchical, with branches from more to less important concepts and with more links among the concepts. This suggests tighter relationships among the concepts. In the social sciences, webs or clusters of concepts linked to a pivot concept constituted the most common format. Among the humanities courses, a linear or loose block was more common; concepts exhibited greater independence. Differences were also noted in the types of relationships depicted. There was a higher percentage of dependency (procedural, logical, or causal) relationships among major course concepts in the knowledge structures of science courses. In contrast, in both the social sciences and the humanities courses, a higher percentage of similarity (associative, functional, or structural) relationships was found among key course concepts.

There are learning implications that follow from this research for students who become cognizant of the conceptual structure of their courses. Analysis of the relationships among concepts suggests that the preferred learning strategy in physical science courses, for instance, would be one of learning all of the concepts in order to understand the tightly linked structure of knowledge. Students in social science courses, on the other hand, would have an important learning cue if they recognized a pivot concept and grouped others around it. Students in humanities courses would be wise to focus on individual concepts that are less closely linked to each other. These findings suggest that if professors share with students their understanding of the structure of the course content, student learning will be enhanced. Many of the professors who have participated in the Workshop have done just that. They have told us of using the concept maps (or a form of them) that they developed in the Workshop with their students in a variety of ways. Some have used the concept map on the first day of class to provide an overview of the course to students. Others have first presented a "bare bones" version of the concept map to students, then added to the map progressively as they moved through the course. Still others have asked students to contribute to "fleshing out" a basic concept map so the course can be tailored in various degrees to the background knowledge, experience, and learning goals of the particular group of students taking the course each semester. One professor noted that it was like a light went on for his students when he explained his concept map to them.

Many participants in the Workshop have noted that the clarity in their thinking that results from identifying key course concepts often has profound implications for how they view teaching the course. Donald's work suggests why this may be the case. In each course investigated, Donald (1983) undertook a detailed examination of all course materials, lectures, assignments, and examinations to find frequently mentioned ideas or concepts that appeared to serve a main or linking purpose in the course. The professor then selected all those that he or she considered relevant to the course. From these, the most important or key concepts in terms of their main or linking role in the course were selected. Then, using a tree structuring procedure (Shavelson & Geeslin, 1974), the professor identified the closest or most dominant relationships among the key concepts. The task involved first linking the two most closely related key concepts, then linking the key concept most closely related to one of these, and so on, until all key concepts were represented on the map. Participating professors found this procedure one of the most useful clarification techniques in the study.

In her program of research, Donald (1986, 1987, 2002) also uncovered connections between characteristics of key course concepts and the level of difficulty of the course for students. The sheer number of concepts students were expected to learn and the degree to which concepts were concrete or abstract affected course difficulty. This work suggests that for an individual professor, a deeper understanding of the nature of the concepts in the discipline, and specifically in his or her courses, might well support a better understanding of student learning difficulties.

In the Workshop, our primary purpose in using concept mapping is to support participants in clarifying the course content for themselves and potentially for their students. Yet we know that the value of this activity is far greater for most participants. Over the years, we have been fascinated by observing that most participants produce multiple drafts of their concept map throughout the five days of the Workshop, and sometimes after its conclusion. We are curious to know what motivates and encourages this repeated revision and reconceptualization. The concept mapping process described in most of the literature employs procedures that lead to highly structured maps rather than the procedure we use that leads to unstructured maps. Still, some clues are offered by the existing literature. For instance, Trochim (1989), who has extensively examined the restructuring of knowledge depicted in successively constructed concept maps, describes concept mapping as not only a pictorial representation of thinking but also a tool the map creator can use to determine the relevance, importance, and appropriateness of her or his portrayed thinking. Certainly, we have observed that when participants engage in the concept mapping activity, they inevitably become engaged in a discourse with themselves as they try to sort out what is important and what is not. New insights often result. Adler (1996) suggests that the activity of concept mapping in itself may assist the development of complex conceptual frameworks about teaching and learning.

We now turn to the process of how we go about teaching participants in the Workshop the utility of concept mapping for analyzing course content and the steps we suggest they follow in constructing their maps. The large-group session, which takes place each morning of the Workshop, provides an introduction to the concept mapping process. Participants actually develop their concept maps in the small-group sessions that follow later in the morning and continue in the afternoon.

Large-Group Session

In this first large-group session of the Workshop, we ask participants to focus on the step in the course design process that involves representing course content (Figure 3.1). We explain that although there are several approaches to representing course content described in the literature, we will use a relatively unstructured form of concept mapping. We introduce concept mapping as a visual map of the key ideas in a course.

One of the co-instructors then presents a concept map he or she has developed. Typically, the multiple drafts that have led to the final one are also shown. This shows how the mapper's thinking changed from one draft to the next. The presenter may also emphasize that the map is never considered "final" or static because thinking will evolve with time and subsequent offerings of the course. These presentations by co-instructors are critically important for a number of reasons. Concept mapping is a hands-on, manipulative activity that some participants initially do not feel comfortable doing. Discussion of concept mapping by other professors clearly lends credibility to the nature of the exercise. Co-instructors refer to their own experience in developing their maps—both the travails, since this is not an easy task, and the rewards. Seeing multiple drafts of the presenter's concept map and not just the completed "polished" product provides a realistic idea of what participants can expect from their own initial efforts (Figure 3.2). All of this generally makes the task seem more manageable. Simply listening to another professor describe the process of analysis followed and the meaning derived from the exercise is reassuring. Participants generally sense from the co-instructor that clarifying one's personal orientation toward course content and using it as the basis for course planning—rather than using textbook materials or another instructor's syllabus—is liberating and highly motivating.

We then present three more examples of concept maps with highly differing formats from previous years. These are reproduced in the participants' binders (Figure 3.3, Figure 3.4, and Figure 3.5) for use as guides throughout (and after) the Workshop. The same examples are referred to again as the design process progresses. The discussion that arises around these examples sets the scene for the day's task. The first thing that participants note is that the process produces very different-looking concept maps. The openness and fluidity of our concept mapping process generally becomes even more obvious by hearing the co-instructor's presentation and by seeing these three examples.

Participants start to understand that their particular disciplinary perspective as well as their unique view of the course under development can be accommodated—and so they are encouraged. We have become convinced that this individual orientation to the course content is vital to a participant since it is from this personal perspective that a professor will be able to most meaningfully engage with students in the learning process. We tell participants that we have repeatedly observed two professors from the same discipline express differences in how they would construct a concept map for the same course and consider this to be a positive situation.

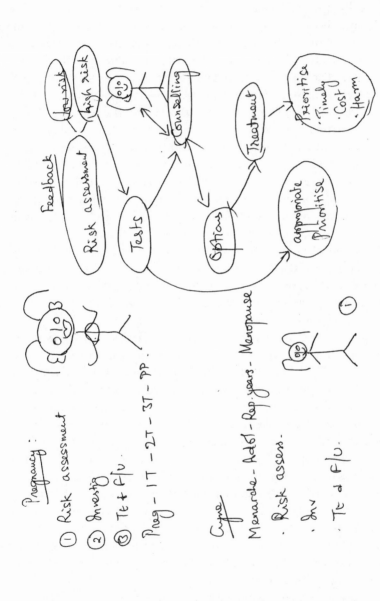

Figure 3.2 Multiple drafts of concept map of course in gynecology, *Introduction to Risk Assessment*, by Srinivasan Krishnavurthy. (*Reprinted with written permission from Dr. Srinivasan Krishnavurthy*)

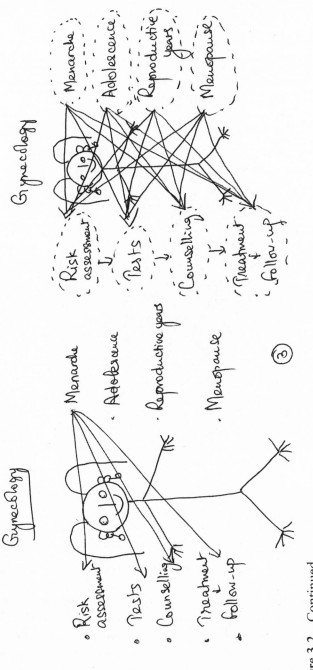

Figure 3.2 Continued

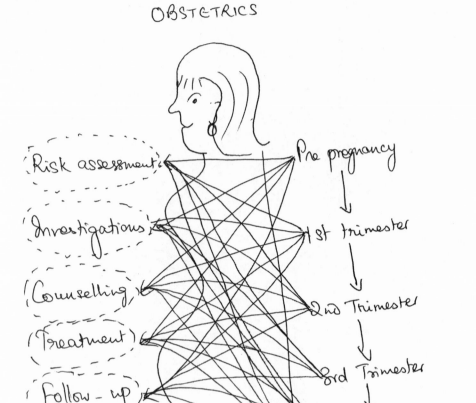

OBSTETRICS

Figure 3.2   Continued

We want participants to leave the large-group session with the understanding that the *process* of developing the concept map is of primary importance, more so than the *product* of the activity, the map itself. At the close of the large-group session, discussion drifts out into the hallway as participants help themselves to coffee, tea, or juice and head off to their first small-group session.

Figure 3.2 Continued

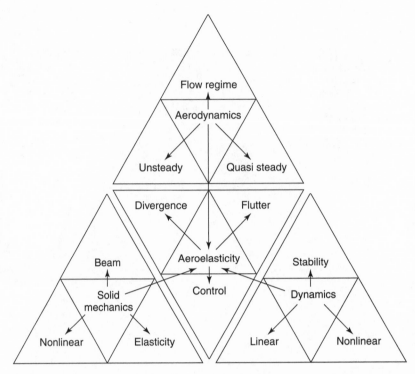

Figure 3.3 Concept map of course, Aeroelasticity, by Hekmat Alighanbari. (*Reprinted with written permission from Professor Hekmat Alighanbari*)

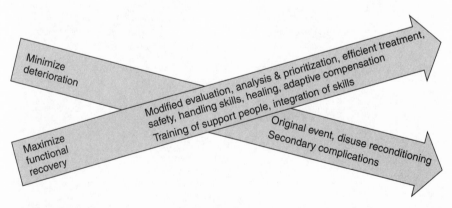

Figure 3.4 Concept map for *Physical Therapy Course on Advanced Neurology* by Karen Koopferstock. (*Reprinted with written permission from Karen Koopferstock, PT*)

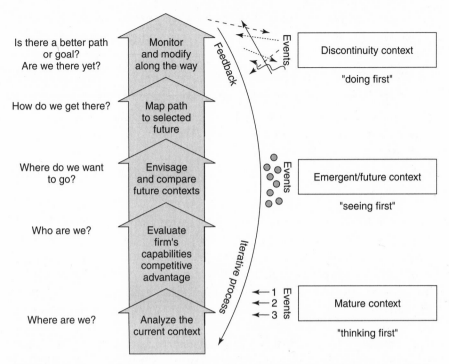

Figure 3.5   Concept map of course, *Navigating in a World of Organizations,* by Jan Jorgensen. (*Reprinted with written permission from Professor Jan Jorgensen*)

Small-Group Session: Morning

The first small-group session follows the large-group session and continues until lunchtime. We generally try to limit the size of the small groups to no more than six participants to allow for maximum discussion and adequate peer feedback. Time is given this first day to personal introductions, going beyond what was possible in the large-group ice-breaker activity. Typically, these small working groups become very cohesive and supportive, to the extent that participants are often disappointed to leave their groups at the end of the week. (Some groups continue to meet periodically after the conclusion of the Workshop.)

We begin the concept mapping activity by suggesting that participants follow some initial steps. The text of the handout we provide is as follows:

1. Write down everything that comes to mind that you consider important in the course you are designing.

2. Go back and read through what you have written and try to reduce the number of ideas or concepts by circling those you consider most important.

3. Write each of the circled concepts on a Post-it note.

4. Sort the Post-it notes into meaningful clusters or groupings.

5. Label each cluster and write the labels on a Post-it note. These labels will probably reflect the key concepts you will use in your map, but this may change.

6. Arrange these labels (key concepts) in a way that is meaningful to you on a file folder.

(We use file folders rather than the table or paper for portability and sturdiness.) The importance here is the relationship among the concepts, so decide how best to represent these relationships. You may want to use lines to connect one or more concepts. You may also want to label the connecting lines to more precisely describe the relationships. Use any of the other terms that you have written on Post-it notes in your arrangement, if this makes sense to you.

The majority of participants follow these steps, although some may proceed in an idiosyncratic manner. As previously mentioned, some individuals find concept mapping incongruent with the way they think and they elect to follow another process to analyze the content of their course. This is not a problem. Our focus throughout the Workshop is to describe the goal (in this case, analysis of course content), the rationale behind the goal, and suggested steps for achieving the goal. We want participants, however, to make their own sense of the exercise, put it into their own words, and use a process meaningful to them to achieve the goal. Broadly speaking, we want to encourage participants to move from thinking about a list of lecture topics in a course syllabus to thinking in ways that better reflect course content as an integrated whole.

The instructor and co-instructor begin to circulate among participants once they have something down on paper and probe for explanation and justification. We listen for consistency between what is said and what is reflected on the concept map. Some get "stuck" with the process. For instance, they may feel that the complexity of a map renders it incomprehensible to others, or conversely, that a simplistic map may no longer be an accurate representation of the course. Some struggle with deciding whether to include more minor concepts and deliberate as to how best to depict them. Usually this happens when a decision has to be made concerning reasonable breadth and depth for a course at a particular level (e.g., introductory, undergraduate). Some may create a structure that, upon further reflection, they do not see as an accurate characterization of the nature of their course content. This often happens when the first attempt results in a listlike or hierarchical structure. The problem then is to find an alternative way of representation. Others find deciding on concepts relatively easy but representing the relationships among concepts more difficult. A simple line connecting two or more concepts may be seen as insufficient to represent the complexity of the relationship. We may ask, in this case, for reconsideration of the overall structure or shape of the map, and encourage the use of this aspect of the map to further communicate relationships among key concepts or in the nature of the course content. Often by returning to the three examples in the binders (Figure 3.3, Figure 3.4, and Figure 3.5) and being reminded that there is both internal and external integrity to these three examples, participants have sufficient food for thought to be able to continue. Issues like these can be resolved, in most cases, by asking for further explanation about what the participant is trying to depict.

Some participants are delighted with their first draft; others are neutral, perhaps deep in thought about the changes or refinements they want to make. Some may be unsatisfied. In our experience, the unstructured nature of the exercise appeals to most, but this is never an easy task. The exercise can be particularly difficult for those who are developing a course for the first time or those who have taught the same course for many years without having made many changes.

The next step is for participants to pair up and explain their concept maps to a colleague in the small group. We display the following suggested progression for this activity:

1. Explain the thinking behind your concept map to your partner.
2. Your partner should listen to determine how well your explanation fits with what is represented in your concept map. Inconsistencies should be pointed out and suggestions to address them discussed.
3. Switch partners and repeat the process.

This activity typically results in lively discussion. The small groups are intentionally composed of participants from different disciplines. Discussion is therefore almost always between a subject-matter expert (the map creator) and a colleague who is not an expert in the same subject matter and who has a perspective more akin to that of a student. This is the first occasion in the Workshop when we intentionally set up a teacher-learner dynamic. Activities such as this that place participants in the role of both "instructor" and "learner" in the course design process occur throughout the Workshop and are essential in helping participants to see through the eyes of their students.

Participants are asked to use the remaining time before lunch to revise their maps as they see appropriate, taking into consideration the comments and questions of their colleagues. We explain that in the small-group session after lunch, they will be asked to present and explain their concept maps to the small group as a whole. Each participant is asked to prepare an overhead transparency of his or her concept map for projection onto a screen for all to see. Some participants prefer to reconstruct their concept maps using software applications on their laptop computers.

We have experimented with various software applications designed for concept mapping and we make these available to interested participants. Several Workshop facilitators are conversant with these applications and can offer examples of concept maps developed using them. We do not, however, routinely use software applications in the Workshop for two reasons. First, if participants have no experience with these applications, the time required to become sufficiently skilled to produce a first concept map would take us beyond the one day devoted to concept mapping. Second, unless participants are fairly experienced with these applications, initial drafts of the concept maps tend to be in the traditional form (i.e., hierarchical, or depicting several lesser concepts clustered around key concepts). In other words, the limitations imposed by the software applications themselves may lead a user into certain kinds of formats. These formats or structures may result in a first concept map that is less true to the nature of the course content than one that is first developed on paper. For some individuals, however, moving to an electronic version once the initial draft is done on paper seems productive. This may enable easier depiction of aspects that would be more difficult to do by hand. In this case, the map creator still begins with his or her own structure rather than one imposed by a software application.

Monday's lunch is hosted by CUTL, allowing all participants to become better acquainted and move closer to developing a sense of community.

Small-Group Session: Afternoon

The afternoon session is devoted to microteaching, an activity in which each participant has five to ten minutes to show and explain his or her concept map to the small group while being videotaped. (Microteaching takes place on each of the first four days of the Workshop.) During this afternoon session on Monday, the procedures for microteaching and for providing feedback are explained. We particularly emphasize the significance of giving and receiving constructive feedback to ensure that group members function well as a support group (see Appendix C).

Each presentation is videotaped so that both the presentation and the discussion about the concept map are included. (In correspondence sent to participants prior to the Workshop, they are asked to bring a blank videotape for use during their microteaching sessions.) These presentations always create much interest. The opportunity to see how colleagues have decided to depict the content of their course and hear their explanation for what they have done is fascinating—for all concerned. Moreover, experiencing an array of courses from multiple disciplines is interesting in itself. Almost always members of the small group (including the instructor and co-instructor) have suggestions on how to bring the visual representation (the concept map) into closer alignment with the verbal explanation. Frequently, members of the group go to the chalkboard to draw possible changes—sometimes it is the presenter, inspired by comments from the group. Many participants express surprise that they can learn so much about their own course from the questions and comments of those in other disciplines and from listening to other presentations. In addition to verbal comments, group members also fill in feedback sheets that are passed along to the presenter (see Appendix D). Keeping to the timetable so that everyone has a chance to present—in the face of such enthusiastic discussion—is a challenge for the instructor and co-instructor!

Participants are asked to take home their videotape and feedback sheets for private review and reflection. Each participant will have revisions to consider based on comments and questions from members of the small group—recorded on the videotape and written on the feedback sheets. Equally important, all presenters have their own reflective writing to do. They are asked to record their impressions and note aspects to which they want to pay particular attention in subsequent presentations as they review their tapes that evening (see Appendix E). Participants are also asked to complete readings (listed in their binders) to further their knowledge about the analysis of course content.

The following day, many participants report that they have generated several more drafts of their concept map. Time is always allotted in the small groups to share and discuss evolving drafts. Typically, at least a few individuals change the entire focus of the course they are designing as a result of the concept mapping activity. We recall one professor of anthropology who discovered, with the help of his small-group colleagues, that he wanted to focus on process rather than information. He revised his concept map to highlight the process of analyzing hunter-gatherer societies rather than focusing on information about the hunter-gatherer societies. Through the analytic process, he surmised, students would uncover the information they needed to understand these societies. Many individuals continue to revise their map throughout the five days of the Workshop as they consider other aspects of the course design process. We encourage this as consistent with the critical notion of checks and balances within the design process. In fact, throughout the five days of the Workshop, participants are asked to consider the coherence or alignment between the design step on which they are currently working and those that have come before. We encourage participants to number the various iterations of their concept map so they have a record of the progression of their thinking. We have experimented in the last two years with an activity to both highlight the usefulness of concept mapping in clarifying thinking and promote more interaction among the small-group members. On Thursday, we ask for the first and last versions of maps from those willing to provide them. These are complemented with others we have saved from past Workshops. The first drafts are put up in the large-group meeting room and participants are invited there for refreshments. Each participant gets a copy of a last draft corresponding to one that is on the wall. (We are careful not to give an individual a map from his or her own small group.) Matching first and last drafts is sometimes easy and sometimes difficult—but the activity always clearly shows the extent to which thinking can change in just a few days.

The first day ends with a great surge of energy and enthusiasm. The small groups have begun to "form," and there is a general sense that expectations of this Workshop will be met and the days ahead will be fruitful. One of the observations we have made in conducting this Workshop is that many participants have not had much opportunity to examine their own teaching and discuss teaching with colleagues. Many describe discussions about teaching in their departments as being perfunctory—not really discussions at all. Others report that the teaching norms are quite explicit in their units, and there is little interest in thinking outside them. So the workshop is for some the first time they have engaged in a teaching development activity as an intellectual endeavor, enriched by discussions with colleagues who are also grappling with the intricacies of course design and teaching.

References

Adler, S. A. (1996). On case method and classroom management. *Action in Teacher Education, 18*(3), 33–43.

Donald, J. G. (1983). Knowledge structures: Methods for exploring course content. *Journal of Higher Education, 54*(1), 31–41.

Donald, J. G. (1986). Knowledge and the university curriculum. *Higher Education,* *15*(3-4), 267–282.

Donald, J. G. (1987). Learning schemata: Methods of representing cognitive, content and curriculum structures in education. *Instructional Science, 16,* 187–211.

Donald, J. G. (2002). *Learning to think: Disciplinary perspectives.* San Francisco: Jossey-Bass.

Novak, J. (1998). *Learning, creating and using knowledge.* Mahwah, NJ: Lawrence Erlbaum.

Novak, J., & Gowin, D. B. (1984). *Learning how to learn.* New York: Cambridge University Press.

Shavelson, R. J., & Geeslin, W. E. (1974). A method for examining subject matter structure in instruction. *Journal of Instructional Learning, 4,* 199–218.

Trochim, W. M. K. (1989). An introduction to concept mapping for planning and evaluation. *Evaluation and Program Planning, 12,* 1–16.

4

CLARIFYING LEARNING

Janet Donald

On Tuesday, anticipation is evident in the high decibel level as participants arrive discussing the development of their concept map and the experience of viewing their videotaped presentation from Monday. For Workshop facilitators and participants, today's task is difficult: to combine the perspective of the subject-matter expert with the role of the instructor as a facilitator of learning. To do this, we must first examine the instructional environment from the point of view of students. Instructors need a sense of who their students are, their level of preparedness, and their expectations. The general question posed is, How does a professor help students become responsible learners?

Our goals are, first, to understand what our students' priorities are and to situate them in comparison with those of other North American post-secondary students. We then want to articulate learning outcomes that are consistent with the subject matter of the course and with student preparedness. Finally, we want to discuss potential higher-order learning outcomes and the kinds of instructional and learning strategies needed to achieve them. To reach these goals requires that participants

- Examine and possibly change their conception of teaching.
- Assume broadened responsibility by taking into account the many factors affecting student learning.
- Begin to create a framework for facilitating learning in their course (which will be further developed on Wednesday and Thursday).

The assigned readings for participants on Monday address the characteristics of undergraduate students and introduce the topic of learning goals. These readings act as a stimulus for the discussion in the large-group session. We define learning outcomes for participants as "statements describing the learning students are expected to achieve in the course." The purpose of learning outcomes is to

- Clarify instructors' expectations of their students' learning.
- Convey to students clear expectations about their learning.

Large-Group Session

The large-group session begins by introducing the need to match course content to what the learner should know and be able to do by the end of the course. The shift in focus from course content, which was addressed on Monday, to student learning requires several steps. We pose this initial question: What is the most important learning students should accomplish in your course? Participants are asked to take five minutes to think about what this question means to them, then to write down their thoughts. They are then asked to discuss their results with the person sitting next to them and to determine *why* they wrote down what they did.

In the general discussion that follows, participants' responses are recorded by one of the instructors and we attempt to roughly categorize the statements into kinds of learning. These statements will stay posted for the rest of the day so participants can refer to them. We also use these statements to provide an initial framework for talking about learning outcomes in the small working groups that follow. The statements range from specific content-oriented goals such as "understand how policies affect practice in providing healthcare" or "become familiar with compositional techniques used in 20th century music" to more general learning goals such as "involve students in evaluating their own learning." The categories we create to group statements may be as diverse as "knowledge of essential terminology," "application of theories to specific situations," or "student self-regulation." The variety of examples helps participants to see how many different kinds of learning outcomes they might consider; it also provides the opportunity for them to question what kinds of outcomes are appropriate.

We then provide an example by referring to the intended learning outcomes for the Workshop, which are included in each participant's binder.

At the end of this workshop, you should be able to do the following:

1. Describe the entire course development process.

2. Describe in detail one process through which the content of a course could be determined.

3. Articulate clear and appropriate learning outcomes.

4. Assess various teaching strategies and select appropriate ones for your specified learning outcomes.

5. Describe methods of evaluation and select appropriate ones for your specified learning outcomes.

6. Plan at least two methods to evaluate teaching.

7. Demonstrate skill and self-confidence in making instructional decisions.

8. Demonstrate skill and self-confidence in making presentations and leading discussions.

9. Develop a complete course plan.

We also provide the intended learning outcomes for this day of the Workshop so that participants can begin to understand that learning outcomes can range from general (e.g., an entire course) to specific (e.g., a single class session).

At the end of this session, you should be able to

• Establish your responsibility as an instructor.

• Establish the responsibilities of students in your course.

• Choose a suitable framework to guide you in developing learning outcomes.

• Write learning outcomes related to the concept map in your course.

We initially focus on the first two learning outcomes—although more general in scope, they are essential for framing the task on this day of the Workshop. We begin the discussion by using our research on student priorities to describe who our students are and how they actually spend their time.

Knowing Our Students

We use a sample of more than five hundred students at our university in six courses from undergraduate programs in arts, science, engineering, and education as a point of reference (Donald & Dubuc, 1999). Although these students report spending a considerable amount of time per week both on studying and homework (a mean of 13 hours), and only slightly lesser time socializing with friends and partying (9 + 3 hours) (Table 4.1).

Table 4.1   Student Priorities: Mean Time Spent Per Week in Different Activities

Priority	Mean hours per week
Studying/homework	13
Socializing with friends	9
Exercising/sports	4
Watching television	4
Partying	3
Hobbies	3
Paid work	3
Student clubs/groups	1
Volunteer work	<1
Talking with teachers outside of class	<1/2

Other extracurricular activities take up less time per week (3 hours in exercising or playing sports or in watching television; three hours in hobbies). The small amount of time that students spend each week working for pay (3 hours) or volunteering (less than one hour) is atypical for North American students according to the National Survey of Student Engagement (NSSE, 2000), but the time spent talking to teachers (less than one-half hour per week) *is* typical. Differences occur across programs in some extracurricular activities—for example, education students report working for pay six hours per week on average, while science students report working for pay less than two hours per week. However, students do not differ in the time they spend exercising, watching television, in clubs, or in talking with teachers. Showing this table allows participants to confront the reality of their students' lives and take into account other activities that may demand undergraduates' attention.

In response to the data in Table 4.1, participant professors frequently raise questions about differences in academic demands across programs and whether nonacademic activities are more important to students than their academic activities. For example, science and engineering professors note that their students need to spend more than 20 hours per week studying to keep up with their assignments. Science and engineering students report spending more time studying—15 to 16 hours—than other students; arts students report 11 hours of study time per week on average. These same arts students report

Table 4.2   A Framework for Understanding Student Epistemologies

	Most entering students	*Most under- graduates*	*Some seniors*	*Some graduates*
Epistemology	Dualistic	Relativistic	Multiplistic	Committed
	Absolute knowing	Transitional knowing	Independent knowing	Contextual knowing
Knowledge is	Certain or absolute	Partially certain and partially uncertain	Uncertain	Constructed based on evidence
Role of learner	Obtain knowledge from professor	Understand knowledge	Create own perspective	Integrate and apply knowledge
Role of instructor expected by students	Communicate knowledge	Aim for understanding	Promote exchange of evidence	Promote evaluative discussion of perspectives

spending ten hours socializing, while the science and engineering students report spending seven to eight hours. Does socializing with friends include shoptalk or discussion of assignments? Professors of undergraduate courses have wryly noted that students tend to categorize their time into schoolwork, sleep, and social life, and pick only two of the three. Others note that peak time for student online access to the library or teaching assistants is 3 A.M. This discussion has a bonding effect on the participants as they realize that they face similar challenges arising from the life space of their students.

We then describe a framework for understanding student epistemologies, defining these as theories of knowledge and students' roles as learners. The framework is based on the work of William Perry (1970, 1981) and Marcia Baxter Magolda (1992). It is a taxonomy of how students interpret their learning experience and how their ways of knowing or thinking evolve during the undergraduate years (Table 4.2). Perry found that students entering the university had a dualistic view of learning: Knowledge is right or wrong and the professor is the authority. As students experience the university, they move through relativistic and multiplistic stages, where knowledge is uncertain and opinion rules, to a stage of commitment where some ideas are held to be more valid than others based on evidence.

Baxter Magolda uses a slightly different terminology and focuses on changes in students' construction of meaning or ways of knowing—from absolute knowing through transitional and independent knowing to contextual knowing. Baxter Magolda found that most students (68%) at her university entered in a stage of absolute knowing: They considered knowledge to be certain or absolute and conceived their role as learners to be limited to obtaining knowledge from the instructor. The remaining 32% of entering students were in a stage of transitional knowing, considering knowledge to be partially certain and partially uncertain, with their role being to understand knowledge. In these two stages, students depict themselves as passive recipients of their professors' wisdom.

During their senior year, some students (16%) displayed independent knowing, in which knowledge is considered uncertain, everyone has his or her own beliefs, and students are expected to think for themselves, share views with others, and create their own perspective. This percentage increased to 57% the year following graduation. Only in the year following graduation did a small number of students (12%) reach a stage of contextual knowing, in which knowledge is judged on the basis of evidence in context, and the student's role is to think through problems and to integrate and apply knowledge. These findings suggest that two-thirds of entering students limit their role as learners to obtaining knowledge, and the majority will not be actively constructing meaning (independent knowing) until after they have graduated.

The results of these studies are revelatory and alarming to participants, but also highly useful since they describe what students' expectations are likely to be and what students' expectations of professors are therefore likely to be. For example, entering dualistic students may not be prepared to understand and think for themselves. These students may therefore experience considerable distress if called on to argue for a particular point of view and to base the argument on evidence, a challenge beyond their level of intellectual development. Professors' failure to recognize and respond to students' level of intellectual evolution may lead to their disengagement rather than engagement—the task is beyond their comprehension and extant learning strategies.

The pedagogical quandary is how to lead students to develop these capabilities, which is what students claim they expect from their university education (Donald & Denison, 2001). In a study in which we asked students to tell us what criteria described student quality on entry to the university, during time at the university, and on graduation, they affirmed that although they consider the ability to analyze, synthesize, and think critically highly important, the importance increases from the time they enter the university to during their studies and then upon graduation. Students expect gains in quality of their thinking, which has implications for programs of instruction. For example, what assignments are appropriate to develop thinking abilities at different stages in a program? More immediately, the need to provide guidance to students so they know they are expected to think and participate actively in their courses becomes imperative—the importance of helping students learn to learn is brought out here.

There is a certain degree of comfort in knowing that student epistemologies parallel the shift in epistemology that occurred in universities during the period of the enlightenment (Donald, 2002). In the Middle Ages, scholastics had assumed a fixed body of knowledge that they defined and over which they held authority (Johnston, 1998). The scientific revolution challenged the notion of fixed knowledge; the revolution was based on the assumption that knowledge was an expanding and open system. From authority vested in the church, validity was now found in scientific measurement, and dissent was integral to the process of testing hypotheses. The shift in epistemology changed the role of the university from curator or reproducer of knowledge to creator of new knowledge, a major transformation that places value on research and requires a change to what is now known as a constructivist view of knowledge.

For the individual learner, this view means that we each construct our own understanding of larger public bodies of knowledge. Our understanding will be constructed according to and consistent with our available framework of knowledge. It further means that as instructors, we need to take into account the prior knowledge of our students and explain to students the importance of their active participation in the learning process. The challenge is to understand our students' starting point and at the same time work toward a more constructivist view of learning.

The discussion in the large group therefore moves to participants' estimating in pairs what kinds of epistemologies the students might have in the courses they are developing, and what kinds of strategies might be used to explain to students the role they need to play as learners. Often, answers to the question posed at the beginning of the session: "What is the most important learning students should accomplish in your course?" respond to the issue of helping students to participate actively in their learning. For example, the answer written on the chalkboard, "involve students in evaluating their own learning," is directly related to active participation and higher-order learning.

Student Goals and Learning Outcomes

In the large-group discussion participants, having considered students' perspectives on learning and their actual behavior, move on to comparing student and course goals and outcomes. We refer to the North American research literature on postsecondary learning to place in context the need for explaining learning outcomes to students, and we drive home the importance of doing so. For example, in an analysis of trends and implications for learning and teaching in the 21st century, Baxter Magolda and Terenzini (1999) point out that higher-order thinking skills and the ability to make up one's own mind are essential learning outcomes in a world in which multiple perspectives abound and right action is often in dispute. Important learning outcomes at the postsecondary level include not only complex cognitive skills but also an ability to apply knowledge to practical problems, an appreciation of human differences, and an integrated identity.

We know at the same time that students' learning goals have changed markedly over the last 30 years from intellectual to vocational (Astin, 1998). This presents another kind of instructional predicament because student goals mediate between what instructors intend students to learn and what students actually learn. Furthermore, we have found that those students whose goals are vocationally oriented are less likely to pursue goals of thinking and evaluating (Donald & Dubuc, 1999). Vocational goals tend to be negatively related to higher-order learning. In a broadly based study of professors' and students' learning goals in more than 100,000 courses in eight fields, Cashin (1988) found that despite the rhetoric surrounding teaching higher-order skills such as critical thinking and problem solving, many disciplines remain focused on imparting factual knowledge. As might be envisaged, students report that they make progress in learning what their professors emphasize. The most positive finding from this research is that higher-order learning goals, such as problem solving and learning principles, generalizations, or theories, are overall considered important by faculty. Thus, in the large-group discussion, the challenge is thrown out that to have students achieve higher-order learning goals, faculty need to go beyond simply identifying these goals to developing ways to support students in reaching them.

We have found it useful to provide examples of several different frameworks, or taxonomies, of learning goals that participants may find suitable for their courses. Although these may be only briefly introduced in the large-group session due to time limitations, their introduction here allows the participants to register their familiarity with such frameworks or their need for further explanation. We start by describing the classic taxonomy of educational

Table 4.3   Examples of Learning Outcomes Using Taxonomies
of Educational Objectives

Cognitive domain	Learning outcome example
Knowledge	Give a broad definition of aeroelasticity
Comprehension	Explain physically the classic binary flutter
Application	Use the theory of seasonal adaptation to explain insect survival
Analysis	Classify insects into their correct orders and support your choice
Synthesis	Construct a divergent-controlled airfoil
Evaluation	Assess the strengths and weaknesses of various evaluation methods in relationship to your learning outcomes
Affective domain	Learning outcome example
Receiving	Be aware of patient needs
Responding	Participate in class discussion
Valuing commitment	Assume responsibility for organizing study group
Organizing a value system	Weigh alternatives for most effective learning outcomes
Characterization-philosophy	Practice a caring attitude toward clients
Psychomotor domain	Perform skill with proficiency

objectives in the cognitive domain (Bloom, 1956) and provide a handout of verbs such as *explain, interpret, analyze,* and *evaluate* that can be used to describe higher-order outcomes; we then ask participants to create an example from their course. We also provide examples from previously developed courses and examples of learning outcomes in the affective and psychomotor domain (Table 4.3).

To provide practice within a specific framework, we next ask participants to reconsider the most important goals they have for students in their course using this classic framework. We ask them to write at least two learning outcomes for their course, review them in pairs to identify domains and levels, and look for a match with their concept map. We find a wide range of reactions to the use of taxonomies; some participants consider them too explicit, and others want greater detail. The commentary leads us to a discussion of alternative models or frameworks to guide the production of learning outcomes.

As a first contrast to the classic taxonomy, we present a simplified version of learning outcomes in the cognitive domain that divides outcomes into knowing, understanding, and thinking (Erickson & Stommer, 1991). Examples of verbs that describe knowing are *define, label, recall,* and *relate.* Examples of verbs that describe understanding are *classify, explain, identify, interpret, review,* and *report.* Examples of verbs that describe thinking are *analyze, criticize, contrast, evaluate, propose, rate, solve, support,* and *synthesize.* We try to explain the importance of creating higher-order learning outcomes that involve student understanding and thinking. Two other frameworks are included in participant binders and are discussed in the large- or small-group sessions depending on time and interest. One is the working model of thinking processes developed from the postsecondary literature and tested in different disciplines in several universities, such as Stanford and Cambridge (Donald, 1992, 2002). It is a more detailed operational set of examples that apply directly to courses at the postsecondary level (Table 4.4).

Participants are able to see from this framework that they have choices in the detail or specificity with which they produce learning outcomes and that some outcomes may be more closely linked to their own discipline. The other framework is taken from the studies by Cashin and Downey (1995) on learning goals in different fields (Table 4.5). This set of learning goals is more broadly based but takes into account higher-order outcomes such as learning fundamental principles and generalizations or theories or learning to apply course material to improve rational thinking, problem solving, and decision making. Since this set of learning goals has been used to evaluate the level of instruction in many American universities, background is also provided on the emphasis different discipline place of these learning outcomes.

We have not quite finished in the large-group session. We have found it critical to return to the idea of why learning outcomes are important: because they focus on learning rather than teaching, and because they provide a lens for examining the mutual responsibilities of teacher and students. We also point out that there are different levels of learning outcomes for a program, for a course, for a class, or for an activity within a class—at increasing levels of detail. We note that we will focus on course and activity outcomes in the small-group session to follow.

Table 4.4 Working Model of Thinking Processes in Higher Education

DESCRIPTION (**PS, SM**)	Delineation or definition of a situation or form of a thing
Identify context (**E**)	Establish surrounding environment to create total picture
State conditions	State essential parts, prerequisites, or requirements
State facts	State known information, events that have occurred
State functions	State normal or proper activity of thing or specific duties
State assumptions (**CT**)	State suppositions, postulates, or propositions assumed
State goal	State ends, aims, objectives
SELECTION (**PS**)	Choice in preference to another or others
Choose relevant information (**E**)	Select information that is pertinent to the issue in question
Order information in importance	Rank, arrange in importance or according to significance
Identify critical elements	Determine units, parts, components that are important
Identify critical relations	Determine connections between things that are important
REPRESENTATION (**PS**)	Depiction through enactive, iconic, or symbolic means
Recognize organizing principles	Identify laws, methods, rules that arrange in systematic whole
Organize elements and relations	Arrange parts, connections between things into systematic whole
Illustrate elements and relations	Make clear by examples, the parts, connections between things

(*Continued*)

Table 4.4 (Continued)

Modify elements and relations	Change, alter, or qualify the parts, connections between things
INFERENCE (**E, H, CT, PS**)	Process of drawing conclusions from premises or evidence
Discover new relations between elements	Detect or expose connections between parts, units, components
Discover new relations between relations	Detect or expose connections between connections of things
Discover equivalences	Detect or expose equality in value, force, or significance
Categorize	Classify, arrange into parts
Order	Rank, sequence, arrange methodically
Change perspective	Alter view, vista, interrelations, significance of facts or info
Hypothesize	Suppose or form a proposition as basis for reasoning
SYNTHESIS (**PS**)	Composition of parts or elements into a complex whole
Combine parts to form a whole	Join, associate elements, components into system or pattern
Elaborate	Work out, complete with great detail, exactness, or complexity
Generate missing links	Produce or create what is lacking in sequence; fill in gap
Develop course of action	Work out or expand path, route, or direction to be taken
VERIFICATION (**E, H, CT, PS, SM**)	Confirmation of accuracy, coherence, consistency, correspondence
Compare alternative outcomes	Examine similarities or differences of results, consequences
Compare outcome to standard	Examine similarities, differences of results to a criterion

Table 4.4   (Continued)

Judge validity	Critically examine soundness, effectiveness by actual fact
Use feedback	Employ results to regulate, adjust, adapt
Confirm results	Establish or ratify conclusions, effects, outcomes or products

E: Expertise, **H:** Hermeneutics, **CT:** Critical Thinking, **PS:** Problem Solving, **SM:** Scientific Method.

Table 4.5   Examples of Learning Goals

Gaining factual knowledge

Learning fundamental principles, generalizations, or theories

Learning to apply course material to improve rational thinking, problem solving, and decision making

Discovering the implications of course material for understanding oneself

Developing specific competencies and points of view needed by professionals in the field

Developing skill in oral and written expression

Gaining a broader understanding and appreciation of intellectual-cultural activity

Developing creative capacities

Source: Adapted from Cashin & Downey, 1995.

Small-Group Session: Morning

The instructor and co-instructor support participants in developing a set of learning outcomes for their course in the small-group session. The discussion revolves first around the kind of framework they find most suitable for their course and discipline. For example, Are there affective or psychomotor outcomes in the course? Is the course introductory or advanced, and to what extent will this affect the choice of level of outcomes? What resources are available? This part of the course development process introduces a reality check and uncovers conditions and limitations to be taken into account. This is the first demand for alignment within the broader learning environment and calls on participants to go beyond personal disciplinary frameworks, which some have not done before.

To begin the task, participants are asked to individually develop two learning outcomes, taking into consideration the following four criteria:

1. Is the learning outcome stated from the learner's perspective (e.g., the learner will be able to. . . .)?

2. Is the learning outcome measurable in some way? (What will you accept as evidence that learning has occurred?)

3. Is the learning outcome related to the structure of your course (e.g., your concept map)?

4. Is the learning outcome clear to you and will it be clear to your students?

The participants have previously discussed the most important learning to be accomplished in their course in the large group, and have practiced writing two outcomes, but the small-group discussion evokes a reconsideration of three trial outcomes. Once participants have tested the frameworks and developed the learning outcomes, they select one and transfer it to an overhead transparency or their computer for presentation to the small group. The group then critiques each learning outcome presented using the four criteria for evaluating learning outcomes.

The first issue that arises is whether the outcome has been written so that it shows what the learner is expected to do. Often participants frame classroom activities in terms of what they expect themselves to do because they think of this as their responsibility as teachers. However, we are interested in being able to explain to students from *their* perspective what they will be able to do, turning them into responsible learners. This change in perspective also requires that participants begin to consider the activities students will undertake in order to achieve the learning outcome, so the ground is laid for considering instructional strategies, the next step in the course design process.

The second issue, whether the learning outcome is measurable, evokes further discussion since within the traditional administration of courses, evaluation is usually not linked specifically to learning but has its own pattern of midterms and finals. We find that through this process of course design, the participants begin to see the necessity for different forms of evaluation, particularly assignments that require different kinds of performance on the part of students. This raises the further issue of the complexity of evaluating student learning, and the mismatch between learning and evaluation as it has commonly been administered in the university. The evaluation of learning will be the theme for Thursday, so this discussion starts participants pondering what possible methods of evaluation would fulfill the criterion of measurable learning outcome.

The third issue is whether the learning outcome matches or is consistent with the concept map designed by the participant the previous day and possibly redesigned the previous evening. If the learning outcome has no reference to the concept map, there must be a reconsideration of the outcome or the concept map, and we make the point that course concept maps may evolve over the entire five days of the Workshop and over years in the individual course design process. The participants engage in heated discussion about the extent to which the concept map can take into account the learning outcomes without becoming unwieldy, and some time is spent in this coordination and alignment process.

Finally, the criterion of clarity is a more general demand for simple and direct language that is consistent with text, concept map, and the language or discourse that is used in the discipline. Early definition of terms is a collateral requirement in achieving clarity, but another is recognition that a vocabulary must be built in any course, and that the learning outcomes and concept map should highlight the critical or essential vocabulary to be learned.

Following this extended discussion, participants work on their respective outcomes. They often refer to the examples in their binder; several examples of concept maps and the related course learning outcomes are included. The examples demonstrate that outcomes may vary in number (examples in the binder range from seven to twelve learning outcomes), may be grouped around course concepts, and make immediate reference to course concepts.

If time permits, participants share learning outcomes with one another to obtain feedback. Since participants will be presenting their learning outcomes in the afternoon microteaching session, concentrated effort goes into the production of their outcomes so they can receive feedback on them.

Small-Group Session: Afternoon

The first activity is for participants to review their microteaching presentation on their concept map from Monday, then discuss revisions to the maps. The revisions may be minor or major, and some participants bring a series of attempts to show how their thinking about the principal concepts in their course changed as they worked the previous evening. The morning's activities in creating learning outcomes will also be juxtaposed to the concept map review.

The discussion gives participants the opportunity to note things they liked and did not like about their presentation, and how they might vary their approach and provide clarification for their own students. This discussion also allows them to express their reaction to the process, and in particular, to their self-evaluation. Often members of participants' families will have provided feedback as well, and confirmation of what participants are doing well or could improve. The remainder of the session is given to participants' presentations of their learning outcomes while being videotaped. Presentations are typically five to ten minutes, followed by questions and comments. Since participants have had the opportunity to be videotaped the previous day and to see their own tape, they tend to have explicit goals about what they want from this session. Often they will ask the other participants for specific feedback on certain aspects of their presentation.

Few restrictions are put on the kind of presentation to be made. One model is to give a lecture or presentation as if to a large class. If this model is followed, however, several suggestions are made. The first is based on the fact that in a formal lecture, the challenge of presentation often provides a "high" to the presenter, but very little may be retained by the students. Therefore, is the instructor making optimal use of class time? The issue is one of salience or memorability. Thus, participants are asked to consider how they will make their presentation memorable, and what in their presentation is most important for students to remember. A major strategy for memorability is to highlight what is critical to focus on—whether a key concept that relates different ideas in the presentation or a puzzle or problem that prompts thinking in tandem with the presenter.

The presentations are thus focused, and yet the participants are attempting to accomplish several things at once, some familiar and some novel. Because for the most part participants will have already lectured to large classes, they may bring a set of expectations about what a lecture or presentation should be. Moreover, they will be comparing their expectations with information from the morning large-group session as well as from the critiques of colleagues in their small groups. They may preface their presentation by explaining what group of students they are speaking to, and they may ask participants to take on the role of these students. The presentations thus tend to be more succinct and directed than those of the previous day, yet they can yield surprises and sometimes point to general concerns, such as making eye contact or speaking to the audience.

Preparation for the Following Day

At the end of the small-group session, we review what participants need to do in preparation for Wednesday. Participants are asked to once again view their videotape and complete the follow-up form (Appendix E) in the evening. They are asked to revise their learning outcomes based on the feedback received from other members of the group and recorded on the videotape directly after the presentation. Two articles on teaching strategies are provided in the binders; they focus on ways to increase student participation and develop thinking skills. The readings are intended to prime participants for the Wednesday session. Finally, participants must begin to think about Wednesday's microteaching session, which will be a longer presentation of ten to fifteen minutes. In this microteaching session, participants will choose content from their course to teach a small group, using a teaching strategy that is appropriate to the type of learning they wish to foster. They will learn more about selecting teaching and learning activities that are appropriate to various kinds and levels of learning in both the large- and small-group sessions on Wednesday. They will also have time to put finishing touches on their microteaching session to be presented that afternoon.

References

Astin, A. W. (1998). The changing American college student: Thirty-year trends, 1966–1996. *The Review of Higher Education, 21*(2), 115–135.

Baxter Magolda, M. (1992). *Knowing and reasoning in college: Gender related patterns in students' intellectual development.* San Francisco: Jossey-Bass.

Baxter Magolda, M., & Terenzini, P. (1999). *Learning and teaching in the 21st century: Trends and implications for practice.* Retrieved in October 2002 from www.acpa.nche.edu/srsch

Bloom, B. S. (Ed.). (1956). *Taxonomy of educational objectives: Handbook I-Cognitive domain.* New York: David McKay.

Cashin, W. (1988). *Student ratings of teaching: A summary of research* (IDEA Paper No. 20). Manhattan, KS: Kansas State University, Center for Faculty Evaluation and Development.

Cashin, W., & Downey, R. (1995). Disciplinary differences in what is taught and in students' perceptions of what they learn and how they are taught. In N. Hativa and M. Marincovich (Eds.), *Disciplinary differences in teaching and learning,* New Directions in Teaching and Learning (Vol. 64, pp. 81–92). San Francisco: Jossey-Bass.

Donald, J. G. (1992). The development of thinking process in postsecondary education: Application of a working model. *Higher Education, 24*(4), 413–430.

Donald, J. G. (2002). *Learning to think: Disciplinary perspectives.* San Francisco: Jossey-Bass.

Donald, J. G., & Denison, D. B. (2001). Quality assessment of university students: Student perceptions of quality criteria. *Journal of Higher Education, 72,* 478–501.

Donald, J. G., & Dubuc, P. (1999). *Report on students' conceptualizations of learning, 1994–1995 .* Montréal, Canada: McGill University.

Erickson, B. L., & Stommer, D. W. (1991). Knowing, understanding and thinking: The goals of freshman instruction. *Teaching college freshmen* (pp. 65–77). San Francisco: Jossey-Bass.

Johnston, R. (1998). The university of the future: Boyer revisited. *Higher Education, 36,* 253–272.

NSSE. (2000). *National survey of student engagement: The college student report.* Bloomington: Indiana University Center for Postsecondary Research and Planning.

Perry, W. G. (1970). *Forms of intellectual and ethical development in the college years: A scheme.* Troy, MO: Holt, Rinehart & Winston.

Perry, W. G. (1981). Intellectual and ethical development. In A. W. Chickering & Associates (Eds.), *The modern American college: Responding to the new realities of diverse students and a changing society* (pp. 76–116). San Francisco: Jossey-Bass.

5

DESIGNING TEACHING
FOR STUDENT LEARNING

Cheryl Amundsen, Laura Winer, and Terry Gandell

We turn our attention in the Course Design and Teaching Workshop on Wednesday to designing teaching that will support, encourage, and motivate student learning. The focus for participants will be to consciously align their course content and learning outcomes with teaching and learning activities in class, outside of class, and online. This task has a different feel from those we engaged in on Monday and Tuesday. Making reasoned decisions about appropriate teaching and learning activities may directly imply changes in actions as a teacher. This is very different from analyzing course content or developing learning outcomes. The course design process becomes more "real" as participants begin to picture themselves actually carrying out the plans they are developing.

We want to encourage participants to view teaching as a stimulating and creative design process with many decision points. We continue to ask them to reframe their teaching to a learning-centered perspective. On this particular day, we ask them to make reasoned decisions about which teaching and learning activities will best accomplish the desired student learning. These are not black-and-white decisions. A learning-centered perspective is not embodied by one or two particular teaching methods or activities, nor does it necessarily exclude any particular method or activity. We draw participants into a process of analysis whereby they do not judge any teaching method (e.g., lecturing) as intrinsically good or bad. We ask them instead to consider the characteristics of various teaching and learning methods, and to then determine their appropriateness relative to the learning they want students to achieve. This may seem, at first glance, like a straightforward matching task, but for a variety of reasons, most Workshop participants find the exercise much more complex than that.

Most professors have little practice or experience with teaching methods other than traditional lecture or discussion formats that are common in graduate level seminar courses. Some professors have a particular teaching style that they use in every teaching context, regardless of the type or level of student learning they expect. Professors are increasingly encouraged or required at many universities to integrate technology into their teaching, and this is a source of stress and discomfort for some of them. Others may already use various technology applications, but their decisions may not be based on sound pedagogy. Contextual constraints (e.g., inadequate classroom space, limited technical support) may also discourage a professor from employing a different teaching approach. Finally, a number of professors are concerned that students will respond negatively to teaching and learning activities that are new to them. Any of these situations can make it difficult for a professor to reframe teaching to a learning-centered perspective. The following paragraphs discuss how we support Workshop participants in working through these potential impediments. We will first discuss the rationale behind our approach, and then we will provide detailed descriptions of the activities that take place in the large- and small-group sessions on Wednesday.

A World Beyond Lecturing

It is an accepted fact that most professors have very little preparation for their teaching roles. Their graduate school experience stresses scholarship and research (Boyer, 1990; Schuster, 1990). It is not surprising, then, that most professors who come to the Workshop employ traditional, lecture-based instruction, essentially following the teaching that was modeled for them in their own university studies (Singer, 1996). We do not try to dissuade Workshop participants from lecturing. Rather, we engage them in a discussion and inform them of the literature, which suggests that certain instructional strategies are more or less appropriate for different types of learning. Broadly speaking, lecture-based instruction has been shown to be most effective when the goal is to transmit information, and when organization and clarity are desired (Saroyan, 2000). Other, more interactive methods are effective when the goal is higher-order thinking and developing a deeper understanding (McKeachie, 1999; Morrison, Ross, & Kemp, 2001). We share with participants a number of ways in which different researchers have organized learning outcomes with appropriate teaching and learning activities; these appear as Table 5.1, Table 5.2, and Table 5.3. We submit that since disciplinary context matters and learning tasks vary, a variety of instructional approaches have a place in higher education instruction, both separately and in articulation.

We encourage participants to judge the merits of a particular teaching or learning strategy based on how well it will support a particular type of learning for a specific student group in a specific context.

The conversation about teaching methods is complemented by our intentional modeling of a wide variety of teaching methods in the Workshop. We use this as another way to broaden participants' familiarity with less traditional ways of teaching. We often introduce these methods by taking a few minutes to describe the method and we briefly explain how it supports what we want participants to learn. At other times, we create more formal opportunities to deconstruct some of the methods we model. After identifying what we see as the relevant characteristics of a method, we explain why we think it is appropriate to the learning we want to support and encourage, and we discuss how it fits with what we know of participants as learners and with the Workshop context. This allows us also to model the decision-making process that we ask participants to engage in as they develop this part of their own course. For their part, they let us know if and what they learn from this, sometimes sharing how they might use or adapt a method to better fit their subject matter and their instructional context. They also tell us why they would not use some methods. The process often provides participants with a chance to experience at least one new method that they can readily see themselves using in their own classroom teaching, and this is when we see "light bulbs come on"—we sometimes hear a distinct "aha" or a quiet "hmmm."

We also share with participants the additional criteria we use in choosing methods to model in the Workshop. These are consistent with the learning-centered approach that we explicitly and openly support. The first criterion is that the method must include active involvement of the participants. By this we mean there must be the possibility for the participant to be engaged and not simply remain a passive receiver of information. We do give explanations or mini-lectures, but there are always embedded or follow-up questions. We make a point to model a number of strategies that can be used to add an active involvement component to lectures (e.g., minute papers, intensive writing, pair share). We also model more interactive strategies with participants engaging in peer discussion, critique, and demonstrations. Sometimes this leads to considerable movement around the teaching space and generally results in a noisy environment. This, too, is intentional since participants must be able to anticipate that more active participation will generate a livelier environment—though it need not be chaotic.

The second criterion we employ in choosing methods to model is that the method must provide participants with opportunities to practice the desired learning. There must also be the potential for feedback about this learning to both the participants and to us, the instructors and co-instructors. We explain to the participants that we have a debriefing session every day after the Workshop is over. Part of what we discuss during these sessions is the effectiveness of our instruction that day, sharing our own impressions and using the oral and written feedback of participants to assess what went well, what did not go so well, and why. The same activity sometimes works well in one small group but not in another, which speaks volumes about group dynamics and why this should be taken into consideration when selecting a particular method of teaching. As a result of discussions in the debriefing session, we sometimes decide not to use a particular activity again because it may be a poor fit with our learning goals, the Workshop context, or certain groupings of professors as learners. We might also decide that the activity requires too much time relative to the learning benefits derived. Our hope is that making our thinking process transparent will help participants to think about teaching in a more systemic way. We want them to learn how to use their teaching and learning activities as indicators of how well their students are learning, and by implication, how well they are teaching. The participants consider on Thursday how to evaluate student learning, and this provides an opportunity to revisit the importance of providing opportunities for practice and feedback.

The third criterion we use in choosing methods to model is variety. We ask participants in the large-group session on Wednesday to list all of the different teaching methods or activities that have been used to date in the Workshop. The participants are generally surprised at the variety, and as learners, they appreciate it. The ensuing discussion helps them to identify variety as an important aspect of the quality of the instruction they are experiencing.

Why Do We Teach the Way We Do?

We want to engage Workshop participants in thinking about how they teach and why they teach that way. Many participants describe a particular teaching style that they have adopted for themselves. We intentionally lead them to question the appropriateness of their style to all situations. Letting go of a preferred style, however, is often not easy and usually takes time, even when doing so makes sense intellectually. Some participants become keen about a particular approach after attending the Workshop, abandoning their old style for this new one. This, of course, is equally problematic: An approach appropriate for the particular course they design in the Workshop may not be so for other courses. We recall one participant, for example, who worked very hard as a result of this Workshop to develop an online and in-class project-based discussion format for his undergraduate course of 40 to 50 students. His "new approach" (as he called it) worked very well: It provided better support for student learning; the students produced papers and projects he now enjoyed marking rather than dreaded marking; more students attended class on a regular basis than ever before; and student feedback on the whole was very positive. One day he phoned to relate the following: Another professor, whose teaching ability he highly respected, had asked him to take over teaching her graduate level course because she had heard such good things about his teaching. When he sat down to plan the new course, however, he realized that his new approach would not work for this other course and its students. The discovery was distressing to him, but he worked through the same decision process that we follow in the Workshop. This aided his analysis of the situation, and he was able to identify methods that would be a better fit with the learning expected in a graduate course and with the level and experience of these particular students.

Participants in the Workshop often refer to certain teaching "norms" that exist in their respective departments or faculties, and express a feeling that they need to conform to these. We encourage them to question these norms. We want participants to think about, for example, "Why do I assign a term paper in every course I teach? What is the learning purpose of that term paper?" We have found stereotypes and expectations regarding teaching to be very strong in some disciplines. We recall, for example, the microteaching presentation of a professor from mathematics. During the critique of his presentation, other members of the small group asked why he wrote and talked so quickly; why he continuously stood right beside the overhead projector, making it impossible for half of the group to see what he was writing; and why he never looked at any of them. He told us that many of his own professors had taught in this way. He had, in fact, decided to use the overhead projector so that he would be facing students. He said he just did not realize that he needed to change more than the technology. For him, this model of teaching was strongly associated with what mathematics professors do, and even though he could intellectually understand that student learning was not being well supported, teaching that way felt natural.

We have also had professors from arts and humanities who are accustomed to relatively small seminar courses in which students typically are assigned readings and then expected to discuss them in class. They often complain about the quality of the discussions or the uneven contributions from students. Upon examination, we often find out that the perceived "ideal" of a professor is one who enters the seminar room, greets students, and launches into an interesting and stimulating discussion. This ideal is wonderful and worth trying to achieve, so we try to reframe it for participants. We suggest different activities that can be done ahead of time so students feel ready to enter discussion (e.g., reading guides, focus questions), and what can be done during the discussion (e.g., respecting wait time, not dominating discussion, dealing with students who talk too much or not enough). Participants may not have thought of preparing students in ways other than telling them to "read the chapter." We also ask them to examine the learning purpose of these discussions and consider different formats for discussion, such as small-group presentations, summaries, or debates. These strategies also have the benefit of using and focusing the professor's expertise to design assignments and activities. At the same time, they mediate the shift in the professor's role from dominating the discussion to one of supporting and encouraging it.

Our experience as faculty developers and our reflections on our own teaching have shown us that questioning one's practice is difficult. It may involve an adjustment of one's self-image, a questioning of deeply held values, and a readiness to take some risks. The intellectual acceptance of a reasoned approach to decision making about teaching and learning strategies is only one part of the process of changing the way one teaches (Amundsen, Saroyan, & Frankman, 1996). Linking what we know with what we do is not always straightforward or easy. The theory of transformative learning (Mezirow, 1991), as interpreted by Cranton for faculty development in higher education (Cranton, 1994, 1996), posits that a change in practice occurs for most adults only when there is a change in their basic assumptions about themselves as learners, the role of the teacher, and the goal of education.

The microteaching sessions that Workshop participants engage in on Monday through Thursday are intended to engage them in an examination of assumptions. Moreover, the sessions provide participants with the opportunity to link what they are learning with their own teaching practice. Two of these microteaching sessions involve participants teaching other members of the small group some content from the course they are developing. First, participants explain the process they followed to select the particular teaching method or activity. They then describe the learning they want each member of the group to achieve. This is the intellectual part of the activity and is almost always the easiest. Myron Frankman, a professor of economics and the author of Chapter 9 in this book, put it this way, "I knew the learning benefits of using small-group discussions; I just didn't know *how* to do it. No one had ever modeled this for me. Where do I stand [in the room]? Do I listen in on the small-group discussions—won't the students stop talking? What if a student gives wrong information? What if the discussion becomes too loud?"

These are all legitimate concerns, and resolving them is necessary to reach a state of comfort with implementing the activity. The microteaching session also provides a safe and supportive environment for this type of practice. While the activity constitutes only a small step toward actually doing what would be done in the classroom, for many participants it is enough to allow them to take the next step. As we discussed in Chapter 2, change that is sustained is most often slow, and characterized by small, but significant departures from current practice. The process of change is also often iterative, and we remind participants that an occasional step backward need not be a source of worry but rather should be accepted as part of the process.

I Cannot Change My Teaching Because the Chairs and Tables Are Fixed

We acknowledge that professors may not have a completely free hand in deciding what teaching and learning activities they will use. Large classes and inflexible physical spaces can certainly limit choices. For example, some classrooms may have tables or desks that are anchored to the floor and cannot be rearranged. Many university instructors are assigned to a large hall that is set up to accommodate lectures, with the focus toward the front and low or minimal lighting in the rest of the room. Use of a variety of teaching and learning activities is possible even in these situations, but some creative rethinking of the space and the way it is used is needed. Finding solutions sometimes involves locating and requesting a classroom (perhaps in another building) that will accommodate what the professor wants to do. It may involve going in before class starts and rearranging the furniture, or asking students to help with this once they arrive. Students can be asked as they enter the classroom, for example, to sit in groups of three or four to accommodate small-group work. Involving students has the advantage of letting them see that their professor is intentional about creating a space conducive to their learning. It also provides an opportunity to discuss with students what the intended goal is and what role they need to play to make it work.

Lack of time and resources may also inhibit a free hand in selecting and implementing some teaching methods. The professorial roles of scholar, teacher, and contributor to university governance and the wider community make for a busy professional life. This cannot be disputed. Changing one's teaching, therefore, requires careful consideration of the small steps that are the most meaningful to both the professor and the students' learning. Fortunately, these small steps often open the door to more significant changes.

Some professors, especially those experienced with various computer technologies, bemoan the lack of adequate hardware, software, or technical support. Some have identified incredible resources that they would like to share with their students, but they are stymied for a number of reasons, including not having enough time to make all this technology work the way they want. This problem is decreasing somewhat as universities provide more resources and technical support and as more and more students acquire and learn to use sophisticated systems that allow them to do much more than word processing. Some professors describe the pressure they feel to integrate technology into their teaching but admit they do not know where to start. We applaud the learning opportunities that technological support has made possible. We do not, however, subscribe to the rhetoric that claims learning will necessarily improve with the presence of technology.

Computers Are Not Teaching Strategies

Arguments for the integration of computer technologies into university teaching are, upon careful inspection, often convoluted. Reasons for technology integration based on economics, efficiency, or currency are often mixed up with or disguised as rationales based on student learning. We agree there is some merit to arguments that focus on keeping pace with innovation; that students should acquire the technological capabilities that will be required for the professional contexts in which they will work; and that the university should be within the same technological sphere as its societal context. We also agree that under certain circumstances and in consideration of pedagogical principles, creating online courses or programs to accommodate students who cannot regularly be on campus is an appropriate use of technology for learning. These positions, however, should not be confused with arguments that claim learning is enhanced simply by using computer technologies.

We do not consider computers as teaching and learning strategies or methods. We believe technologies can be used to enable particular teaching and learning strategies that may otherwise be difficult, less efficiently implemented, or even impossible without these technologies. Clark (1983, 1994), among others, first made this argument two decades ago. He argued that research studies that pit instruction enabled by technology against traditional instruction are misguided and the findings misleading because they may well be comparing different instructional strategies. The benefits that apparently derive from one strategy may also be due to the more careful design process that technology-supported instruction requires. Papert (1987) made a similar argument when he compared a technocentric perspective with a perspective that views learning technologies as "building materials" that must be studied in relation to the learning context in which they are used.

In the rush to get faculty "up to speed" in using technology, many universities have launched workshops that often focus on technical skills and overlook the implicit assumptions about learning that underlie the technology being used (Houseman, 1997). Teaching and learning activities, if they are even addressed in these workshops, are often generic and are divorced from the professors' subject-matter expertise and their understanding of student learning in their discipline. The outcome of this approach is that most uses of technology in higher education today are simply for course management or to support traditional lecture-based instruction (e.g., posted course outlines, lecture notes and readings, electronic submission of assignments, class mailing lists, e-mail contact with instructor or teaching assistant) (Amundsen, Sohbat, & Bures, 2000; Bures, Amundsen, & Abrami, 2002). This may partially reflect the newness of these technologies, but we maintain it also reflects the predominant views of learning and teaching in higher education. Much of the instructional potential offered by technology will be wasted until these are addressed. We posit that it is mistaken to expect much about teaching (and learning) will change simply by providing computer technologies and teaching professors how to use them.

We consider instructional methods that are supported or enabled by computer technologies in the same way in which we consider those that are not supported by technology. We approach the decision to use them from the same reasoned perspective that begins with consideration of student learning goals, the subject matter, and the learners' characteristics, and then with consideration of other factors such as available resources and the time to implement relative to the learning benefit achieved. We do not spend time in the Workshop teaching participants to use specific computer applications. We do, however, provide information on where such training may be obtained. Some of the instructional methods that are modeled in the Workshop are enabled by various computer applications (e.g., presentation software, concept mapping software, online discussion forums, examples of course web sites). The discussion about why we use these focuses on the learning rationale, just as it does with any other teaching and learning method. We refer to examples of professors who use computer technologies to create interactive learning experiences for students in class, out of class, and in online courses (e.g., interactive course web sites, online conferencing and small-group discussions, online research and project groups, discipline-specific interactive software). One of these professors will often be the featured speaker at a brown-bag lunch during one day of the Workshop. These discussions serve to juxtapose the uses of computer technologies modeled by the presenters with other uses that simply replicate traditional lecture-based courses.

There are two ways in which we see computer-based instructional technologies offering an opportunity for the development of teaching. One strictly pragmatic effect arises from the fact that instructional methods involving computer technology may somehow be seen as more worthy of investment in the eyes of both professors and their administrators than those considered more traditional or less innovative. Second, computer technologies clearly provide an ideal environment for experimenting with more interactive and student-centered teaching approaches because of the potential for creating collaborative environments for student learning outside of the classroom (Gandell, Weston, Finkelstein, & Winer, 2000).

Based on their research with secondary schoolteachers, Becker and Ravitz (1999) speculate that "effective staff development helps produce change in teachers' objectives, goals, and teaching philosophies and that under these circumstances, the introduction of computers and similar technologies provides these teachers with an opportunity to test out their new understandings and pedagogical points of view" (p. 376). Frankman (author of Chapter 9) considers e-mail and online conferencing two tools that provided a catalyst and enabled him to finally link changes he wanted to make in his teaching with his actual teaching practice. His 20-plus years of professorial career had been characterized by very formal classroom practice, in which he used a traditional lecture method, addressed students only by last names, and was addressed in turn as Professor Frankman. The first breakthrough, as he describes it, was when he started using e-mail to contact his students.

> It was a confrontation when I was about to send my first e-mail message to a student. You know, I'm of the old school timewise . . . I never addressed students by their first name, not even graduate students. So when I was about to send my first e-mail message to a student . . . I wrote, "Dear Joan," or whatever, and that was the first time I addressed a student by the first name. This was my twenty-fourth year of teaching . . . but the next year, I made the break and I started calling students by their first names, even in class . . . this changed the classroom dynamics. (Amundsen et al., 1996, pp. 14–15)

From this seemingly simple change came many more, both in the classroom and enabled by technology. On reflection, Myron spoke about the satisfaction that came from bringing his teaching in line, little by little, with his values. A couple of years later, he was featured in a university publication as a professor using technology in innovative and pedagogically sound ways.

Wednesday of the Workshop finds many participants quite pleased with the possible changes they are contemplating making to their teaching. Many of them have been exposed for the first time to a variety of methods as a result of what they have seen modeled, what is described in their readings, and what has been presented by previous participants. For many, there is also concern that the changes they want to make will not be greeted positively by their students. We invite the discussion of these concerns because professors absolutely need to consider the students' views of learning and the learning habits their students bring with them.

Students Have Habits, Too!

Students have developed habits in the ways they approach their studies, just as professors have developed their habits of teaching on the basis of, among other things, how they themselves were taught. The predominant model in higher education is characterized by lectures, term papers, and exams, so it is not surprising that students' habits are built around these predictable aspects of the courses they take. They may not greet changes that render their habitual behaviors less effective. They may, in fact, strongly resist changes. There is no doubt that more learning-centered and interactive approaches require more time and intellectual effort from students (Entwistle, Entwistle, & Tait, 1993), and even more when computer technologies are involved (Laurillard, 1993, 2002; Perkins, 1991). We advise that professors start with small changes, or "baby steps," both for their own comfort and for that of their students. This may require time and a supportive environment for students as they become aware of the goals and potential learning benefits of directions their professor wants to take.

The notion of "transparent teaching" (Hunkins, 1987) has provided a useful basis for discussion. The idea here is that professors share their decision processes with students, explaining the learning rationale behind various teaching and learning approaches. We encourage professors to discuss with their students how they arrived at the decision to use a particular teaching or learning strategy—just as they do in their microteaching sessions in the Workshop. The learning purpose for a lecture, a small-group discussion, online study groups, a term paper, a reflective study guide, virtual field trips, or any other teaching/learning method should be clear to students from the onset. The other important element behind the notion of transparent teaching that will put students more at ease is to make sure that students understand what they are supposed to do. This may require direct instruction about how to do something, or it may require opportunities for practice that will not significantly affect their grades (e.g., instruction and practice on how to use a particular piece of software or application, clear expectations of the various roles in a project group). Students are remarkably forgiving when new teaching methods do not work out as planned if they understand the learning purpose behind their professor's actions and if they are not personally penalized.

We now turn to a description of how we actually go about supporting Workshop participants to make decisions about teaching and learning strategies, and how microteaching serves as an opportunity to put these decisions into action. The large-group session, which takes place first thing in the morning, provides an introduction to the reasoned decision-making process. In the small-group sessions that follow, participants consider various teaching strategies and the fit of these strategies with the learning outcomes they have identified. They then select a portion of their course content to teach in the microteaching session to their small-group colleagues using an appropriate strategy.

Large-Group Session

The large-group session on Wednesday begins by again displaying our representation of the course design process (Figure 3.1). We call attention on this morning to the placement of instructional strategies in the graphic. We note that instructional strategies in the graphic are directly linked first to learning (at the center), then to learning as reflected in the other course design elements: content analysis, learning outcomes, and evaluation of learning. The stated goal of the day is to try out a decision-making process in which participants will consciously and specifically link their classroom and online teaching, and the assignments they design, with the learning outcomes they have identified for the course they are developing.

Most Workshop participants have not thought of teaching as broader than what they do in the classroom, nor have they consciously linked the way they teach or the assignments students do to particular types of learning they want to foster.

One of the members of the Centre of University Teaching and Learning (CUTL) and a co-author of this book, Lynn McAlpine, has developed the metaphor of an iceberg to illustrate that designing learning is just as important as designing teaching (McAlpine, 2001). We have begun to use this metaphor to broaden professors' ideas about their teaching role and, in particular, to call their attention to the aspects of student learning that they may have overlooked or of which they have not even been aware. The part of the iceberg that we can see represents only about 10% to 15% of its total mass. Since we cannot see what is underwater, we have little idea what it looks like, yet we know that there is a direct, although imperfect, correlation between what appears above water and what is below water. It is suggested that this is the case with student learning,

> What we as professors can "see" of the process of student learning is largely what we view in class (e.g., students looking at us, asking questions, and

participating in discussions; student writing), as well as, sometimes, out of class (e.g., visiting our office, e-mailing a question). However, these observations are just the tip of the iceberg. We have little insight into the invisible aspects of the learning process: how the students conceive of the learning task, and what strategies they use both inside and outside of class to achieve what they believe they should be learning. Yet, ultimately, this largely invisible learning results in some products (e.g., essays, exams, assignments) that we then grade. (McAlpine, 2001, p. 10)

This part of student learning that is largely invisible to professors may in fact be the most important aspect of learning, and so it should be intentionally considered by professors. That is why we stress in the Workshop that we want to design teaching strategies that go beyond the classroom and will consciously design what students will do outside of the classroom and in online environments. The essential idea is coherence among what the professor does, what the students do, and the learning outcomes.

We introduce the idea of selecting teaching methods that are appropriate to different kinds of learning by discussing three charts that are consistent with the learning outcome frameworks we discussed the day before (see Chapter 4). We discuss each of these in turn. The first, Table 5.1 (Weston & Cranton, 1986), uses Bloom's taxonomy of the cognitive domain and links this to appropriate instructional strategies and methods. This chart typically accomplishes two things: First, it gives Workshop participants "cause for pause"; many say it makes sense but that they simply have never thought of teaching in this way. Second, the chart provides a vocabulary for beginning the discussion of different categories of teaching approaches in terms of the learning they best foster. We do not present this chart as a strict relational classification but rather as a way of thinking about learning and instructional strategies and methods that are supported by research findings.

The second and third charts, Table 5.2 and Table 5.3 (Gandell et al., 2000), are based on the learning classification proposed by LaSere Erickson and Weltner Strommer (1991). These researchers found that the terms *knowing, understanding,* and *thinking* were the terms most commonly used to describe student learning by the professors they interviewed. We have used this classification of learning and, as with the chart based on Bloom's taxonomy, made links to appropriate teaching and learning strategies; we referred to them in Chapter 4. Our intention in sharing these classifications is to encourage participants to think about student learning and, more specifically, the learning outcomes they have developed on the previous day, in relationship to how class time is spent and assignments and activities they design for students.

Table 5.1 Overview of Instructional Strategies

	Instructor-centered	Interactive	Individualized
Domain of learning	Tends to highlight cognitive	Usually effective for higher cognitive and affective learning; may include psychomotor, e.g., nursing stage	Cognitive, but may stress psychomotor, e.g., lab work—may emphasize lower levels, e.g., programmed instruction
Nature of activity	a. Lecture—students are passive; efficient for lower cognitive levels b. Questioning—encourages student involvement; may cause anxiety; relatively effective to monitor student learning c. Demonstration—students are passive; relatively effective to illustrate application of a skill or concept	a. Class discussion—encourages student involvement; may cause anxiety and be difficult in larger classes; requires time b. Discussion groups—encourages all students to participate; requires time c. Group projects—encourages active student participation; may cause interpersonal difficulties; requires careful planning and monitoring; students learn how to work co-operatively d. Field or clinical—students are actively involved; management and evaluation may be difficult; occurs in natural setting so approximates authentic task	a. Out-of-class preparation for class—students are actively involved; can be done at time and speed convenient to student b. Independent projects—students are actively involved at time and speed convenient to them; can be time-consuming; may be difficult to assess c. Lab work—students actively involved; management and evaluation may be difficult; can involve relatively authentic setting and tasks

e. Role playing/simulations—requires active participation; may produce anxiety; provides practice in "safe" setting

f. Peer teaching—encourages student involvement; may cause interpersonal difficulties; requires careful planning and monitoring; uses differences in student expertise

d. Modularized instruction (workbook or online)—can be used at time and speed convenient to student; may not be motivating for some; requires time and expense to create

e. Programmed instruction (workbook or online)—very structured (drill and practice) at time and speed convenient to student; may not be motivating for some; requires considerable time and expense to create; can provide extensive feedback; most effective at lower levels

Source: Adapted from Weston, C., & Cranton, P. (1986). Selecting instructional strategies. *Journal of Higher Education, 57*(3), 259–288.

Table 5.2   Classification of Learning Outcomes in the Cognitive Domain

Knowing	
Define	Memorize
Label	Recall
List	Relate
Understanding	
Classify	Interpret
Explain	Review
Identify	Report
Thinking	
Analyze	Rate
Criticize	Solve
Contrast	Support
Evaluate	Synthesize
Propose	

Sources: Adapted from Kemp, J., Morrison, G., & Ross, S. (1994). *Designing effective instruction.* New York: Macmillan; LaSere Erickson, B., & Weltner Strommer, D. (1991). *Teaching college freshmen* (pp. 65–80). San Francisco: Jossey-Bass.

Next, we ask participants to generate a list of all of the different teaching methods or strategies they have seen us, the instructors, and co-instructors, use in both the large- and small-group sessions of the Workshop as well as any that they have seen used in other contexts. They are encouraged not to worry about the specific or proper name of the strategy; they simply need to describe it. This exercise produces an interesting discussion because for many participants, this is the first time they have examined instruction so closely. They generally have no trouble remembering what we have modeled in the Workshop, even though they may not have thought of these as "instructional strategies" or "teaching methods." We then take as examples some of the strategies identified by participants and discuss the purpose behind them or how they were related to the intended learning. Participants thus begin to formulate for themselves the "why" behind different approaches to teaching. Usually, we invite a past participant of the Workshop to present a strategy or method that he or she has developed and is currently using. For example, a

Table 5.3   Appropriate Use of Web Features for Facilitating Types of Student Learning

→ Types of learning ↓ Features of the Web	Knowing (e.g., memorize, list, define)	Understanding (e.g., explain, identify, classify)	Thinking (e.g., analyze, evaluate, synthesize)
Content presentation (e.g., course outline, course notes, references, demos)	Usually	Possibly	Not usually
Searchable information (e.g, articles, journals)	Usually	Possibly	Not usually
Information exchange (e.g., e-mail)	Usually	Possibly	Possibly
Guidance, practice, and feedback (e.g., quizzes, self testing, exercises, Q&A)	Usually	Usually	Usually
Discussions (e.g., online conferences, list serve, video-conferencing)	Not usually	Usually	Usually
Simulations (e.g., interactive tutorials, models, labs)	Not usually	Possibly	Usually

Source: Adapted from Weston, C., & Cranton, P. A. (1986). Selecting instructional strategies. *Journal of Higher Education, 57,* 259–288; LaSere Erickson, B., & Weltner Strommer, D. (1991). *Teaching college freshmen.* San Francisco: Jossey-Bass.

professor from agriculture demonstrated how she used an adapted form of a popular word game to teach technical vocabulary. A professor from engineering demonstrated how he used his course concept map as a learning and assessment tool. Not only did he use the concept map as a strategy to organize student thinking at the beginning of each lecture, he then had the students create their own concept maps at the end of the course to demonstrate their understanding of the concepts and the relationships.

Participants next move on to the small-group setting to begin the consideration of teaching strategies that may be appropriate to the learning outcomes of their courses.

Small-Group Session: Morning

The small-group session generally begins with lots of questions from participants. They have concerns about whether some of the teaching methods discussed in the large-group session are actually used or could be used in their discipline and how students would react to them. They always have issues about how much time it takes both to prepare and to use methods other than lectures. Linked to this is the question of how they will be able to cover the required content if they use a more time-consuming approach. We invite the discussion of these concerns. Stories often emerge from participants or instructors about when they used a particular method or strategy and the successes or failures they experienced. These stories illustrate how small changes are a prudent way to proceed; change need not be "all or nothing." For example, one may effectively use a particular method or strategy in addition to a lecture or within a lecture (e.g., minute paper, pair and share) to address a particular type of learning. Participants normally settle down to the task at hand after a few minutes. Once this reasoned approach to selecting instructional strategies "clicks" for participants, many become very enthusiastic because they now have a rationale, one that makes sense to them, for deciding how they are going to teach. It was at this point in one small-group session that an engineering professor exclaimed, "Oh, this is just like a design process! It is so logical. Once you think about it, it makes sense."

We ask participants to consider the following questions and discuss their responses with others. This is displayed on an overhead projector:

1. What teaching methods or strategies appeal to you? Which ones can you see yourself using?

2. Look back over your learning outcomes and concept map. Which of the methods or strategies that attract you lend themselves best to the course you are designing? Why?

3. Pick one method or strategy and link it specifically to a particular learning outcome or set of outcomes.

4. Now, visualize yourself using the method or strategy. Are there any issues that make it difficult to implement this method or strategy (e.g., classroom configuration, resources, attitudes of students or colleagues)? Can you address the issue directly (e.g., find another classroom) or adapt the strategy so the issue is resolved?

We provide participants with a simple three-column handout to note their thinking as they discuss these questions. The three columns are strategy name or description; type of learning supported; advantages, disadvantages, and adaptations.

Once participants have made at least a few decisions about teaching strategies, we ask them to prepare a ten- to fifteen-minute microteaching session using a strategy with which they have some comfort. Participants are told about this activity the day before and so many have already done some initial planning. Most choose a learning outcome that can be addressed using a lecture approach or a modified lecture approach. The remainder of the morning session is spent preparing this teaching session, which they will present after lunch.

Small-Group Session: Afternoon

Each participant is encouraged in the afternoon small-group session to arrange the classroom before beginning to teach so it best supports the learning that is wanted for their small-group colleagues to experience. This can range from the mundane to the creative: It may involve moving furniture; positioning and focusing the overhead projector, and deciding where to stand; and organizing other materials, supplies, or resources. Essentially, we want participants to think about their teaching session from the perspective of the learner rather than focusing on themselves. For some, this paradoxically turns out to be a great relief. Ralph Harris, an engineering professor and the author of Chapter 8 in this book, expressed his relief when he made what he termed the paradigm shift from thinking about teaching to thinking about learning. Much of the anxiety that he had associated with teaching disappeared because in his mind the spotlight was now on the learners and not on him.

Participants begin their microteaching session by clearly outlining the learning they want members of their small group to achieve; they note any particular aspect about which they would like feedback. Peer critique follows each microteaching session in the same way as on other days of the Workshop.

Participants by this time are much more comfortable with the notion of getting up in front of their peers and being videotaped. This is apparent in the relative ease with which they react to questions and comments at the conclusion of their teaching sessions. As stated above, most participants vary little from the lecture format, although they often incorporate a short questioning activity. There are, however, those who are bolder and may even invent their own method or strategy. The variations are instructive, and there is ample opportunity to discuss the learning rationale behind each individual's teaching session.

At the end of the day we call participants' attention to the readings for that evening and ask them to review the videotape of their microteaching session. We then pose the *BIG* challenge, that of another ten- to fifteen-minute teaching session to be presented the next day. This time we ask participants to use a teaching method or strategy that is new for them and appropriate for the learning outcome they have in mind. We stress that this is their opportunity to experiment, to take a risk in the context of a small supportive group of colleagues. Amid groans, furrowed brows, but also smiles, the participants leave the Workshop for the day.

We often discuss in this day's debriefing session what we have come to call the "Wednesday phenomenon." We have consistently noticed that "things come together" for most participants on Wednesday as they make their own sense of the reasoned approach to instructional decision making that we support. This is not to say that they discontinue their critique of the ideas presented, but the mid-Workshop mark seems to be the threshold for making a deeper sense of the meaning of what they have learned. The real skeptics—and there are always a few—sometimes experience a "flip" in their attitude and become counted among those who are enthusiastic supporters of instructional change. This is also the point at which those who are inclined to drop out do so, but this number is very small. To this day, the Wednesday phenomenon remains a bit of a mystery to us.

Conclusion

The primary goal of the Workshop is to teach participants to follow a reasoned approach to instructional decision making. Rather than promote a "right way to teach," we emphasize the importance of using a variety of methods that are more likely to promote intended learning. Following a reasoned approach may sometimes not require any change in teaching practice. Coherence among content, learning outcomes, and teaching practice may already exist. More often, however, a change is implicated.

Nowhere is our understanding of change brought more to bear than in working with instructional methods and strategies. This is because in deciding on instructional methods and strategies, professors make decisions that have direct implications for their own behavior and what they do as a teacher. The part that is relatively easy is supporting Workshop participants in understanding, at an intellectual level, that making an appropriate match between strategies or methods and types of learning is a reasonable and sensible thing to do. What is a big challenge is helping them translate this intellectual understanding into teaching practice. We can all appreciate this better if we only review the areas in our own lives where what we do is not necessarily a reflection of what we know.

Kozma's (1985) grounded theory of instructional innovation describes teaching change as a personal process and describes new teaching behaviors as evolving slowly from past practices. The psychological literature on personal change suggests the same thing (Tien, 1991). The generally incremental process of change is also recognized in a number of frameworks that characterize professors' evolving thinking and practice as they become more knowledgeable and experienced teachers (Ramsden, 1992; Sherman, Armistead, Fowler, Barksdale, & Reif, 1987). The question for us is how best to prompt change, given its slow, incremental nature.

We try to address this in the Workshop by first leading participants to question why they teach as they do and developing an understanding of the link between teaching strategies and learning as supported by research. Participants then practice a decision-making process based on the appropriateness of various methods and strategies to encourage and support different types of learning. Practice in putting their decisions into practice is provided through the microteaching experience. Finally, through discussions, we encourage a continuing process of reflection on what they do as teachers.

We recognize that there are limitations in the very "planful" way in which we structure the Workshop. We emphasize thinking before doing, and planning before teaching. We defend this as a reasonable way to structure the Workshop because, for the most part, it provides participants with reasons that make sense to them, and the analytical process is one they are accustomed to and comfortable with. There is, of course, the possibility that if professors move away from using only a lecture-based approach and have more and closer interactions with students, they and their students will be able to build valuable learning from spontaneous questions, discussions, and observations inside and outside the classroom. We also identify *doing* before *thinking* as a potentially powerful process. For example, a professor may simply be attracted to trying a particular method or approach without understanding all of the learning implications and, in so doing, may come to better understand how this method supports learning. We have found this to be especially true with computer-enabled methods. We admit that it is often difficult to really know the learning value of a particular method or approach, and, therefore, to be able to "select" it until it has been used. Knowing comes from doing as well as from thinking.

References

Amundsen, C., Saroyan, A., & Frankman, M. (1996). Changing methods and metaphors: A case study of growth in university teaching. *Journal of Excellence in College Teaching, 7*(3), 3–42.

Amundsen, C., Sohbat, E., & Bures, E. (2000, April). *Comparing instructor and student perceptions of the use and learning benefits of computer conferencing.* Paper presented at the American Educational Research Association, New Orleans, LA.

Becker, H. J., & Ravitz, J. (1999). The influence of computer and internet use on teachers' pedagogical practices and perceptions. *Journal of Research on Computing in Education, 31*(4), 356–384.

Boyer, E. L. (1990). *Scholarship reconsidered: Priorities of the professoriate.* Princeton, NJ: Carnegie Foundation for the Advancement of Teaching.

Bures, E., Amundsen, C., & Abrami, P. (2002). Motivation to learn via computer conferencing: Exploring how task specific motivation and CC expectations are related to student acceptance of learning via CC. *Journal of Educational Computing Research, 27*(3), 247–262.

Clark, R. (1983). Reconsidering research on learning from media. *Review of Educational Research, 53*(4), 445–459.

Clark, R. (1994). Media will never influence learning. *Educational Technology Research and Development, 42*(2), 21–29.

Cranton, P. (1994). *Understanding and promoting transformative learning.* San Francisco: Jossey-Bass.

Cranton, P. (1996). *Professional development as transformative learning: New perspectives for teachers of adults.* San Francisco: Jossey-Bass.

Entwistle, N., Entwistle, A., & Tait, H. (1993). Academic understanding and contexts to enhance it: A perspective from research on student learning. In T. M. Duffy, J. Lowyck, & D. Jonassen (Eds.), *Designing environments for constructive learning* (pp. 331–357). Berlin: Springer-Verlag.

Gandell, T., Weston, C., Finkelstein, A., & Winer, L. (2000). Appropriate use of the web in teaching higher education. In B. Mann (Ed.), *Perspectives in web course management* (pp. 61–68). Toronto: Canadian Scholars' Press.

Houseman, J. (1997). Infusion, not diffusion: A strategy for incorporating information technology into higher education. *Journal of Distance Education, 13*(1/2), 15–28.

Hunkins, F. (1987). Sharing our instructional secrets. *Educational Leadership, 45,* 65–67.

Kemp, J., Morrison, G., & Ross, S. (1994). *Designing effective instruction,* New York: Macmillan.

Kozma, R. (1985). A grounded theory of instructional innovation in higher education. *Journal of Higher Education, 56*(3), 300–319.

LaSere Erickson, B., & Weltner Strommer, D. (1991). *Teaching college freshmen.* San Francisco: Jossey-Bass.

Laurillard, D. (1993). *Rethinking university teaching: A framework for the effective use of educational technology.* London: Routledge.

Laurillard, D. (2002). *Rethinking University Teaching* (2nd ed.). London: Routledge, Chapman, & Hall.

McAlpine, L. (2001). Les étudiants bénéficient-ils de la recherche en pédagogie universitaire? In L. Winer, D. Fyson, & Y. Giroux (Eds.), *Actes du Colloque Recherche en Pédagogie Universitaire* (pp. 10–13). Quebec City, Canada: CREPUQ.

McAlpine, L. (2004). Designing learning rather than designing teaching: A model of instruction for higher education that emphasizes learner practice. *Active Learning in Higher Education, 5.*

McAlpine, L., & Weston, C. (2002, July). *Reflection on teaching. Using an empirical model to analyze, improve and learn about your own practice.* Paper presented at the Higher Education Research and Development Society of Australia, Perth.

McKeachie, W. (1999). *Teaching tips* (10th ed.). Boston: Houghton Mifflin Co.

Mezirow, J. (1991). *Transformative dimensions of adult learning.* San Francisco: Jossey-Bass.

Morrison, G., Ross, S., & Kemp, J. (2001). *Designing effective instruction* (3rd ed.). New York: John Wiley.

Papert, S. (1987, January/February). Computer criticism vs technocentric thinking. *Information Technology and Education,* 22–30.

Perkins, D. (1991). Technology meets constructivism: Do they make a marriage? *Educational Technology, 31*(5), 18–23.

Ramsden, P. (1992). *Learning to teach in higher education.* London: Routledge.

Saroyan, A. (2000). Addressing the needs of large groups: The lecturer. In J. Bess (Ed.), *Teaching alone/teaching together: Transforming the structure of teams for teaching* (pp. 87–107). San Francisco: Jossey-Bass.

Schuster, J. H. (1990). Strengthening career preparation for prospective professors. In J. H. Schuster & S. W. Wheeler (Eds.), *Enhancing faculty careers: Strategies for development and renewal* (pp. 65–83). San Francisco: Jossey-Bass.

Sherman, T. M., Armistead, L. P., Fowler, F., Barksdale, M. A., & Reif, G. (1987). The quest for excellence in university teaching. *Journal of Higher Education, 58,* 66–84.

Singer, E. (1996). Espoused teaching paradigms of college faculty. *Research in Higher Education, 37*(6), 659–679.

Tien, S. S. (1991). The self in transformation: Dialectical processes in long-term psychotherapy. *Journal of Contemporary Psychotherapy, 21*(2), 135–147.

Weston, C., & Cranton, P. (1986). Selecting instructional strategies. *Journal of Higher Education, 57*(3), 260–288.

6

EVALUATING STUDENT LEARNING

Cynthia Weston and Lynn McAlpine

Evaluating student learning, one of the most complex areas of course design, is the focus of the day on Thursday in the Course Design and Teaching Workshop. Although this is an area of teaching in which professors have substantial experience, such as grading papers and exams, much of this experience is neither satisfying nor positive. In the needs assessment questionnaires completed before the Workshop, professors name many of their concerns about evaluating student learning. Some of the most common are these:

- How to evaluate learning in large classes
- How to grade group work and participation in smaller classes
- How to increase reliability among multiple graders (TAs)
- How to deal with requests for remarking
- How to increase objectivity when marking

Concurrent with these evaluation concerns, Workshop participants are also struggling on Thursday to develop evaluation plans for the specific courses they are designing. This plan is to be included in the course outline presented to their small-group members on Friday. At minimum, this means specifying the assignments and/or tests they will use to evaluate learning and the weight they will give to each in the course plan.

The range of participants' concerns, their individual needs regarding evaluation for their own course design, and the complexity of the topic of evaluation make Thursday a particularly challenging day. Our goal is to arm participants with a framework that will assist them in assessing the strengths and weaknesses of evaluation methods for the course they are designing and for learning situations in general. Thus, we undertake to place concerns and questions within a larger context of major evaluation concepts. We do this in several ways. First, before coming to the Workshop on Thursday, participants are encouraged to read the articles on evaluation included in their binder. These focus on evaluation as a mechanism for getting to know the quality of student learning, evaluation plans for different disciplines, and criteria and standards for grading (Ramsden, 1992; Walvoord & Johnson Anderson, 1998). Second, Thursday morning begins with a presentation in the large group of selected major evaluation concepts. Third, we move into the small groups for individual coaching on evaluation plans and for initial work on assembling course outlines. Fourth, throughout the Workshop we model evaluation techniques that participants experience as learners, and thus we are able to draw on these as examples of evaluation concepts.

In the following pages, we define major evaluation concepts we have chosen to focus on in the Workshop and indicate how these are touched on in the large-group session on Thursday morning (the emphasis may change slightly each year depending on the facilitators and questions that emerge earlier in the Workshop). We then describe how these concepts are explored in small-group activities. We later describe how, throughout the Workshop, we model techniques to formatively assess learning. We conclude by reflecting on where we are in our thinking about evaluation of student learning.

Introduction to Major Evaluation Concepts

Large-Group Session

Evaluation of student learning can be approached at many levels. In the large-group session, we choose to focus on several major evaluation concepts that link to participants' concerns and provide conceptual tools for guiding principled decisions in relation to course design. Following are the focus points for this session:

- Coherence or alignment of evaluation and learning outcomes
- Formative and summative evaluation
- Informal and formal evaluation
- Reliability and validity
- Norm- and criterion-referenced approaches
- Traditional and alternative methods
- Evaluation and grading

In the needs assessment that they complete prior to the Workshop, many participants express concerns related to evaluation and grading. This is not surprising; our experience suggests that professors generally think of evaluation as creating tests or assignments that can be graded and used to arrive at a mark for students at the end of a course. One of our major goals is to expand the thinking of participants beyond grading.

Coherence of Evaluation and Learning Outcomes

The Concept

What we evaluate, signals what we want students to learn (Fenwick & Parsons, 2000); it defines the actual curriculum from the students' point of view (Ramsden, 1992); it is the most significant prompt for learning (Boud, 1995). In this sense, the evaluation plan for a course actually defines the learning goals from the students' perspective because it communicates what students should focus on during the course. For example, if an evaluation plan consists primarily of multiple-choice tests requiring recall of information, this tells students to focus on learning specific information. If an evaluation plan requires students to work through cases in which they propose not only solutions but also their rationales, this sends a message that critical thinking is important. Rowntree (1977) reminds us that evaluation, for professors, often extends beyond the content and includes affective outcomes such as values and commitment to a subject.

Coherence in course design means that what is stated in learning outcomes is explicitly and intentionally supported with content, instructional strategies, and evaluation. Our evaluation procedures often show where lack of coherence or misalignment among course design components occurs. Many of us can recall a professor who spent a lot of time or went into great detail about a topic in class. Thus, we assumed the topic was important and would be on the exam; when it was not, we may have felt confused or tricked. An experience in a history of education course in graduate school is still vividly remembered by one Workshop facilitator: The students sat around a table and had engaging discussions about issues in education. These were really enjoyable and productive discussions. Given what was going on in class, the expectation was an essay type exam requiring the kind of critical analysis and interpretation that had been practiced weekly. Imagine the students' shock when the exam required recall of specific facts from readings listed on the course outline but never mentioned during the course. Totally unprepared for this kind of evaluation, the reaction was confusion and upset, and performance on the exam was disappointing. It would have been better, of course, if the instructor had designed an evaluation appropriate to the discussions from which students learned so much more than facts. This is an example of incoherence in course design, a misalignment between what was being practiced and what was evaluated. This professor probably never thought about evaluation as connected to the rest of the learning process, nor the impact that such lack of coherence can have on students.

Addressing the Concept of Evaluation

We begin the large-group session on Thursday morning by presenting the Workshop concept map (Figure 3.1). We describe briefly how evaluation fits with the other components of the course design process and how it must be aligned with the learning outcomes. We emphasize that evaluation and learning outcomes are flip sides of the same coin. For evaluation measures to be valid, they must measure the learning stated in the outcomes. Outcomes and evaluation drive the selection of instructional strategies. We stress that in a course that is designed coherently, the instructional strategies provide students with sufficient practice and feedback to enable them to accomplish the desired learning and be prepared for evaluation activities. Our most consistent and prominent message on Thursday morning is this: What is evaluated must be directly and intentionally based on learning outcomes, and what is stated in learning outcomes defines what is to be evaluated.

Formative and Summative Evaluations

The Concepts

Scriven's (1981) description of formative and summative evaluation provides a useful way of thinking about the purposes for evaluating student learning. The purpose of formative evaluation is diagnosis, growth, and improvement in learning. It is usually done in an ongoing way during the learning process and commonly (but not always) associated with evaluation techniques that do not involve grading. Included in formative evaluation are current notions of ongoing, dynamic, educative assessment in which feedback given during learning becomes a more important aspect of evaluation than an audit or judgment given only after learning activities are over (e.g., Brown & Knight, 1994; Shepard, 2000; Wiggins, 1998).

Summative evaluation is done for the purpose of reporting, decision making, or making a final judgment about the learning at a particular point in time. It is usually done at the end of the learning process and is usually (but not always) associated with a grade or mark. In this sense, summative evaluation implies a verdict. Thus, concerns such as reliability and validity are paramount, and these will be discussed further in the section entitled Evaluation and Grading.

Addressing the Concepts of Formative and Summative Evaluations

The concepts of formative and summative evaluation are usually introduced explicitly in the large-group session. This may be done by eliciting concerns and linking them to these concepts or by encouraging participants to think about the purposes for which they evaluate student learning. They usually name purposes such as the need to give grades, report marks, determine whether a student should move on to another level of study, motivate students to study, and improve student learning.

When participants consider the purposes of evaluation, some realize that, for example, they are using summative evaluations (e.g., a series of quizzes worth 50% of the course mark), but their purpose is actually formative: letting students know how well they are doing. Others have mentioned that they use grades to motivate students. We suggest that summative evaluation not be used for motivational purposes and that a more formative approach be taken.

The distinction between formative and summative evaluation helps participants to articulate the purposes for which they assess learning and facilitates realigning their evaluation methods to more directly accomplish their purposes.

We encourage professors to incorporate ongoing, dynamic, formative evaluation that guides student learning into their more prevalent practice of summative grading of student work after it is completed. This move—from thinking about assessment as something done to students, to something done with students, and finally to assessment as something done for students (Brown & Knight, 1994)—requires changing thinking and practice so that participants and their students see evaluation as a source of insight and help instead of an occasion for meting out rewards and punishments (Shepard, 2000).

Formal and Informal Evaluations

The Concepts

Formal and informal evaluations can be distinguished in terms of degree of structure, awareness of both parties that the evaluation is occurring, and documentation of results. Formal evaluation methods are structured tools and procedures for assessing learning that are devised in advance. Both students and teachers are aware that evaluation is occurring and that there is some kind of documentation of results. Examples include assignments, term papers, projects, presentations, midterms, finals, quizzes, thesis defenses, and comprehensive exams. Informal evaluations, on the other hand, may be devised in advance or created spontaneously; often they do not have structured tools or procedures. Sometimes only the evaluator is aware the evaluation is occurring, and there is not usually documentation of results. Examples include instructors' perceptions of questions and answers during class, conversations during office visits, nonverbal behavior, and class participation. Informal evaluations are not necessarily unplanned; they may be very intentional, such as monitoring the kinds of questions asked or answers given during class as a means to redirect instruction if necessary.

Formal and informal evaluations can be used for both formative and summative purposes. Common in higher education are formal summative evaluations, such as tests or papers, and formal formative evaluations, such as feedback on graded quizzes or ungraded drafts of papers. Also common are informal formative evaluations, such as suggestions given to a student regarding how an idea for a paper might be developed or revised, or adjustments made to a student's response to a question. The most worrisome evaluations are those informal summative evaluations we as professors may make without realization, such as the silent judgments that particular individuals are "good" or "bad" students. Another example of informal summative evaluation is judgments made about class participation based on perception, without benefit of clear procedures or criteria. These can lead to faulty or unfair conclusions about students. Being aware of these distinctions helps professors be more intentional about when and where to use formal and informal techniques in the assessment of student learning.

Addressing the Concepts of Formal and Informal Evaluations

In the morning large-group session, the concepts of formal and informal evaluation usually arise in response to participants' questions about whether all learning outcomes have to be formally evaluated. We try to add to participants' use of infrequent formal evaluations (usually graded) by encouraging increased use of frequent informal formative methods (not graded) to provide continuous feedback to students on their progress toward learning goals— such as a one-minute paper to informally assess learning at the end of a class or an option to resubmit work after feedback.

Evaluation and Grading

The Concepts

Evaluation is a judgment about student progress toward learning goals. Grading consists of placing a value, usually a number or a letter, on that judgment. Ramsden's (1992) conception of evaluation "for learning first and grading second implies the use of a spectrum of methods" (p. 191). Evaluation done at

the beginning of the instructional process can be useful for diagnostic purposes and as a point of reference for later evaluation of student progress. Evaluation done during instruction is useful for formative purposes to facilitate
development and for gathering information about student progress and
process. Evaluations done at the end of the learning process are most often for
summative purposes, commonly assess products of learning, and are usually
tied to grading. Many participants come to the Workshop assuming that every
evaluation should be graded. An important goal for us in the Workshop is to
recognize that evaluation is much more than grading.

Addressing the Concepts of Evaluation and Grading

In the large-group session of the Workshop, we try to make explicit the distinction between evaluation and grading. This may be done through presentation and examples or by eliciting participants' definitions of the two terms
and trying to come to a consensus on the distinction as a group. For many
participants who have never before considered evaluating student progress
toward learning without giving a mark, the distinction can be a revelation.

We try to encourage thinking about evaluation as an ongoing formative
process integrated with instruction that continuously guides learners as to their
progress and the professor as to how well teaching is achieving what is intended.
During the large-group session, participants often ask if and how ongoing formative evaluation can be done in large classes. We believe that it can, and one of
our favorite techniques that can be used in a class of any size is the one-minute
paper (e.g., Angelo & Cross, 1993). Students are asked, for example, to summarize what they have learned at a certain point during the class by writing for one
minute. These papers may be handed in to the professor who can evaluate (and
preferably not grade) what is being learned and get a sense of what the next
steps in teaching should be, or they can be kept by the students to make judgments about their own learning. Among other informal evaluation techniques,
we model the use of the one-minute paper in the Workshop so participants will
have a sense of its usefulness from the learner's perspective for consolidating
learning. Participants recognize that one-minute papers take little time away
from teaching and thus can easily imagine using them in their own classes.

Reliability and Validity

The Concepts

There are several types of reliability to consider when evaluating learning in
higher education. We concentrate on two aspects in the Workshop: inter-rater
reliability, or the extent to which different individuals marking the same work
would assign the same mark; and intra-rater reliability, or the extent to which

a professor is consistent in marking across papers. While there are various ways to ensure inter- and intra-reliability, we focus on the definition and the use of clear criteria and standards as an effective mechanism for ensuring both.

Validity is a critical issue in course design: More than any other factor, the quality of an evaluation measure depends on its validity (Oosterhof, 1994). The type of validity most relevant to participants in the Workshop is content validity. Content validity establishes how well questions, tasks, observations, or other elements of an evaluation relate to the content domain being assessed (Oosterhof, 1994). In the course design process, this translates into making sure that the evaluation is coherent with the learning outcomes.

Addressing the Concepts of Reliability and Validity

In the large-group session, the concept of reliability may be defined directly by the Workshop facilitators, but the subject is usually raised first by participants as one of their greatest concerns. They seldom use the term *reliability*; they wonder how to increase "consistency" among multiple markers (inter-rater reliability) or their own "objectivity" when grading essay papers (intra-rater reliability). The facilitators listen for these questions and seize the opportunity to define the concept of reliability and introduce the notion of criteria as a way of increasing consistency and objectivity. We generally recommend that participants develop a set of criteria and standards that characterize the levels of performance (e.g., an "A" paper or a "C" paper) and then use these to guide their own marking and to train multiple markers. The use of criteria enhances reliability among multiple markers and reliability for the professor across a set of papers since expectations are made explicit, and performance or lack of it is easier to detect.

The concept of validity may or may not be defined directly by the facilitators in the large-group session. However, we know that content validity, which we call coherence, can be a problem, most notably when evaluation methods require a different kind of learning from what has been stated in the outcomes and practiced in instructional strategies. For this reason, when we introduce the concept of coherence at the start of the Thursday morning session, we are indirectly addressing content validity—emphasizing the importance of evaluating what is intended to be evaluated. This is usually addressed more directly in the small-group sessions on Thursday afternoon when participants set up the grading systems for the courses they are designing. As they decide how much weight to assign to different evaluation methods, they are essentially struggling with content validity through matching the importance ascribed to learning outcomes with the measures used to evaluate learning.

Norm- and Criterion-Referenced Approaches

The Concepts

Most professors in higher education are accustomed to a norm-referenced approach to evaluation—that is, the practice of comparing students to others within the group as a frame of reference for making a judgment or putting value on students' work. Some assumptions related to norm-referenced evaluation are that grading should be on a curve, and that regardless of how much students have learned there will be a normal grade distribution, with the majority of students in the middle and progressively fewer at the top and the bottom. In this approach, it is possible that two students taking the same course in two different semesters, but who have achieved the same level of learning, will receive different final marks, clearly demonstrating the lack of connection between learning and evaluation. Less common in higher education is a criterion-referenced approach to evaluation, where student work is compared to a predefined benchmark, such as a set of criteria. Some assumptions here are that all students can get an "A" if they have achieved the course criteria, or conversely all could fail, and that students are more motivated by such an approach.

Addressing the Concepts of Norm- and Criterion-Referenced Approaches

In the large-group session, the concepts and assumptions of norm- and criterion-referenced evaluation are presented. We favor a criterion-referenced approach—and say so. We suggest that defining criteria stimulates and clarifies thinking as professors are forced to articulate the specific features expected to be present in students' work. Establishing these in advance helps the professor guide the work, clarifies expectations when communicated to students, and can greatly facilitate marking when shared with teaching assistants (TAs) or others charged with the responsibility of evaluating student work.

Traditional and Alternative Methods

The Concepts

Traditional evaluations are those most commonly considered and used in higher education, such as tests, term papers, and exams. Traditional methods tend to evaluate the *products* of learning through artifacts that demonstrate students' acquisition of declarative knowledge (the "what"), usually in cumulative, summative ways. These include term papers that synthesize what has been learned about a topic, or exams that assess facts, concepts, and principles learned. These methods also tend to assign traditional roles to teacher and student in the evaluation process, when the professor is the evaluator and decision maker and the student is the recipient of the decision.

Alternative methods, those less commonly used in higher education, move beyond evaluating learning products toward evaluating students' thinking and ability to apply in authentic situations what they have learned. Student acquisition of cognitive *processes* may be evaluated through artifacts that provide evidence of student thinking, such as case solutions, portfolios, and journals. For example, asking students to show how they did their work when solving a math equation allows evaluation of the process as well as the product (the solution) of learning. When cases are used as part of an evaluation method, and students are asked to explain why their decision is appropriate, particularly when there are a number of credible and acceptable decisions, their thinking process, as well as the resulting decision, can be evaluated. Alternative methods may also evaluate *progress* in learning—that is, the development, growth, and advancement of learning—through artifacts such as student journals or portfolios in which development is documented over an extended period. As well, two products separated in time can be compared to evaluate progress, or observations of a process at two points in time can be compared to evaluate improvement.

Alternative methods may also assign less traditional roles to teacher and student in terms of who does the evaluation, who gives feedback, and who makes the decisions. In evaluation, there is always a power situation. Whoever is the giver of feedback and/or the decision maker is in the position of power, and the recipient becomes the object of scrutiny. Instructor-directed evaluation, in which the professor is the giver of feedback and/or the decision maker and the student is the recipient, is most familiar in higher education. Since instructor-directed evaluation is most familiar to participants in our Workshop, we focus on introducing notions of peer evaluation and self-evaluation.

In peer-directed evaluations, students give feedback and make decisions, and the recipients are other students. This is evaluation of work by people of equal status and power. Fenwick and Parsons (2000) talk about peer evaluators as "critical friends" who show appreciation and value for what is being attempted, but who also are trained to discuss the observed experience. Since peer evaluation is an unusual situation for most students, its use is usually recommended first for lower-impact evaluations, such as giving formative feedback, rather than for summative evaluations when marks are given. If students are to be involved in marking their peers' work, it is useful for them to have some involvement in the process of creating the tool and the criteria used to evaluate. In this way, they have ownership in the process and become very clear about what is expected in their work. An important part of peer evaluation is preparing students to both give and receive feedback in a way that is constructive and leads to improvement (e.g., Brown, Bull, & Pendlebury, 1997; Fenwick & Parsons, 2000). This can be done through practice using criteria to observe, interpret, and assess the work of others. In self-evaluation, students are responsible for assessing their own work: they give feedback to themselves, make decisions, and are the recipient. This is particularly useful for helping students to think about and reflect on their own learning, thus developing metacognitive, or reflective, abilities.

Choosing the ways to evaluate learning products, process, or progress and determining the roles of participants in the evaluation process depend in part on professors' beliefs about teaching and learning and the institutional structure within which the individual operates. If there is a set of declarative or procedural knowledge that has to be achieved, and/or the individual is operating within a formal educational structure where grading or accreditation is required, then evaluation would tend to focus certainly on products of learning, perhaps on process; but assessing progress alone may not be sufficient. Roles in the evaluation process would likely be traditional but could also incorporate peer evaluation and self-evaluation. If operating within an adult or continuing education context where the prevailing attitude supports individual growth or favors graduate supervision, a focus on progress may be most appropriate and satisfying for the learners, and individual input into the focus of evaluation as well as self-evaluation of achievement may be most appropriate.

Addressing the Concepts of Traditional and Alternative Methods

In the morning large-group session, we might not define traditional and alternative methods explicitly, although the concepts would be introduced where appropriate in response to questions raised. Throughout the Workshop, we encourage participants, through examples and suggestions, to expand beyond the traditional and incorporate alternative evaluation methods when these appropriately support the goals of the course and parallel the methods used in instructional strategies and practice.

The roles of participants in the evaluation process are not normally addressed explicitly during the large-group session but do come up for discussion in the small groups. We have modeled and participants have experienced peer evaluation and self-evaluation throughout the Workshop, so we draw upon these experiences as examples.

Small-Group Session

At the end of the large-group session, participants move as usual into their small groups. At this point, participants have made many cascading decisions about their particular course in terms of content, learning outcomes, and instructional strategies. We work in small groups in the morning for about two hours, selecting evaluation methods appropriate to course learning outcomes. The afternoon, as is the case every day, is dedicated to microteaching. Thus, our goal is that by lunch break on Thursday, each participant will have a draft evaluation plan. This can be elaborated on later Thursday evening and incorporated into the course outline presented on Friday morning to the small group. The evaluation portion of the course outline should specify assignments and/or exams required for successful completion of the course and the weight that each is given.

Because of the individual specificity of course decisions, evaluation concepts tend to be developed most explicitly and in most detail in the small groups. The sequence of topics and the depth with which they are explored depend on the small group; discussion evolves, driven by the participants' needs. Sometimes, we give mini-lectures; more often, group members are engaged in interactive questions and discussion with the facilitators and among themselves. Thus, what is described following is but one possible scenario and is intended to provide a flavor of the discussion that might occur in a small group.

Coherence

When we sit down in the small groups on Thursday, participants' greatest interest is in settling on methods they will use to assess their learning outcomes: "Can I continue to use my current evaluation methods?" "What other methods might be used?" "How can I evaluate some of the attitudes and values I have included in my learning outcomes?"

We begin by guiding participants through a thinking process for selecting evaluation approaches that correspond to learning outcomes. We ask participants to study tables included in their course pack (e.g., Cranton, 1989) that analyze the appropriateness of common evaluation techniques for each level and domain of learning. For instance, one table suggests short-answer tests as appropriate for evaluating lower levels of learning in the cognitive domain and essays as more appropriate for evaluating higher cognitive levels such as analysis and synthesis. We ask participants to think about why different evaluation techniques need to be considered for different types of learning. This has been a successful activity for engaging participants in thinking about the extent to which their evaluation methods are aligned with their learning outcomes.

Participants usually notice that the techniques for evaluating lower-level cognitive outcomes are more familiar to them than those for evaluating higher cognitive levels or affective learning. As well, they frequently recognize that familiar evaluation methods may no longer be appropriate for the outcomes newly defined for their courses.

Traditional Versus Alternative Approaches

Discussion about coherence often prompts reassessment of the types of learning desired. Participants may at first enthusiastically recognize their own interest in evaluating thinking processes (e.g., problem solving or critical thinking) or progress (e.g., growth and advancement of learning) in addition to content knowledge. Some may then be reluctant to move outside the familiar "box" of traditional evaluation methods. They wonder: "Is it legitimate to evaluate thinking processes instead of just the 'answer'?" "How can covert processes be evaluated?" "Wouldn't it all just be subjective?"

At this point, participants may voice discomfort or concern. In this situation, small-group interaction and multidisciplinary perspective is crucial. By this time, small-group members are quite familiar with one another's courses and thus are able to act as sounding boards for each other. Because they all are struggling with new concepts and know firsthand the difficulties others are experiencing, small-group members invariably step in to support one another in a positive, sensitive manner. (We never cease to be inspired by this.) For example, as "Jane" from Biology starts to feel overwhelmed and annoyed by the prospect of moving away from traditional methods such as multiple-choice exams toward an alternative method for evaluating students' problem-solving processes, "Jack" from Management describes a case-based approach he has used in the past to evaluate this kind of learning. The others of the small group, sensing Jane's resistance and frustration to the idea, try to encourage her by exploring how a case-based evaluation method might be adapted for her content and context. Jane listens, perhaps with arms tightly crossed, while the group members work through how the evaluation might be constructed, even what might be the wording of the assignment. We have seen time and again how through group expertise and support in this way, participants begin to move outside of their comfort zones toward evaluation methods that are more in line with their learning outcomes.

As a part of this discussion, the issue of group work and participation usually arises since it is perceived as a way of evaluating many aspects of learning. In some faculties, it is the norm to give a certain percentage of the course grade for student participation; however participants begin to question the meaningfulness of this. They disclose that a mark may be assigned based on their "sense" of a student's participation. We encourage articulation by participants of how participation relates to the goals of their course. Frequently their learning outcomes do not require evaluation of participation, but they identify implicit expectations about students' ability to ask questions and articulate their thinking process or to contribute constructively to a group. We recommend that these expectations be made explicit, and as participants do this, some may add new learning outcomes to communicate their expectations about participation to their students.

The evaluation of participation and group work provides a platform to prompt consideration of alternative evaluation roles for teacher and student. Who will do the evaluating? Does it have to be the professor? Could peer evaluation be used for group work? Could self-evaluation be used for individual contributions? If so, who will decide on the guidelines for evaluation? As these decisions are considered, we again raise the importance of criteria. Regardless of who is doing the evaluation, expectations must be made explicit, by the professor alone in concert with the learners or by the learners themselves, and these expectations must guide the evaluation process.

Reliability, Criteria, and Standards

The notion of criteria addresses a number of participant concerns. Criteria provide guidance for evaluating group work or participation. Criteria increase objectivity and reliability when the evaluator is marking a set of papers or increase reliability across multiple markers, and they can help professors respond to requests for remarking.

It is not unusual at this point for participants who have similar evaluation concerns to break into pairs or threes to work, for example, on elaborating specific criteria to guide evaluation of participation, term papers, or journal contributions. We have at hand sample rubrics from our own courses and other sources (e.g., Bean & Peterson, 1998; Fenwick & Parsons, 2000) to share with them when the moment arises.

We suggest that participants make explicit the criteria and standards they will use to assess quality of work. First, they clearly define the parameters of the task (e.g., assignment, paper, or project), which usually results in revealing the criteria. Then, they try to distinguish the characteristics of top performance, middle performance, and weak performance, which results in the standards that will be applied in evaluating work according to criteria. We suggest that written criteria and standards be shared with students in advance to provide clarity and guide their studying behavior. If the criteria and standards are to be used by teaching assistants or markers, thus individuals should be trained by the professor, perhaps by marking a set of papers together, sharing the feedback and marks they would give, and adjusting their interpretation of the criteria until a shared understanding is attained.

Norm- and Criterion-Referenced Approaches

Participants often ask "Will giving criteria and standards in advance make learning too easy?" "Will course grades end up being too high?" This provides an opportunity to revisit the concepts of norm- and criterion-referenced approaches to evaluation. We acknowledge their concerns: Criterion-referenced evaluation may reduce variability in marks since criteria are clearer and thus may be more readily achieved by a greater number of students. Participants usually raise questions about how to deal with this in a system that exerts pressure to produce a normal distribution of marks in a course. We do not have easy answers for this. On the one hand, a change in culture is likely required for units to accept a shift in approach. On the other hand, since university education is supposed to be about learning, we are puzzled by resistance to a concept that enhances it. We share our own personal stories of discussions we've had with administrators and committees over the years defending our use of a criterion-referenced approach. We also provide examples from our own courses and those of others that emphasize the learning purpose of evaluation: detailed descriptions of assignments and the criteria used to evaluate them, options to resubmit work after formative feedback, and contract grading.

Formative and Summative, Formal and Informal

In some faculties, such as Law, it is not uncommon for the final exam to count for 100% of the course grade. In other faculties, a midterm and a final exam are the standard. As the discussion progresses in the small group, participants begin to see that evaluation is a more central and crucial aspect of the teaching and learning process than most of them had recognized. Some feel daunted by the prospect of evaluating everything they have named in their learning outcomes. Common questions include "Do all learning outcomes have to be evaluated or graded?" "How many evaluation measures should there be?" One of our guiding principles is that changes to teaching are best made in small, incremental steps, adding one or two new bits at a time rather than undertaking huge leaps. Thus, we might explore the possibility of adding one new formal assignment to be evaluated summatively and find one or two opportunities for informal formative feedback (e.g., from peers and/or the instructor) that is not graded. Conceiving of evaluation as an educative rather than judgmental or auditing process (Wiggins, 1998) requires a substantial shift in thinking and practice for most professors. We endeavor to support this evolution through discussion and multiplicity of examples.

Evaluation, Grading, and Validity

As the two hours in the small group on Thursday draw to a close, participants still have many pressing questions before making their evaluation plan concrete: "How should evaluations be distributed across the course?" "Which ones should get the most weight?" In response to how evaluation measures should be distributed across a course, we revisit the notion of ongoing evaluation. We recommend that students have regular opportunities to practice what they are supposed to be learning and get feedback on that practice. We further suggest that the most important learning outcomes should be given the most practice in the learning process and the most weight in the evaluation plan. Upon reflection, participants often recognize their tendency to give most weight to types of learning that are easier to assess, such as knowledge of facts or principles, and to avoid assessing more important, usually complex, higher-level outcomes because they are uncertain how to measure them.

One technique we use to ensure validity is the creation of a matrix in which participants' course learning outcomes are listed down one side and evaluation methods selected are listed across the top (e.g., Oosterhof, 1994). By checking off which methods address each learning outcome, participants can readily see which outcomes are emphasized (or overemphasized) and which are not evaluated at all. They can also quickly see from this visual display whether the different aspects of their evaluation plan reflect the relative importance of what students are to learn. First, the participant can think about weight given to learning outcomes in each assignment or evaluation during the term. For example, on a 25-item test, which of the course learning outcomes are being evaluated? Are just a few outcomes being measured? Are they the outcomes that are of most concern to the professor at that time? Sometimes professors find that a certain test emphasizes a few lower-level outcomes because those are easier to evaluate when they really want to evaluate higher-order outcomes. At a second level, professors can think about the weight given to learning outcomes in the overall evaluation plan for the course. When looking across assignments and exams, are the most important outcomes given adequate weight? Again, professors sometimes find that the overall plan puts more weight on less important outcomes, such as recall of information, than on the most important outcomes, such as thinking, which would be evident through papers, projects, or case studies.

Lunch Break (What? Already?)

Usually no one is ready to break for lunch when the time comes. We have opened up Pandora's evaluation box, and after a mere three hours—one in large group and two in small group—the participants are just beginning to form their evaluation plans. They have been introduced to major evaluation concepts: coherence, formative and summative, informal and formal, evaluation and grading, reliability and validity, norm- and criterion-referenced approaches, and traditional and alternative methods.

There are several messages we hope they take away (and we think they do, judging from the evaluation plans they bring in on Friday): that evaluation be coherent with learning outcomes; that weight given to evaluation measures reflect relative importance of learning outcomes; that they ensure practice and feedback before grading; that they be more intentional about ongoing formative feedback; and that they realize not everything has to be graded. We have looked for opportunities to link their questions to these concepts and build on them so discussion evolves naturally. And most important, we have not underplayed the complexity of evaluating student learning but have tried to point out how information gained through various evaluation methods concurrently provides feedback on the effectiveness of teaching.

Reflections on Evaluation: Where We Are in Our Thinking?

We are continuously developing a more complex understanding of evaluation of student learning. In fact, although we have referred to this component as "evaluation of student learning," we are now introducing the term *assessment,* which emphasizes the outcomes of learning as "more complex and more closely aligned with life than with an individual performance measure in an antiseptic context using sanitized instruments" (Eisner, 1993, p. 224). In this sense, assessment moves beyond evaluation to concerns of understanding learning tasks and learners as inherently complex and to designing assessments that represent and honor those characteristics. Assessment becomes increasingly integrated with instruction. The purpose becomes primarily educative (Wiggins, 1998), and students have a greater role in the process through self- and peer assessment.

This notion of assessment fits with cognitive and constructivist views of learning, which we espouse: Knowledge is socially and culturally developed, intelligent thought involves self-monitoring and deep understanding of principles, and transfer of learning is supported (Shepard, 2000). But assessing higher-order learning is time-intensive. Although we consider it essential in higher education, we worry whether what we are suggesting to professors is feasible within the current situation in higher education in North America: increasing class size and decreasing resources.

The new technologies show much promise in the area of evaluation and are of increasing interest to professors and the university. We think of online assessment as an alternative method that can facilitate measuring process and progress through features such as conferencing, which provides opportunities for formative feedback, self-assessment, and peer assessment. Unfortunately, some professors tend to use online assessment in traditional ways such as multiple-choice tests or quizzes. Issues exacerbated in online assessment include authentication of respondents, validity of results, and controlled access.

We recognize that understanding evaluation requires in-depth work beyond the Workshop. Grading often represents the greatest concern of the participants, and we do not spend as much time on this or construction of evaluation tools as they might like, nor do we model more formal summative methods that are often of basic concern to the participants. We realize that the ongoing formative evaluation and alternative methods of evaluation, such as providing formative feedback and allowing resubmissions, requires considerable time. So we have to work through how to make this manageable for participants who teach large classes. Recognizing this, we have developed follow-up sessions to the Workshop. We now give an annual three-hour workshop on evaluating written work, such as essays, in which multiple examples of criteria for evaluation are provided for specific disciplines.

References

Angelo, T. A., & Cross, K. P. (1993). *Classroom assessment techniques* (2nd ed.). San Francisco: Jossey-Bass.

Bean, J. C., & Peterson, D. (Eds.). (1998). *Changing the way we grade student performance: Classroom assessment and the new learning paradigm* (Vol. 74). San Francisco: Jossey-Bass.

Boud, D. (1995). Assessment and learning: Contradictory or complementary? In P. Knight (Ed.), *Assessment for learning in higher education* (pp. 35–48). London: Kogan Page.

Brown, G., Bull, J., & Pendlebury, M. (1997). *Assessing student learning in higher education*. London: Routledge.

Brown, S., & Knight, P. (1994). *Assessing learners in higher education*. London: Kogan Page.

Cranton, P. (1989). *Planning instruction for adult learners*. Toronto: Wall and Emerson.

Eisner, E. W. (1993). Reshaping assessment in education: Some criteria in search of practice. *Journal of Curriculum Studies, 25*(3), 219–233.

Fenwick, T., & Parsons, J. (2000). *The art of evaluation: A handbook for educators and trainers.* Toronto: Thompson Educational Publishing.

Oosterhof, A. (1994). *Classroom applications of educational measurement* (2nd ed.). New York: Macmillan.

Ramsden, P. (1992). *Learning to teach in higher education.* London: Routledge.

Rowntree, D. (1977). *Assessing students.* London: Kogan Page.

Scriven, M. (1981). *Evaluation thesaurus* (3rd ed.). Inverness, CA: Edgepress.

Shepard, L. A. (2000). The role of assessment in learning culture. *Educational Researcher, 29*(7), 4–14.

Walvoord, B., & Johnson Anderson, V. (1998). *A tool for learning and assessment* (pp. 9–16). San Francisco: Jossey-Bass.

Wiggins, G. (1998). *Educative assessment.* San Francisco: Jossey-Bass.

7

THE FINAL STEP

EVALUATION OF TEACHING

Alenoush Saroyan, Cynthia Weston, Lynn McAlpine,
and Susan Cowan

The last day of the Course Design and Teaching Workshop is the time to reflect on the entire design process and think of ways in which classroom experience can be used formatively to improve teaching. Designing a solid course and improving course evaluation are possibly the two most compelling reasons that initially attract participants to the Workshop. We know this from responses to the needs assessment that we send out a few weeks prior to the Workshop. The concerns about student course ratings and teaching portfolios pertain to the two policies that are in place for the evaluation of teaching in our university. The policy to evaluate all undergraduate courses using student course rating questionnaires was introduced at McGill in the early 1980s. Since then, professors have always had questions about their use and validity. The teaching portfolio is a more recent policy that was introduced in 1994. Questions voiced about it usually pertain to the creation of the document itself and the criteria used to evaluate portfolios and, by extension, teaching in a given department.

We address these concerns only on a general and somewhat superficial level in the large-group session on this last day. However, as with the other topics of this Workshop, activities and related discussions that occur during the five days in the small and large groups appear to sufficiently address participants' queries. The indication to us is that the same kinds of questions and individual concerns are not voiced again when we ask the group to fill out the post-Workshop evaluation questionnaire. Moreover, we believe that participants realize that if they design their course with student learning in mind, they can utilize student feedback formatively to improve their teaching. For many participants, this is the first time they have "engineered" the learning process of their students. They do this by clarifying for themselves what they want students to learn, how they will support this learning, and how they will know if students have attained the level and type of learning intended. This in itself brings many participants closer to their students. They become more familiar with the way students think and what they value and expect from a course. Consequently, they feel less threatened by students' evaluation of their course and their teaching.

Conditions for Improving Teaching

The success of the Workshop and its apparent relevance to the needs of participants can be better explained by the teaching development model proposed by Centra (1993). In this model, Centra refers to four conditions that need to be present for teaching improvement to take place:

1. The process of improvement must result in some newly gained knowledge.
2. The individual investing time in the process must perceive the improvement as having some value.
3. Support systems and appropriate mechanisms must be available to assist the individual in the process of improvement and change.
4. Finally, sufficient intrinsic or extrinsic motivation (rewards, promotions, salary increments, and the like) must be present.

In our view, the Workshop meets all four conditions. For McGill University professors, the fourth condition is a particularly strong and appealing factor, given the context of our institution and the teaching policies therein. The quality of teaching, as determined by existing evaluation policies, has fairly serious implications for career advancement and remuneration. Both tenure and promotion necessitate, at a minimum, a rating of *reasonable* in the category of teaching.[1] Many departments would actually hesitate to forward a tenure dossier beyond their unit if the evaluation of teaching was not *superior,* and certainly not if it was *unsatisfactory.* Another important factor is that our teaching portfolio policy applies to all ranks: Every academic, including a full professor, is expected to document teaching and related activities.

---

[1]The other two categories are research and service. The ratings in each category are superior, reasonable, unsatisfactory.

Furthermore, teaching performance, together with performance in research and service, provide the basis for determining merit pay, which for most is the principal mechanism for salary increase.

Our primary goal with respect to the evaluation of teaching is to help participants develop an appreciation for its formative aspect and for ways in which information about the quality of teaching can be gleaned from multiple sources. These include students as well as peers and the individual professor himself or herself. To promote peer evaluation and self-evaluation, the Workshop offers a supportive environment where individuals can practice giving and receiving constructive feedback. The multidisciplinary composition of the small groups helps in heightening sensitivity to input from others. In these groups, each individual is the expert in his or her own subject area but a student with respect to all others. The microteaching activities cast participants in a dual role: as professor and as student. The result is that as the "subject expert," the participant receives immediate "student" feedback about learning, and as "students," participants come to appreciate some of the difficulties their own students might experience as learners in the classroom.

Our discussion of the evaluation of teaching is always anchored in a broader discussion concerning the complex task of teaching. By the last day of the Workshop, participants have experienced in different ways through activities how every teaching episode forces an individual to face a number of demands concurrently. They begin to better appreciate the relevance of a knowledge base that extends beyond subject matter. They become more aware that teaching necessitates dealing with a number of constraints, such as the immediacy, unpredictability, and public nature of the task (Leinhardt, 1993; Shulman, 1993). By the last day, the Workshop activities have also reinforced the Centre for University Teaching and Learning's (CUTL's) view of teaching and its components (see Chapter 2).

Definition of Effective Teaching

Classical Definition

With our particular conceptualization of teaching, how do we specifically define effective teaching, and is this definition similar to or different from what the literature has to offer? A classical definition, for instance, is provided by Chickering and Gamson (1991). Their list of principles of good teaching consists of the following:

1. Encouraging student/faculty contact and cooperation among students
2. Active learning

3. Giving prompt feedback

4. Emphasizing time on task

5. Communicating high expectations

6. Respecting diversity

The distinction between this particular definition and others is associated with the theoretical lens through which teaching is viewed, and this has been elaborated on in detail elsewhere (Saroyan & Amundsen, 2001). Each of the two prominent paradigmatic views, behavioral and cognitive, places emphasis on different aspects of teaching.

Behavioral Definition

From a behavioral perspective, effective teaching is defined in terms of overt behaviors, or visible actions, that lead to effective learning as measured by student achievement on some test. This, also known as the process/product paradigm (Shulman, 1986), draws on empirical findings showing that particular teaching behaviors (input) lead to certain kinds of learning (product). The focus of this perspective is teacher action and not the process involved in teaching, student learning, or other mediating factors such as the social context of learning. From this point of reference, actions such as expressive use of gestures and movement during the delivery of instruction, eye contact, and appropriate humor can lead to increased student achievement and self-confidence and a larger number of completed assignments. Other observable attributes—such as organization and clarity of presentations, and use of outlines, diagrams, and different kinds of examples—help students better integrate new material with what they already know. This helps facilitate both the storing and the retrieval of information.

Cognitive Definition

The cognitive perspective, on the other hand, looks at the psychological processes invoked during teaching or learning. In this context, research into effectiveness examines what it would take for students to process information at different levels and acquire complex, cognitive thinking skills such as reasoning, problem solving, and analytical thinking. With respect to teaching, effectiveness pertains to the processes involved in transforming content knowledge into instruction (Shulman, 1986). This transformation requires adapting, altering, and enriching content based on past experiences of teaching the same content. To this end, empirical studies have examined the thought processes of master teachers and have compared them to those of novices, with the aim of delineating dimensions along which these two groups can be differentiated. Availability of complex knowledge schemas, the ability to see relationships between lessons and overall curriculum, a rich knowledge base and the ability to link teaching actions to a large number of instructional goals, and a more profound interpretation of classroom situations (e.g., Copeland, Birmingham, DeMeulle, D'Emidio-Caston, & Natal, 1994) are a few of these dimensions.

Feedback, Reflection, and Practice

Using the model of teaching expertise proposed in Chapter 2 (Figure 2.1) as our point of reference, we inevitably return to the question we asked earlier: What would effective teaching mean in this context, and would the evaluation of teaching necessitate evaluating every component of the model? As discussed in Chapter 2, in our model, convergence in perceptions and actions is one measure of competency. Another measure is the degree to which relevant knowledge is used to inform perceptions and actions. It follows that actions, perceptions, knowledge, reflection, and the context in which the instruction takes place are all elements that need to be taken into account for evaluating teaching, particularly if the purpose of evaluation is improvement. How can this be done? What means and methods are currently available that can produce both valid and reliable measures of effectiveness and standards of competency? Admittedly, there is no single instrument or process that can evaluate teaching in this complex form, though various activities can provide insight into the different elements of the model. Some of these activities are used expressly in this Workshop for formative evaluation because they force participants to examine their own thoughts and actions. The microteaching activity is one such example. This experience allows participants to view their teaching captured on videotape and to think back about their instructional decisions, making explicit the unobservable aspects of their teaching. This is possible because the Workshop set-up is unthreatening, and the feedback given by peers is received by participants with an open mind for the most part. Most important, all participants are on equal footing in respect to their familiarity with a newly acquired language about teaching and learning.

There is no question in our collective mind that this way of going about evaluating teaching—examining one's thoughts, assumptions, and actions—ought to be built into every professor's academic repertoire and should be an aspect of the evaluation process. We believe that evaluation followed by reflection can lead to change, and this can best be done when input is received from multiple sources. With this in mind, we use every opportunity throughout the Workshop to engage participants in thinking about their teaching actions, thoughts, and assumptions.

In the remainder of this chapter, we describe ways in which the evaluation of teaching is introduced and practiced during the Workshop.

A Little Bit of Theory

It should be clear by now that for us, teaching is not a set of actions that can be mastered and promptly ticked off on a checklist. This view is manifest in all the activities we plan and implement during this Workshop and in our broader approach to faculty development discussed in Chapter 12 and Chapter 13. To develop teaching, we need to be cognizant of all the elements comprising teaching and the way they interact with one another. Similarly, to evaluate teaching for the purpose of improvement, we need to think of ways in which the evaluation can take into account all of these elements. It is obvious, then, that in the Workshop, we put as much emphasis on the thinking behind teaching as we do on observable teaching actions.

The "Iceberg" Metaphor

In the opening chapter of this book we noted that we conceptualize the teaching process as an interplay between the unobservable and the observable—that is, perceptions, knowledge, reflection, and action in which each element informs the other. One analogy we have used effectively to describe teaching in our Workshop is the iceberg metaphor (McAlpine & Harris, 1999). The one-eighth of the iceberg that is visible above the surface of the water can be compared to the observable teaching actions seen in the classroom as well as those actions revolving around the planning and organization of the course and interactions with students. The remaining seven-eighths of the iceberg is below the surface of the water and not visible to the naked eye. We liken this part of the iceberg to the cognitive and affective processes invoked during the dynamic activity of teaching.

In this Workshop, we attempt to make the invisible aspects of teaching visible. We draw on adult learning theory to justify the activities included in the Workshop and highlight the relevance of these to the evaluation of teaching. This theory posits that as adults, we can begin the change process only if we know what our assumptions are and if we are ready to question them. This view is particularly prominent in the theory of transformative learning (Mezirow, 1991). This theory purports that examining assumptions candidly and identifying "distorted" views held on teaching and learning is the first step in the change process. Questions that can lead adults to reflect on the source of a problem include "What is the assumption; How did we come to hold this assumption; Why does this assumption matter; Are there alternative ways to address the situation?" (Cranton, 1994, p. 731).

How can the change process be best mediated? Again, the same literature highlights the following:

1. The importance of structured reflection (Schön, 1983)
2. The support and critique of peers (Sherman, Armistead, Fowler, Barksdale, & Reif, 1987)
3. A better understanding of the subject matter (Shulman, 1987)
4. A willingness to experiment and take risks in teaching (Saroyan, Amundsen, & Cao, 1997; Van Note Chism & Sanders, 1986)

Ramsden (1992) also contends that any activity aimed at improving teaching needs to engage instructors in ways that are appropriate to the development of their understanding of teaching. One way to make learning about teaching meaningful to instructors is to place the experience in the context of their specific subject area and then to encourage them to make thinking about their actions explicit. The activities of the Workshop are planned accordingly. They aim to engage participants in an ongoing process of evaluating teaching-related thoughts and actions. The multidisciplinary small-group context affords the opportunity to practice new and perhaps alternative approaches based on input from peers and self-evaluation.

When and How Do We Address the Evaluation of Teaching?

During the Workshop, we emphasize and model ways in which individuals can examine their course, and their teaching actions and related thoughts, and by which they can glean relevant information that will help them improve their teaching. As has been the case with all the topics discussed in the chapters so far, activities occur in the large group, in the small groups, and at the individual level. In the following, we discuss how each of these contexts helps us engage our participants in the continuous process of the evaluation of teaching.

In the Large Group

In the large group on the last day of the Workshop, we briefly discuss student course ratings and teaching portfolios, the two teaching-related policies currently in effect in our university. We also bring to the attention of the participants the newly introduced policy on the evaluation of graduate student supervision.[2] With respect to student course ratings, participants come to the Workshop with questions about the validity and reliability of data generated by student course ratings; whether students, given their limited subject knowledge, are actually in a position to evaluate the teaching of "experts"; and whether the context of instruction (e.g., large class, multiple sections, liberal grading) can bias the evaluation. They also seek advice for specific actions to redress weaknesses that their students might have already identified in a previously taught course.

We anchor our discussions about student course ratings in empirical findings of related research. Participants find interesting the evidence to support the contention that the greater the number of student raters, the more reliable the rating: 10 raters=.69; 40 raters=.89 (Cashin, 1988). Similarly, studies show that highly rated classes are also classes where students learn more (i.e., get higher grades in exams), and that there is a relatively strong correlation of student ratings with instructors' self-rating and with the ratings of others (e.g., peers). Finally, participants find revealing that grading leniency, class size, and instructor enthusiasm may be a potential source of bias for student rating (Greenwald, 1997; Greenwald & Gillmore, 1997).

The items that typically appear on student course ratings are derived from research on student learning. For instance, overall course effectiveness (e.g., compared to other courses, I learned . . .), teacher skill dimension (e.g., explains clearly), student perceptions of learning (e.g., I learned a lot), and ratings of instructor structure (e.g., manages time well) are all correlated with student learning. Discussions lead to the general understanding that student course ratings provide fairly stable data concerning teaching actions and students' perceptions of the effectiveness of those actions (Braskamp & Ory, 1994; Cohen, 1981; Feldman, 1988; Marsh, 1984, 1987; Saroyan & Donald, 1994; Seldin, 1984). Participants also become aware that the types of items used in student course ratings typically involve instructor actions; as such, the information can hardly help change instructors' thinking. Moreover, because student questionnaires are typically administered during the last few weeks of the course, they can hardly be used formatively. This is why many institutions in recent years have begun to gradually adopt a variety of new teaching evaluation methods, including portfolios, microteaching and self-evaluation, evaluation by peers and administrators, and student journals, to offset the limitations of student course ratings. This is the case in our institution where teaching portfolios are used as well as student ratings to evaluate teaching. In addition to being a product, the portfolio engages individuals in an ongoing

---

[2]Supervision is considered teaching at McGill University.

process of thinking about teaching, which is an integral part of every academic's professional responsibility.

Regarding the teaching portfolio, the questions that interest our participants most evolve around the policy itself and how it is actually implemented. We discuss, at some length, the four sections that make up the portfolio and elaborate on the types of documents that can be submitted in support of each of the four sections. These are categorized under the following general headings:

1. Statement of teaching philosophy
2. Description of teaching responsibilities
3. Evidence of effectiveness
4. Description of teaching development activities—undertaken for personal and professional development or as an academic leader

If participants require further details, they are referred to specific workshops on these topics organized by CUTL during the year. Alternatively, they can arrange for individual consultation with a CUTL counselor. Our discussion concerning the evaluation of teaching is enriched and complemented by the relevant readings included in the course pack specifically selected to address the broad range of participant concerns.

Summative Versus Formative Evaluation of Teaching

In the large group, we highlight the summative aspect of teaching evaluation. Summative as compared to formative implies a judgment by someone else, followed by a decision based on that judgment. With regard to teaching, summative evaluation would involve judging the quality of teaching for administrative decisions such as tenure and promotion. In contrast, formative evaluation of teaching is carried out for the purpose of improvement. The possibility of using informal and formative ways to evaluate teaching are new ideas for most participants and something that is very different from experiences related to their actual teaching. In real life, professors seldom evaluate their own teaching informally, particularly while their courses are still in progress. Typically, their experience is limited to being evaluated by their students at the end of term. However, one component of the teaching portfolio, namely the teaching philosophy statement, is intended to be a formative exercise. In the Workshop, we try to complement this process by providing our participants with other tools so that they can evaluate their teaching for the purpose of improvement. Why this focus on the formative aspect? We strongly believe that an important goal of the evaluation of teaching ought to be the improvement of teaching.

Starting from the very first day of the Workshop, participants have the opportunity to observe and experience ways in which the facilitators evaluate their own teaching formatively. For instance, twice during the Workshop (at the end of the first and third days), we collect a very short questionnaire that elicits feedback from participants concerning the Workshop in general and our teaching in particular. The questionnaire is basically three short questions:

1. What did you learn today?
2. What did you learn that you use in your teaching?
3. What would be one suggestion to make the workshop better?

The data generated by these questions are compiled and reported back to the group on each of the following days. Here, our intent is to model one way in which evaluative feedback can be elicited from the learners (in this case, our learners—i.e., the participants), acknowledged, and incorporated into practice.

In the Small Groups

As might be expected, much of the work concerning formative evaluation of teaching happens in the small groups. The unthreatening and supportive environment of these groups encourages participants to try out new ideas and new ways of teaching, for which they receive immediate feedback from other participants and the facilitators. The feedback is given following both microteaching presentations and other informal presentations on work in progress.

Microteaching

Earlier we noted that microteaching sessions are built into every day of the Workshop, and since the focus of each session is different, different kinds of formative feedback are elicited. In general, each participant is allotted ten to fifteen minutes for the microteaching presentation after which the individual is asked to provide the group with his or her own initial impressions of the presentation. The presentations are related to the course that is being developed: Initially, they involve the description of the course, its concept map, and related learning outcomes. Later on, the focus is on teaching (delivery), using actual content from the course material being developed. The idea is that each individual will be able to try at least two different strategies, preferably ones with which they are less familiar, keeping in mind that they must facilitate intended learning. Each individual is thus able to experiment within a personal comfort zone. For some, this may be using an overhead projector to accompany a lecture. For others, it may be trying out collaborative learning techniques. Presentations are followed by peer feedback including comments from the facilitators. This is a guided process that builds as the five days progress. Presentations and feedback are videotaped, leaving participants with a complete record of presentations, teaching, and peer feedback for the entire Workshop.

Encouraging Peer Evaluation

Structured peer evaluation of teaching ensues in the small groups following each microteaching session. Our knowledge of group dynamics and group formation has directed us in determining how to structure feedback, particularly on the first two days when groups are still going through the "storming" and "norming" stages. Once the groups are formed and comfortable, which in our case generally appears to take place by the third day, we engage participants in the actual evaluation of teaching. To further prepare the participants, the first session is preceded by a discussion on principles involved in giving and receiving constructive feedback. Handouts provided in the course pack, which participants have been asked to read in preparation for this activity, provide a useful framework for our discussion. Peers are asked to put themselves in the place of learners and communicate the impact of the microteaching on their own learning, the extent to which they attained the intended learning outcome, and what might have helped them learn better. An aspect of receiving feedback that we particularly stress is to be open to all comments, even those that may seem completely idiosyncratic. Though participants are encouraged to explain the thoughts underlying their actions, they are advised against justifying their actions in response to a particular criticism. We emphasize that feedback is only for consideration. Whether particular feedback is accepted or incorporated in a subsequent teaching episode is left entirely up to the presenter.

The sequence of developing skills to formatively evaluate teaching is as follows: On the first day, the microteaching presentation is limited to a brief description of the course selected to be developed in the Workshop. We know that the experience of being videotaped and the first impression of seeing oneself on tape is a big shock to many, regardless of the quality of the teaching. Since this impression is likely to color an individual's views and comments about the teaching, we have built in a "practice run" at the outset. That is, on the first day when participants briefly present their selected course (an assignment that they have been asked to prepare for the first day of the

Workshop), they are videotaped. This practice run makes the videotaping nonintrusive and diminishes the chance that the activity itself becomes a distracting factor.

The evaluation criterion given to participants for this activity is whether the course description meets university requirements for inclusion in the program calendar. Both the presenter and the small-group members are asked to give feedback with this criterion in mind.

When participants present their concept maps in the afternoon, delineating the main concepts and their relationships to one another, they are provided with a number of questions that again guide them in the peer evaluation and feedback process. These questions include the following:

- What is the specific relationship between/among each of the concepts?
- Have any relationships been overlooked?
- What would happen if concept "x" were removed?
- Is it easily apparent which concepts are peripheral/less important?
- Is it easily apparent which concepts are central/important?

On the second day, the microteaching involves the presentation of a revised concept map as well as learning outcomes. Here again, the feedback is framed by specific questions concerning the learning outcomes. Are they

1. learner oriented?
2. measurable?
3. clear and concise?
4. derived directly from the concept map?

On the third and fourth days, the assignments involve teaching a small part of the course being developed, each time using a different and preferably new instructional strategy. For the evaluation of this assignment, more specific comments concerning the teaching are elicited. First, the presenter is invited to say what he or she finds effective or ineffective in the presentation and identify areas on which feedback would be personally useful. The peers are then invited to provide feedback. By this time in the Workshop, the participants have had sufficient time to bond and create functional groups. They are also at a stage when they can appreciate critical comments.

While we provide specific criteria for providing feedback on the effectiveness of teaching, we are cognizant that in this evaluation process another referent for participants is their personal mental model of good teaching. This model, in most instances, is shaped by past experiences of teaching as well as memorable learning experiences and teachers or professors associated with these particular memories. As Workshop facilitators, we also have similar references. However, our view is tempered by the theoretical and empirical literature on teaching and learning. It is this latter aspect that we intentionally highlight during feedback sessions.

In the small-group interactions, specifically when individuals engage in peer evaluation, the advantage of multidisciplinary groups once again becomes apparent. Comments generated during these sessions seldom address the subject matter and almost always relate to teaching and pedagogical concepts. We can safely say that the identity of the individual as a "subject-matter expert" is rarely challenged because comments almost never become personal. Moreover, the multidisciplinary composition provides participants the unique opportunity of being exposed to different and perhaps new perspectives on teaching and learning. As participants observe their colleagues teach in ways that to them might appear to be completely innovative, their experiences are enriched and their imaginations nurtured. And if their own learning is facilitated when innovative teaching approaches are used, they are likely to be more inclined to try out new ideas when they themselves teach.

Individual Work and Self-Evaluation

An activity that runs parallel to receiving feedback from peers is self-evaluation, and this, too, is a process participants engage in from the very first day of the Workshop. The activity is loosely structured. After the microteaching presentation, participants are given the videotape of their own teaching to view in private and to write a reflective piece on. The specific writing task is for participants to identify aspects that seem to be effective and ineffective in their teaching, and one or two things that they will do differently in the next microteaching presentation. The requirement to look back at one's own actions, articulate the rationale for instructional decisions and held assumptions about teaching and learning, ask questions of oneself about these assumptions, and, finally, evaluate the effect of actions taken on student learning invokes metacognitive processes. We are particularly keen on creating a context for developing this capacity so individuals can become more reflective because, in our view, this is how adults learn. Viewing the videotape and completing the ensuing reflective writing activity invoke the examination of one's assumptions, and this we find is a powerful process and a critical step that can lead to change.

So far in the book, we have repeatedly stated that the goal of the Workshop is to promote a principled approach to course design. In addition to achieving this goal, we find that there are tangential outcomes. One such outcome is the development of a new vocabulary that enables participants to talk about teaching and think about it more precisely. Once in command of a commonly understood language, participants are in a position to provide an explanation for their instructional decisions to their peers. For instance, they can specify what kind of learning outcomes they have in mind, why a given strategy is likely to foster a specific kind of learning, and what and why aspects of their microteaching session need to be fine-tuned. Once the tacit is made explicit, others have something to which they can respond, and thus the foundation of formative evaluation is laid. This particular aspect is reflected on in Chapter 9 by dik Harris, one of our past participants.

Conclusion

By the last day of the Workshop, participants have gained new insights into ways they can develop and teach their course and formatively evaluate their teaching. This leads them to ask different kinds of questions concerning teaching and learning. For instance, they want to know if it is possible to try out new teaching strategies, particularly those that are unfamiliar to students, without jeopardizing their course ratings. They also want to know what role they need to play to make students more responsive to teaching strategies and more active and responsible in their own learning. This is a particular challenge in disciplines where traditionally a student's role has been that of passive recipient of information. Most important, they want to know how to avoid jeopardizing student learning when they try out different teaching approaches. While the Workshop affords participants and facilitators an environment to explore new opportunities and challenges involved in improving teaching, the reality where newly developed ideas have to be tested is not always flexible. Making substantive changes to teaching necessarily takes time, requires experimentation, and may, in some instances, provoke student dissatisfaction and perhaps yield lower than expected course ratings. In such instances, faculty developers, as change agents, need to be able to provide the necessary support and resources to ensure success. We need to engage departmental chairs in the process so they in turn can be supportive of initiatives taken to improve teaching. New and innovative ways of thinking about teaching and learning-centered teaching strategies are more likely to blossom if the paralyzing concern about short-term consequences of poor evaluations is minimized. Clearly, a strong partnership among the professor, the students, the departmental chair, and the faculty developer is one sure way to advance the shared goal of promoting student-centered learning and effective teaching.

References

Braskamp, L. A., & Ory, J. C. (1994). *Assessing faculty work*. San Francisco: Jossey-Bass.

Cashin, W. (1988). *Student ratings of teaching: A summary of research* (IDEA Paper No. 20). Manhatten, KS: Kansas State University, Center for Faculty Evaluation and Development.

Centra, J. (1993). *Reflective faculty evaluation*. San Francisco: Jossey-Bass.

Chickering, A. W., & Gamson, Z. F. (1991). Appendix A: Seven principles for good teaching. *New Directions for Teaching and Learning, 47*, 63–69.

Cohen, P. A. (1981). Student ratings of instruction and student achievement: A meta-analysis of multi-section validity studies. *Review of Educational Research, 51*, 281–309.

Copeland, W. C., Birmingham, C., DeMeulle, L., D'Emidio-Caston, M., & Natal, D. (1994). Making meaning in classrooms: An investigation of cognitive process in aspiring teachers, experienced teachers, and their peers. *American Educational Research Journal, 31*(1), 166–196.

Cranton, P. (1994). *Understanding and promoting transformative learning*. San Francisco: Jossey-Bass.

Feldman, K. A. (1988). Effective college teaching from the students and faculty view: Matched or mismatched priorities? *Research in Higher Education, 28*, 291–344.

Greenwald, A. G. (1997). Validity concerns and usefulness of student ratings of instruction. *American Psychologist, 52*(11), 1182–1186.

Greenwald, A. G., & Gillmore, G. M. (1997). Grading leniency is a removable contaminant of student ratings. *American Psychologist, 52*(11), 1209–1217.

Leinhardt, G. (1993). On teaching. In R. Glaser (Ed.), *Advances in instructional psychology* (Vol. 4, pp. 1–54). Hillsdale, NJ: Erlbaum.

Marsh, H. (1984). Students' evaluation of university teaching: Dimensionality, reliability, validity, potential biases, and utility. *Journal of Educational Psychology, 76*, 707–754.

Marsh, H. (1987). Students' evaluations of university teaching. Research findings, methodological issues and directions for future research. *International Journal of Educational Research, 11*(3), 253–388.

McAlpine, L., & Harris, R. (1999). Lessons learned. Faculty developer and engineer working as faculty development colleagues. *International Journal of Academic Development, 4*(1), 11–17.

Mezirow, J. (1991). *Transformative dimensions of adult learning*. San Francisco: Jossey-Bass.

Ramsden, P. (1992). *Learning to teach in higher education*. London: Routledge.

Saroyan, A., & Amundsen, C. (2001). Evaluating university teaching: Time to take stock. *Assessment and Evaluation in Higher Education, 26*(4), 337–349.

Saroyan, A., Amundsen, C., & Cao, L. (1997). Incorporating theories of teacher growth and adult education in a faculty development program. *To Improve the Academy, 16*, 93–115.

Saroyan, A., & Donald, J. G. (1994). Evaluating teaching performance in Canadian universities. *Das Hochschulwesen. Forum für hochschulforschung, praxis und politik, 6*(282–291).

Schön, D. A. (1983). *The reflective practitioner: How professionals think in action.* San Francisco: Jossey-Bass.

Seldin, P. (1984). Faculty evaluations: Surveying policy and practices. *Change, 16,* 28–33.

Sherman, T. M., Armistead, L. P., Fowler, F., Barksdale, M. A., & Reif, G. (1987). The quest for excellence in university teaching. *Journal of Higher Education, 58,* 66–84.

Shulman, L. (1993, November/December). Teaching as community property: Putting an end to pedagogical solitude. *Change,* 6–7.

Shulman, L. S. (1986). Those who understand: Knowledge growth in teaching. *Educational Researcher, 15*(2), 4–14.

Shulman, L. S. (1987). Knowledge of teaching: Foundations of the new reform. *Harvard Educational Review, 57*(1), 1–22.

Van Note Chism, N., & Sanders, D. (1986). The place of practice-centered inquiry in a faculty development program. *To Improve the Academy, 5,* 56–64.

PART III

REFLECTIONS OF FOUR WORKSHOP PARTICIPANTS

We are particularly pleased to include the four chapters of Part III in the book. When we decided to invite past participants of the Course Design and Teaching Workshop to contribute a chapter, we thought we should ask those who had gone on to become leaders in promoting teaching in their respective departments. We were fortunate that the first four we approached agreed to take on the task.

Our contributors in the order of their chapters are Ralph Harris, Professor of Mining and Metallurgical Engineering; Myron J. Frankman, Professor of Economics; Richard (dik) Harris, Professor of Physics; and Richard Janda, Associate Professor of Law.

Our invitation was intentionally open-ended. We simply asked the four to think about the way in which the Workshop had influenced their thinking and perhaps actions as teachers and scholars. It is evident from these chapters that each has interpreted the task differently. We have sequenced the chapters in an order that seems to us to go from the more concrete to the more abstract.

Three of the four authors have continued their affiliation with the Centre for University Teaching and Learning (CUTL) and have established formal ties with our unit. They also serve in various roles that further the development of teaching and learning within McGill University. These and many of our alumni have been influential in helping us promote the scholarship of teaching in the disciplines. We continually look to these individuals to inform our own understanding of discipline-based teaching and learning and to forge stronger ties with our colleagues across the university.

8

IMPACT OF THE COURSE DESIGN AND TEACHING WORKSHOP

Ralph Harris

Background

"Teaching is a lot like parenting." This might be an unexpected idea to start a paper about university teaching and learning, but in retrospect it sums up the situation in which I found myself when I started my university teaching career in the early 1980s. Essentially, my then and still employer put me in front of a class and said, "Go," somewhat analogous to a cursory "slap on the bottom." I suppose it was assumed that I knew what to do and that I knew what I wanted to achieve.

When I started teaching, I did not know that it was a lot like parenting. I had nothing to go on but my own notions, and it did not occur to me to get help. I assumed that I was supposed to be on my own. I realize now, looking back, that I did not fully understand many of the things I was about to teach. I had just completed my Ph.D. and I was quite unclear of where I was going with my teaching. This chapter tells the story of my slow evolution as a teacher. It is meant to provide some insight about how I went from a place of inexperience to a place of competence. This chapter is also meant to provide encouragement to others for the effort required in making such a change.

I first present a snapshot of my teaching before exposure to the Centre for University Teaching and Learning (CUTL), their philosophies, and the Course Design and Teaching Workshop. I then describe my involvement with the Workshop and members of CUTL over ten years, and the spinoff activities I have engaged in as a result of the enthusiasm I developed in working with members of CUTL. I hope my story shows how my involvement with CUTL and in particular the Workshop has improved and enriched my life, and as a consequence, improved and enriched my teaching. This chapter is also meant to illustrate how complex the task of teaching is for me personally, and how the impact of the Workshop has extended beyond my own university teaching—to influence, for example, my professional consulting career, my community service activities, and my personal relationships, particularly those with my children.

Prior to my first sabbatical in 1989–1990, my teaching could be described at best as heroic! At worst, it could have been described as chaotic and substandard, at least from the point of view of students being able to do engineering after "learning" from me. Ironically, this did not translate into poor student ratings since the students had a lot of fun getting through a course that was considered a "rite of passage." However, I had an experience during my first sabbatical that shook me up. I had the occasion to work alongside former students of mine in a professional setting and I saw an enormous gap between what I would have had them learn and what, in practice, they did learn.

It has become clear that my own undergraduate learning experiences contributed to teaching being such a challenge for me. The very small classes (two to five students maximum), coupled with the fact that my undergraduate teachers had no more formal training in pedagogy than I did when I became a teacher, meant that my role models provided few clues as to what to do in front of a class. My introverted and anxiety-ridden character and a somewhat distant relationship with my own family compounded these deficiencies.

For reasons outside the scope of this chapter and, in fact, still beyond my own understanding, this combination of factors led me to reinvent my courses each year. I used no guidelines in making these changes and had no basis for explaining the resulting successes and failures. In a related article (Harris, 2000), I chronicle some of the antics I followed trying to cope with the deficiencies I saw. Some of the experiences were fun in a wild, chaotic, manic kind of way, but by and large they were *very* stressful for me and not that effective for the students. However, at the time, it was the best I knew. This last sentiment highlights one of the parallels I see between parenting and teaching.

On return from my first sabbatical, after encouragement from a concerned party, I joined a new CUTL activity, a semester-long faculty discussion group. For me, it was "group therapy" and exactly what I needed. For the facilitators, it was an opportunity to share their passion and insight, and their desire to improve teaching and student learning experiences. At the end of the sessions, I was invited to attend, as an audiovisual assistant, the first CUTL five-day Workshop, with the understanding that I could also participate in the activities.

My Experiences with the Workshop

Over the last several years, I have taken on various instructional roles in the Workshop, including co-instructor for a small group, presenter to the large group, and lunchtime discussion facilitator. The reason I have continued to volunteer for these roles is because I very much enjoy supporting other professors in developing their courses while at the same time having the opportunity to examine and continue to develop my own courses. In the following, I juxtapose my experiences as a member of the instructional team with reflections on my own learning.

My first experience with the Workshop in 1992 allowed me to observe the CUTL instructors' purposeful interventions to get the participants to reflect on what they wanted to achieve through their teaching. I also observed in one particular instructor a highly supportive style during her feedback and the explicitness with which she stated her reasons for saying and doing what she did with the group. I now use this strategy of explicitness frequently so there is as little uncertainty in my students' minds as possible as to the purpose and direction of my courses. I observed the CUTL instructors model some of the strategies that had been described in the faculty discussion group, which had been my first CUTL experience. I learned from this and began to grasp the relationship between the four components of the course design process: content analysis, learning outcomes, strategies, and evaluation.

My second experience with the Workshop was as both registered participant and co-instructor-in-training. I used my course, Technical Report Preparation, which I had just been assigned and which I have now recast as Engineering Communication Skills,[1] to be my case study for the Workshop. I experienced a major personal breakthrough in that Workshop, discovering that I could use humor to combat my anxiety and improve student learning. I continue to use this strategy whenever appropriate.

There is a focus in the Workshop on the purposeful selection of teaching strategies. This aspect remains a challenge for me. In everyday teaching and life today, I continue to struggle to link strategies to outcomes. I have found that one teaching strategy may have a number of learning outcomes, and the way one should use a strategy depends on the priorities placed on the learning outcomes. This has been no more evident for me than in my use of the

---

[1] The name change reflects my broadening and deepening of the learning outcomes to include oral, managerial, and workflow management-type skills. This was a direct result of the lessons and skills learned in the Workshop, in that I was able to identify and put into practice teaching strategies that promoted a much higher and more sophisticated set of learning outcomes than those in place in the course I inherited.

"Mad Professor" routine[2] in my communications course. It was originally used just as an ice-breaker activity in the Workshop, but I now use it to support student learning about presentation skills, the need for purposeful preparation, and the use of specific, purposely chosen strategies—for example, the activities and extent to which one can go to engage a particular audience.

The third year that I was involved with the Workshop, I took on multiple roles as co-instructor of one of the small groups, presenter to the large-group session about active learning strategies, and demonstrator of the "Mad Professor" at the Friday lunchtime wrap-up. The enthusiasm of the CUTL staff in modeling interactive teaching activities that year and the answers they gave to the questions posed by participants proved somewhat overwhelming for some of the participants. This was demonstrated on the Thursday afternoon, when one of the participants, in an outburst, charged that we, the instructors, were engaged in brainwashing. In response, one of the CUTL instructors calmly discussed the CUTL philosophy, and in so doing addressed my own concerns about brainwashing, if not those of this particular individual. It was as tense a moment as I have ever experienced in a classroom, but it was also a remarkable learning experience for me as I had already been described as being overzealous in my enthusiasm for the learning-centered teaching philosophy supported by CUTL. Looking back, I see that I have been very passionate about whatever project I have in the front of my mind at any particular time in my life. This has sometimes been problematic, but more often has led me to positive outcomes. This passion overflows into my teaching and, I believe, adds to the students' interest in my courses.

My personal focus in that particular Workshop was to come to a deeper understanding of the various domains of learning outcomes and levels of learning and the great usefulness of these concepts in selecting appropriate teaching strategies. That year, I also became conscious of incorporating the CUTL material with my own engineering language and experience to provide guidance and leadership to the members of my small group. In my own teaching, I was analyzing my courses and adding strategies to them as appropriate because the learning outcomes for these courses were becoming clearer to me. It is worth noting that the only departmental guidance about the course I was teaching was the published 50-word McGill University calendar course description, along with the comment that if I did not like the description, it was easy to change. It is also worth noting that in 1994 I had not yet

---

[2]The teaching strategy is known at McGill University as my "Mad Professor" routine. In this teaching strategy, I use negative examples of teaching to promote thinking about good public speaking skills in my communications skills course.

produced a course outline for my core, extractive metallurgy course, even though I had been teaching this course for 13 years! This remarkable state of affairs is a simple testament to the extraordinary ad-hocery that is possible in university teaching and the acceptable levels of learning that can follow simply from a combination of an enthusiastic instructor and talented students.

I was a co-instructor in the Workshop again the next year. This time, I worked with a CUTL instructor with different academic training from that of my previous CUTL partners. This instructor's expertise was in the area of evaluation, a subject that was of particular interest to me as an engineer and because of my own self-exploration with respect to moral and ethical standards and behavior. I was still concerned with the "brainwashing" allegation. The experience that year shed new light on my view of teaching and nurturing. I saw that the very difficult subject of evaluating and making decisions about people's level of achievement was exactly that: very difficult. I learned, however, that it is at least possible to go about it in an organized and clear way.

This CUTL instructor's academic approach in the Workshop, coupled with an intense desire for the success of the people with whom she worked, plus an extraordinary capacity for work and running with the ball, left me with a newfound respect for the CUTL group. Her approach to trying to understand the very mechanisms of learning also felt familiar to me as a scientist and practicing engineer. Now, in addition to the feelings of support and nurturing I had received and so needed from the other members of CUTL, I added a feeling of academic collaboration. In fact, this CUTL instructor and I went on in later joint efforts to discuss and define the essential differences between collaboration and cooperation, and these nuances have remained with me and continue to influence my relationships with students, colleagues, myself, and the world at large.

In retrospect, I see that I was developing a feeling of ownership toward the Workshop; and that within the broad outlines of the design of the Workshop, I was specifying the agenda for my small groups and at the same time taking from it what I needed to improve my own teaching. It was also clear from the things I was doing within the McGill community and soon to do on the international scene that I felt that I had mastered the essence of the teachings of the Workshop. I had changed my views about myself and my role as a teacher. I even saw the applicability of these changed views to my work outside of the domain of university teaching per se and extending to the domain of project management.[3]

---

[3]I have successfully applied strategies I have learned in the Workshop to projects as diverse as my editorship of McGill Faculty Association publications and my central involvement in set-up of a potential billion-dollar lithium metal production business.

In 1997 I presented to the large group of the Workshop on the topic of concept mapping. I kicked off by sharing with the participants the ongoing development of the concept map for my course, Extractive Metallurgical Engineering. I decided to use the humor strategy combined with a negative example to show that the key for successful concept mapping is to develop a symbolic representation of the course material that also conveys the purpose and outcomes of the course. My article (Harris, 2000) is a loose description of my presentation that year.

That same year I discovered a new passion, that of information technology (IT) as applied to teaching. I was experimenting with HTML[4] and, in particular, exploring ways to improve my communications course by use of e-mail and web page composition, which I hoped would encourage students to reflect on their mastery of effective communication. The year 1997 was also close to the beginning of McGill's exploration of online learning, and at the time there was particularly strong competition among vendors of teaching and course creation technology. CUTL's perspectives and views on teaching were also somewhat in competition with the proponents of online teaching technologies at McGill. This was because many of those promoting various technologies were not well versed in pedagogy but were, like me, highly enthusiastic about the new possibilities.

The next year, I volunteered to be a co-instructor in the Workshop. This time, I was aware that the reasons were selfish. I wanted the opportunity to explain the use of my chosen online teaching technology and I wanted the acknowledgment of bringing the "tool" to McGill. This iteration of the Workshop was a watershed for me since there happened to be significant and obvious tension between me and the CUTL instructor I was working with for the first time. This was especially true with respect to our personal reactions to one participant in our small group. It was interesting to me that this CUTL instructor focused her time in the small-group session on the particular student with whom I was having so much trouble, while I focused on the rest of the group. I saw that I was damaging the experience for the small group as a whole since I challenged the CUTL instructor and her values. I also found that I enjoyed the experience, not in a malicious sense but rather as evidence that I had finally developed a strong sense of, and conviction in, my own philosophy regarding teaching and learning. It was apparent that my time as a co-instructor was best over, not only because I was challenged to find a middle ground from which to work but also because it was time to move aside and allow other McGill faculty the benefit of being co-instructors.

---

[4]Hyper Text Markup Language in a server/client computer environment. It occurs to me that here also is another loose parallel to the parenting notion of teaching.

My involvement in the Workshop over the next few years included presentations to the large-group sessions and facilitating brown-bag lunch discussions. I enjoyed the opportunities to present my various concept maps. It was clear that the description of my own experiences with concept mapping and the fact that my concept maps for Extractive Metallurgical Engineering had so greatly changed over the years were of value and interest to people. My engagement through this period with the online course design and delivery technology was almost total and somewhat to the detriment of my progression at McGill.[5] I had been sponsored to attend LotusSphere in DisneyWorld, Florida, by Lotus Canada, and my courses, which were developed in Learning-Space, were being considered by Lotus as showcases for marketing their technology. I was keen on showing Workshop participants what the learning experience was like for students of web-facilitated courses, and so I developed an online lab-based exercise for them. It was an exciting time since almost everyone was interested in this new technology.

In 2000 the demands of completing a novel online teaching project (described in more detail below, Utah/Chile/McGill Teaching) left me in need of medical intervention. The rigors of that project, combined with an increased enthusiasm for metallurgical research and the realization that promotion at McGill was not going to follow from my teaching and faculty development activities, left me wishing to disengage from my activities with CUTL. Ironically, that same year I was appointed an Affiliate Member of CUTL, which meant that I received official recognition for my past efforts and also assumed a set of new responsibilities. I had profoundly mixed feelings. McGill had decided not to pursue my novel teaching project, which was disappointing since I had put so much effort into it. Yet in my own engineering courses, I had finally reached something of a balance between teaching and research, having developed an understanding of the appropriate role of technology in teaching.

Spinoffs from the Workshop

The above details my experiences related directly to the Workshop itself. However, my involvement with the Workshop and with CUTL staff led me to undertake a wide range of other teaching-related activities far outside the experience of most engineering professors (Harris, 1998). In the following,

---

[5]On reflection, I now see the outstanding and profound value of my tenure at McGill University. This security gave me the freedom to pursue a passion I now see as highly beneficial to the university and myself. However, without tenure, I would not have been able to take the risks involved in this learning process and to some extent put my metallurgical research activities on hold.

teaching and learning activities that I pursued outside the domain of my regular course instruction are presented chronologically. They span seven years and started before the end of my involvement with the Workshop.

Course Design and Teaching Mini-Workshop

As indicated above, I am a person who likes to have a passion, or even a cause. My idiosyncrasies have led me to do a lot of things, one of which was to develop with one of the members of CUTL a "mini-workshop." We planned a three-hour session to cover the basics of shifting from a paradigm of instructor-oriented teaching to one of learner-oriented teaching.

It was quickly evident that the three-hour session was too intense for the participants, who felt we were far too directive. As mini-workshop co-designers, we were clear about our learning outcomes, but we were not so clear about the best strategies to use. Our decision to try to achieve the outcomes in a three-hour session was deeply flawed, despite the fact that the participants were somewhat familiar with the ideas, all having completed the five-day Workshop. To this day, I remain a little uncomfortable when I meet the professors who participated in the mini-workshop since it was solely my idea. I sincerely thank the CUTL member for her willingness to run with me on this project, and I can say that unless I had done it I might still think that this kind of learning experience could be compressed into a shortened format.

Senate Committee on University Teaching and Learning

I was "elected" to the McGill Senate Committee on University Teaching and Learning (SCUTL) because one of my Engineering colleagues wanted to end his term on the committee. I spent seven enjoyable years on this committee, meeting with and helping and advising staff from across the university on policies relating to faculty evaluation and development in the area of teaching and learning. Most notably, SCUTL developed a requirement and a set of guidelines for the incorporation of a teaching dossier in an academic staff's application for tenure and/or promotion. In those years, the VP Academic chaired SCUTL and members represented all faculties. A change in McGill's senior administration, I believe, resulted in a loss of focus for SCUTL. It became apparent that SCUTL was no longer the correct forum in which to promote CUTL's teaching and learning agenda since SCUTL was no longer chaired by the VP Academic and members were simply nominated by faculties rather than being volunteers keenly interested in promoting teaching and learning at McGill.

Committee on Teaching and Learning in Engineering

A colleague of mine who had also participated in the CUTL Workshop suggested to me that there was a need in Engineering for some kind of Faculty[6]-based effort toward teaching development. Adopting this as another "cause," I put together a proposal for a standing committee of Engineering to be called the Committee on Teaching and Learning in Engineering Faculty (COTLEF). This committee still exists. As founder of the committee, I was named chair and worked with committee members from various departments within Engineering for six years.

COTLEF sponsored a number of activities and developed a presentation series that aimed to provide a forum for Engineering staff to share ideas about teaching. The highlight of the series was a presentation by a student, whom I later hired,[7] who clearly articulated the nature of Engineering students and divided them into three categories: those who cared about grades; those who simply wanted the qualification; and those who put mastery ahead of grades and understood that good grades did not equate to mastery, especially if the grades involved "too cooperative performance." He emphasized the need for instructors to take this reality into account when designing and delivering courses. Another area addressed by COTLEF was information technology. Unfortunately, due to IT's newness, there were at the time few models of how to use technology "better," or even "properly."

COTLEF has been held up university-wide as a model for other faculties to emulate. On its recommendation, the Engineering dean committed a budget for a part-time CUTL faculty developer. This initiative (described in Chapter 12 and Chapter 13) sent a clear message to the entire faculty that the teaching component of responsibilities as Engineering staff was now being given far more credibility than ever before.

Chile Course Design and Teaching Workshop

During a visit to the University of Chile (UoC) to explore establishing ties between its Mining Engineering department and the McGill Department of Mining, Metals and Materials Engineering (then Mining and Metallurgical Engineering), it became evident that the rather formal instructor/student relationship of this premier Latin American institution might benefit from

---

[6]The term *Faculty*, with capital *F*, is synonymous with college or school in the American context.

[7]He undertook a project to create a "virtual-tours" web site for a professional organization; see http://metsoc.cim.org.

CUTL's experience and philosophies. To this end, I proposed with a CUTL member an adapted form of the Workshop (McAlpine & Harris, 1999). Looking back, I am pleased I had the confidence to plan and implement this initiative with UoC. However, my "confidence" also led me to simultaneously attempt to give to a second group of people in the same room a "project management" course since I also saw teaching as a "project." I thought that so long as the managers in the room were quick-witted enough to substitute the concept "project" for the concept "teaching and learning," then a happy outcome would follow. The fit was not as perfect as I had imagined since the language of the discourse was different between teaching and learning and project management. Perhaps the thing that comes through most clearly is my overestimation of others' capacity. I now realize that I expected the concepts I had taken years to master to be self-evident to others after only a 15-minute welcome speech! The result of this workshop was that the project management group was not dissatisfied—they simply did not get out of the experience what I had intended. This dichotomy between intention and results remains a central teaching challenge for me.

Excerpts from an e-mail sent to me by one of the Chilean professors follow. It is interesting to note the significance of the impact of our effort on this one individual.

> I can positively say that your course definitely changed my view about teaching (if I had any before). Understanding teaching as a project focused on certain learning outcomes helped me to understand all the logic behind the teaching process, behind the different teaching activities that I was normally doing just by imitation, tradition, inertia, etc. They became teaching strategies, which needed to be properly planned according to the different planned learning outcomes. Perhaps because of my frame of mind, my enjoyment is very linked to understanding. I also discovered the theatrical possibilities of teaching, and became aware of the immense opportunities of influencing the students in a wider spectrum than that of your specific technical topic.
>
> However, I have to confess, most of these changes are centered in my discourse about teaching, not necessarily in the practice of teaching. In the everyday life at the university I have a lot of pressure on my research outcomes, so I do not dedicate the necessary time to implement all the teaching strategies that come to my mind. I think I am now a better lecturer, but there is much more for me to do just by using the motivation and concepts I learned in your course.
>
> But you know, I have not given up. Just a few days before your e-mail arrived, I was planning to talk to the director to propose to build a practical scheme to help in implementing this teaching approach massively in our

Faculty[8]. I mean introducing some standard procedures, which induce the lecturers to care about learning outcomes. I remember, for instance, some months ago a lecturer complained because the students he receives in one engineering course know nothing about solving differential equations, and all of them have completed a whole cycle of courses on differential equations! Much of this misunderstanding could be avoided, I think, if more emphasis is taken in monitoring learning outcomes of previous courses.

What happened is that teaching today in our Faculty is still a black box. Nobody knows exactly how teaching is carried out in each classroom. The only visible measure is the student opinion at the end of each course, but that is far from enough. I have previously proposed to have some staff specially focused on helping to implement the rules you taught in your course, but there is still a general feeling that any approach in this line is a waste of time; you are born or not born to be a good teacher; you know, nobody is going to accept to be inspected, it is not possible (or not necessary) to interfere in that space, etc.

Well, but I have not talked yet to this new director; perhaps he is different. The important thing is that Engineering won recently a big teaching project and there is now a space (money) for presenting some ideas. I will tell you later of the results of my first interview.

It was during this retreat that the course leader from CUTL and I observed the positive impact and efficiency of my being from the same discipline as the workshop participants (McAlpine & Harris, 1999). It was clear that there was a great benefit to be gained from having an explicit understanding of pedagogical content knowledge in the same discipline as the participants. The benefit of sharing common pedagogical content knowledge is now a feature of some of the spinoff CUTL activities.

Also, since this Chilean version of the CUTL Workshop had the feature that it was held as a five-day retreat at a famous resort high in the Andes, the course leaders were able to run a series of evening discussions with the participants. We suggested the topics the first night but deferred to the groups' wishes after that. The commonality of participant concerns between those in South America and those at McGill provided us with clues about another issue, namely, that the evaluation of teaching is central to the development of a young professor's relationship with teaching. This observation of commonality further encouraged the CUTL instructor and me to expand our collaborative efforts, particularly in the area of evaluation, but not of students, rather of university professors. As a result, we conducted a session for deans

---

[8]College of Engineering.

and chairs at UoC, presenting our vision of how a teaching career could be conceptualized and evaluated. I discuss this in the following paragraph.

Chile Evaluation of Teaching Workshop

Our retreat-based CUTL Workshop in Chile was not only well supported by the Chilean industry that sponsored it but also by the senior administration of the Faculty of Applied Science and Mathematics of the University of Chile, the home of the Mining Engineering department. They were keenly interested in CUTL's ideas and especially eager to make changes to the first-year program that would address the high rate of student attrition. They were also keenly interested in methods by which they could improve the practice of the university's academic staff in general and thus sponsored a two-day workshop about the evaluation of teaching. This two-day workshop was based on the ideas we had previously presented (McAlpine & Harris, 2002), and followed from the discussions that the course leaders had had during our first workshop in Chile.

In a nutshell, the Evaluation of Teaching Workshop conceptualized improvement in teaching as having a progression that follows the natural development of an academic's career. Early in a professor's career, for example, the focus may be on only his or her own teaching; later in the career, he or she may take on much more wide-ranging responsibilities such as curriculum and program development. The central component of our presentation was to stimulate UoC administrators to be explicit about teaching responsibilities and the evaluation of them so they could provide guidance in the manner they wished for their staff. It was an interesting and rewarding experience for me as a young associate professor to be teaching senior administrators how to do their job, and I give much credit to these individuals for being so open to our then recently formed ideas.

Workshop for Improving Teaching in Engineering

A change of dean in McGill Engineering in 1999 resulted in a significantly increased emphasis on teaching development. The new dean was looking at a major restaffing of Engineering and was anticipating the tenure and promotion process for the newly hired professors. As mentioned previously, the new dean accepted a COTLEF recommendation to partially fund a CUTL staff member who would focus on helping newly hired professors. This CUTL staff member and I put together another adapted version of the CUTL Workshop that we called Workshop for Improving Teaching in Engineering (WITE). The planned format was a three-hour session every two weeks over the course of a year rather than a one-week intensive session. The reason for this particular schedule was to provide flexibility for the Engineering participants and give them the opportunity to explore the material presented, mull it over, and perhaps even try it in their classes during the period between workshop sessions.

All five participants in the first workshop had taken the CUTL five-day Workshop and wanted to continue their learning. Thus, the level of the discourse was high. A major focus for these participants was the identification of learning outcomes and the teaching strategies to promote these. It was interesting to see the extent to which these highly talented experts struggled with decisions about what to teach. Also, it was clear that these participants were masters of technology, so there was never a question of how to use technology but rather what were the best ways to use it and why.

Over the years, as the opportunity has arisen, I have informally engaged my own departmental colleagues in various faculty development activities. These have sometimes taken the form of one-on-one coaching sessions on course design, and I have also engaged in informal lunchtime discussion about issues with particular students whom I also know. I feel the greatest impact I have made in my department has been through joint- or team-teaching experiences where I am able to model my adaptation of the course design process and a teaching practice consistent with that process. To my satisfaction, I have seen many of these ideas and teaching strategies adopted by my colleagues. The technology-supported teaching projects I discuss next are the clearest examples of this.

Asynchronous Learning Networks (ALN)

Around the time of my involvement with the University of Chile, a request came from a departmental colleague in relation to more effectively dealing with large classes. He wanted to explore the use of a recently released web-based, server-client knowledge management platform that had been especially designed to deliver "online" courses. The technology proposed by my colleague was Lotus LearningSpace since this particular commercial and proprietary course authoring and delivery software was full-featured and not in need of any HTML programming skills.

It is interesting to note that, in the end, my colleague decided not to apply this particular technology because on inspection we decided it would not address the learning outcomes he had identified. This choice remains a lesson to others that technology is far from being an answer to some teaching challenges. Nevertheless, many other staff adopted the LearningSpace technology in their courses[9] with only my support for the Lotus Domino server and with a very brief demonstration of how to use the technology.

The two most valuable aspects of the ALN project were perhaps the feedback I was able to give CUTL and the participants of several offerings of the Workshop on the use of technology in teaching, and the provision of a "home" and a user-friendly platform as my project was conceptualized in terms of CUTL philosophy.

One group that I particularly wish to mention for their adoption of CUTL's philosophy in implementing technology in teaching is the English and French Language Centre of McGill's Faculty of Arts.[10] This group's decision-making processes consistently placed learning outcomes at the top of priorities, after which the group struggled with the consequences of such decisions. I contrast this to many other deployments of technology that were made simply to lower the burden of the instructor—for example, posting of course notes on a web site.

Intelligent Classroom Project

A complex and far-reaching project that I supported was McGill's "Intelligent Classroom." This project saw the creation of an "automated classroom," designed to lower the burden on instructors using technology in teaching, and, in particular, reduce the challenges associated with use of multiple content delivery mechanisms—for example, presentation software, video, white-board,

---

[9]The ALN project had at one time 500 students online in 20 different courses supported from a technical point of view only by me in a part-time role. I mention this as evidence of the stability and power of the software. The period 1997 through 2001 was one of technology competition at McGill. Software other than that I championed has become preeminent. I remain a fan of the system with which I am most familiar due to its flexibility and power, but I support the decision of McGill to go with the alternative. I am aware that history has not proven some of the claims made against the system I was pushing, and some apparent advantages of the competition have evaporated. It is important to note that for the deployment of technology in teaching on this scale, it was *not* a combination of factors that spoke to the quality of learning that influenced the decision, but rather mundane and uninteresting budgetary and decision-maker knowledge level issues that determined the outcome. This is not to say that the decisions were taken lightly, but rather to emphasize that during this period at McGill there was a significant and regrettable schism between those who ultimately had the resources to take such a huge decision about deploying technology in teaching and CUTL. Luckily, technology constantly improves as a result of competition and I feel that the decision makers were influenced by my small, but rather passionate group of adopters.
[10]College of Arts.

computer animations, software demonstrations, and specimen displays. Also, and more significant, the Intelligent Classroom project recorded and stored in random access on a web-server format audio and video capture of the class along with PowerPoint slides annotated with the ink strokes of the instructor. A special feature of these recordings, based on the ClassRoom2000 technology from Georgia Tech, was that the annotations were linked to the audio and video capture in such a way that clicking an ink stroke on a slide moved the audio and video to that point in the recorded class.

The richness afforded students by so many different forms of engagement whetted students' appetite for learning, and despite many setbacks the project has been extended to other classrooms, with over a fifth of the Engineering faculty at present using the intelligent classroom technology. The Intelligent Classroom project, through close collaboration with CUTL and with input from an Engineering student (mentioned earlier for a presentation to Engineering faculty), has also been designed to offer an asynchronous "online tutor," by which students can post online questions linked to particular slides in the captured classes. The instructors can respond and, if desired, publish the questions and responses so they become part of the online revision and learning tools for the entire class.

Utah/Chile/McGill Teaching

In 1999 I was approached as a result of an international metallurgy conference tradeshow demonstration of my Extractive Metallurgical Engineering course, which at that time had been fully implemented in LearningSpace, to undertake a novel teaching project that would offer this course over the Internet at the University of Utah. The initial interest was for McGill to give a distance education course over the web, but since the Intelligent Classroom was available and capable of broadcasting the class live over the Internet, it was decided to run this course simultaneously at McGill and the University of Utah. We also decided to provide real-time interaction between the students in Utah and the instructor and class at McGill using an additional technology under evaluation from Databeam, now called Learning Server,[11] which allowed multipoint NetMeeting[12] sessions.

---

[11]Now a fully owned subsidiary of Lotus Corporation and offering real-time web-based audio and video connections under the guise of LearningSpace Live.
[12]Databeam's proprietary Internet protocol, Net120, that allows real-time, two-way audio and video conferencing.

My contacts in Chile became aware of this endeavor and their interest in providing education to remote areas of Chile that are well served with web connectivity meant that they, too, wished to participate. Thus, a course was offered in two continents and three countries by one academic staff supported by two teaching assistants, one back-up camera operator, and the creator of the Intelligent Classroom.[13]

It is clear in retrospect that the level of support afforded this project was not sufficient. In fact, the Intelligent Classroom was so early in its infancy that defining what support was necessary was not possible since no one could predict what was going to go wrong next. This was compounded by our being in production—that is, "live"—to Utah three hours per week and there was no alternative or back-up system. Also the Intelligent Classroom could not be "brought down" for repairs since it was being used by many other staff for regular nine-to-five teaching. At night, the Intelligent Classroom creator and I were overwhelmed with other issues, such as digitizing the day's recordings, debugging the software running the entire system, getting McGill personnel to reconfigure the backbone correctly after they had made unannounced changes, preparing classes, marking student work, and so on. To add to the challenge, the basic concept of the Intelligent Classroom was simple; hence it was incomprehensible and unanticipated by the creator that major problems—such as irreproducible, sporadic operating system incompatibilities among the seven required servers; McGill making unannounced changes in VLAN wall socket IP addresses; hardware failures; equipment theft; and so on—would also be an ongoing feature of the Intelligent Classroom.

However, despite all this, back-up manual video recording, digitization, and uploading of the McGill class meant that the remote classes were always able to see the class, albeit not live. In the end, the remote classes most likely had the better learning experience because the McGill class was confronted with the day-to-day real-time classroom problems.

There were also unexpected upsides of the project. For example, students invited their families to log on to classes, especially during student presentations.[14] Another powerful feature of this course was that I had arranged with a group of industry experts to work directly with the students. Industry experts sat in on classes and, as can be expected, expressed disagreement with

---

[13]The cynical reader at this point might be asking about the intelligence of the users of this so-called "intelligent classroom."
[14]This unknown additional load on the servers also caused synchronization and reliability problems.

course content at times,[15] especially my emphasis when I referred in accurate but unflattering ways to the performance of their companies!

It is now clear that the project was far beyond the capacity of those involved to support it. However, a few very useful lessons were provided about students' willingness to be part of innovative projects, and the dangers of losing focus on learning outcomes as a result of enthusiasm for technology were highlighted. It is also fair to say that given sufficient support and with maturity of the technology, high levels of learning should be possible using the setup. Nevertheless, as such teaching activities are outside of McGill's teaching priorities, the project will not be run again in the McGill context.

Current Personal View About Teaching

The period covered in this chapter, 1991 to 2002, describes my complex evolution from a state of profound anxiety about teaching to quite a sophisticated level of practice. I now have a "canned" set of high-quality class presentations supported by interactive quizzes, video, field trips, and external experts acting as consultants to student project teams. In one course, I have decided to print all reading and assignment material rather than have it available online since this is clearly a better means of delivery of material that needs to be read. This decision is significant since it runs counter to the practice of most instructors, but it reflects my opinion that this is the best strategy to achieve the particular learning outcome I desire: students who come to class with the notes read!

Students now seem to expect higher levels of evident technology in classes, and at times they expect that because of all the bells and whistles they should be able to succeed at the course simply by being there. However, my jaded view of this may follow from my experience with one or two groups and may not be generally true. It may also reflect my own struggle trying to understand why students find my courses so challenging after I have made so much effort to make them accessible in every way. Perhaps the answer is *my* high expectations of the students. This is indeed ironic since the center of the CUTL philosophy is to view teaching from the learners' perspective.

I feel that through my efforts I have come closer to having students gain a mastery of my material, a mastery that seems to be hard-won by some, even if it is second nature to me. I hope it is clear from this chapter that the teaching development activities I have led or been a part of have had a great

---

[15]It was indeed stressful to be aware that experts might also be watching a class, as well as other department students, their families, and other instructors.

impact on me, extending beyond my own teaching. I have discussed and disseminated what I have learned through workshops,[16] conference papers, and publications (Blatter, Cooperstock, & Harris, 1999; those previously cited in the chapter).

---

[16]Presentations by the author related to teaching and learning, and faculty development:

- With Saroyan, A. Advances in Teaching and Learning at McGill University. Presentation to a Delegation of Rectors of Brazilian Universities. Office of International Research, McGill University: Montreal, October 16, 1998.
- With Cooperstock, J. Advances in Teaching and Learning in McGill Engineering. Presentation at Homecoming '98. Faculty of Engineering, McGill University: Montreal, November 1, 1998.
- With Saroyan, A., & Cooperstock, J. Applying Pedagogical Principles to Teaching and Learning with Technology: Multicultural Perspectives on the Use of Technology in Education. McGill University: Montreal, October 2000.
- Discussion Strategies: Online Discussion Workshop. Centre for Understanding Teaching and Learning, McGill University: Montreal, January 21, 1999.
- Effect and Affect of Using the Web in Teaching. Education Technology Workgroup. McGill University: Montreal, April 14, 1999.
- Lotus Notes—LearningSpace: Evaluation and Promotion of Student Learning. Faculty of Medicine, McGill University: Montreal, March 15, 1999.
- Lotus Notes—LearningSpace: Promotion of Student Learning. Faculty of Medicine, McGill University: Montreal, December 9, 1998.
- Promoting the Use of Technology in Teaching. McGraw-Hill Education Technology Conference Series: Montreal, November 1–3, 2000.
- With Blatter, J. Real and Metaphorical Bridges for the Teaching of Engineering Communications. INKShed XVI: Mont St. Gabriel, May 6–9, 1999.
- With Beer, A. & Blatter, J. Strangers in Strange Lands: Teaching Engineers/Teaching Communicators. Congress of Social Sciences and Humanities of the Canadian Association of Teachers of Technical Writing Conference. Ottawa, May 27–29, 1998.
- Survey of WWW Teaching. Canadian Materials Science Conference. Montreal, June 1997.
- Teaching Improvement Faculty Case Studies. Senate Subcommittee on University Teaching and Learning, McGill University: Montreal, April 23, 1998.
- Teaching Strategies. New Faculty Orientation. McGill University: Montreal, August 1993 and August 1994.
- Using Lotus LearningSpace as a Teaching and Learning Tool. Centre for Understanding Teaching and Learning, McGill University: Montreal, March 2, 1999.
- Using the Web in Teaching. Centre for Understanding Teaching and Learning, McGill University: Montreal, March 31, 1999.
- Workshop on Online Discussions: Use and Abuse of E-mail. Centre for Understanding Teaching and Learning, McGill University: Montreal, November 8, 1997.

I have also recently seen myself unconsciously using what are essentially teaching strategies in my professional life in situations that involve negotiation. Perhaps this is the core parallel between teaching and parenting. Both are a negotiation between two stakeholders, one of whom has some experience and wisdom about how the other can succeed and the other who has a need and desire to benefit from this guidance to succeed as efficiently as possible. I know from following some of my students through their careers that my teaching has had a far greater impact on them beyond their mastery of extractive metallurgy per se.

My experiences with CUTL and the years I have spent working with the staff of CUTL have shown me how to take a group of people who have very little experience or exposure to a subject and get them understanding and using the material—and, I hope, evaluating the world in terms of the concepts of the subject. The CUTL Workshop has guided and helped me. Since the "slap on the bottom" 22 years ago, I have finally grown and learned how to be a fully functioning parent-teacher. In contrast to my early teaching experiences, I am now much more at ease with my classes and feel that I am successful in having students learn something that they will find of value. My course content has become stable compared with my former annual reinvention, and I now prepare enthusiastically for classes since I know where I want to go and have a broad range of strategies to use to get there. I hope this story shows that there are few quick fixes and that a lot of long-term reflection about what works and what does not work is required. I also hope you can now see that teaching can be a lot like parenting. In my view, this understanding can compensate for the regrettably low prestige society now affords teachers.

References

Blatter, J., Cooperstock, J., & Harris, R. (1999, December). *Designing tools, designing learning opportunities: Issues in developing a CSLC system for the technical communication classroom.* Paper presented at the Computer Supported Collaborative Learning International Conference. Stanford University, Palo Alto, CA.

Harris, R. (1998). Using hard and soft technology in the engineering classroom: The pedagogical challenges. In G. A. Irons & R. Meadowcroft (Eds.), *Challenges in materials education* (pp. 107–120). Montreal, Canada: Metallurgical Society, CIM.

Harris, R. (2000). Anecdotes of teaching engineering: A story in two parts—Personal experiences and innovations. *McGill Journal of Education, 35*(1), 29–39.

McAlpine, L., & Harris, R. (1999). Lessons learned: Faculty developer and engineer working as faculty development colleagues. *International Journal of Educational Development, 4*(1), 11–17.

McAlpine, L., & Harris, R. (2002). Evaluating teaching effectiveness and teaching improvement: A language for institutional policies and practices. *International Journal of Academic Development, 7*(1), 7–17.

9

THE DEVELOPERS'
APPRENTICES

Myron J. Frankman

The very first book that I ever read on teaching (and/or learning) was Highet's (1950) *The Art of Teaching.* I can't recall precisely when I read it, probably during some point in my graduate studies when it appeared to me, against any earlier expectations, that I was likely headed for a career in teaching. At the moment of writing this paper, I am reading *The Elements of Teaching* by James Banner and Harold Cannon (1997). In the third sentence of their preface, they affirm their belief that teaching is an art, and they cite Highet's book on the second page of their preface. Despite the creation of hundreds of journals on education and the creation of the Educational Resources Information Centre (ERIC) database to keep track of tens of thousands of articles on the subject, we find two influential books written 47 years apart putting the emphasis on art and, by implication, the personal element in the relation between teacher and student.

Perfecting Our Art

When I began teaching in the 1960s, like my age-mates and like many since and some still, I had received no instruction on the art of teaching at any time during my formal education. It was assumed, in the words of McGee and Caplow (1965), that "any Ph.D. can teach." Expertise in one's subject was all that was needed. Success in the classroom was taken to require no special knowledge beyond what had been modeled by one's own professors. I brought to my practice of the art of pedagogy the same questioning attitude that was expected of me in the practice of my discipline. It was clear to me that there is much that an artist must learn if he or she is to excel in the chosen craft. I continuously reflect on my practice. Happily, it has not been necessary to rely for insights solely on reflection, nor even extensively on the printed word, as institutional support has been available at McGill for over three decades, first through the Centre for Learning and Development and later through the Centre for Understanding Teaching and Learning (CUTL).

The progress that I made in my persistent quest led to my being asked to be a resource person at the first CUTL spring Course Design and Teaching Workshop in May 1993. As one who is always uneasy with rigid categories and who is convinced that I have more to learn than to teach about pedagogy, I asked to play two roles: resource person and workshop participant. The former role did not exempt me from having to produce a concept map for one of my courses. I am not sure if it was my contrary streak or simply overload that prevented me from making explicit use of the concept map in my subsequent course design. And yet we are often not conscious of what we internalize.

The Workshop brought together professors from across disciplines and faculties. Our one point in common was our desire to engage learners more fully, an outcome promised by the Workshop. A reflection of our diversity of interests is given by the concept maps that I still have in my files: one on the parasite life cycle, another on dental implants, and a third on extractive process metallurgy. One high point of the Workshop that year was a brilliant presentation by Ralph Harris (author of Chapter 8) of the worst that our craft has to offer, which included the inevitable transparency with dozens of numbers in a tiny font of which only one was of relevance and other transparencies that were unintelligible and/or inappropriate. To see some of one's own foibles in a distorting mirror can have a salutary effect.

The most significant aspect of the Workshop was that we were engaged in a common discourse with colleagues who would be available to consult with, and not with a group that would disperse when the event concluded as was the case with a workshop on hypercard that I had attended at Cornell in summer 1993.[1]

Stored on my computer is a copy of the basic concept map that was further elaborated upon by me in the Workshop. Miraculously, I was able to retrieve the full-blown map and successive prior drafts from where they had been buried for several years in the stacks of paper that were supposed to have vanished had the vision of a paperless world not been a deception. My starting point was contrary to the instructions: I have on my first map for my

---

[1]The Cornell Hypercard Workshop led to no tangible direct result, but it did create a readiness to be an early adapter when I first read about the worldwide web in a *New York Times* account in December 1993.

new course every topic to be discussed, grouped under five general headings. With the guidance of my peers and the faculty developers of the CUTL, this metamorphosed into a conceptual template. Although I haven't ever presented the map to any of my classes (yet), that basic template reflects my thinking about all of my courses. Indeed, the schema goes beyond my courses: The basic map captures my holistic approach to my courses and to my understanding of the world. The specific map was for a new course, Data in Economic Analysis, which I was to teach for the first time in the winter semester of the next academic year. The course concepts are contained within an oval, which is intended to be a highly permeable boundary. While certain ideas may be privileged in attempts to understand economic activity, my map emphasizes that context must be taken into account.

Stored on my bookshelf is a copy of the video taken of my microteaching session in the Workshop. In preparing the present contribution, I re-viewed this visual record for the first time since I received it nine years ago. Originally, I had been struck by certain mannerisms of which I had not been aware. Merely seeing those images sufficed to break me of the previously unrecognized pattern. On this viewing, I confess that I was surprised to learn that certain of my lines of argument had not advanced much in the elapsed interval. I blame this on the burdens of the past years. Yet, like first seeing the mannerisms, revisiting the film now has once again had a catalytic effect.

On the final day of the Workshop, we had the opportunity to share our reactions about the week's activities. Mine took the following form of poem, "The Learner Hat."

> I know you won't believe this,
> But it actually happened . . . at McGill!
> Teachers speaking with each other about their craft.
> Teachers suspending judgment,
> Teachers willing to take risks, to consider change.
> In fact, teachers wearing the hat of learners.
>
> The Learner Hat is a magical, transformative adornment.
> Would you believe, these erudite, authoritative, loquacious scholars
> Were actually listening?
> Yes, not merely pausing to catch their breath,
> But truly listening, hearing, reflecting.
> Meeting as equals and accepting critical judgments.
> How did such a thing happen?
> Thanks go to the gang at CUTL.
> Sure there were all the preparatives:

Rounding up the unusual suspects,
Worrying about one thousand logistical details:
No intention of minimizing the weight of all that.
But the secret was in the mix of structure and freedom.

They set the tone, created the framework.
They modeled the very things that we were asked to consider.
They were there to facilitate, to guide,
To help us learn and to learn with us.
And learn we did.
Outcomes, however preliminary, were there for all to see.
The seeds have been planted.
The next crop is likely to bring
The first in a succession of curious, learning-friendly hybrids.

Extending the Conversation

Association with the CUTL certainly conveyed to us that it was safe to talk about teaching—well, at least in certain situations. The Workshop extended the boundaries. The circle of those with whom we could exchange ideas about teaching and learning broadened and we became more inclined to raise such issues. An e-mail discussion list was created at the conclusion of the Workshop to allow us to exchange ideas, but messages were rare (helpful nonetheless on the occasion that I posed a pedagogical query) and the list fell into disuse. The zeal of the moment suffered the inevitable exponential decline as time passed.

Those of us who make our way through the Workshop should be designated as "Apprentice Developers," with the charge to carry on the work of promoting altered approaches to the conduct of learning at McGill and, more broadly, in academia. We should all be expected to report back each semester on at least one way in which we have endeavored to leverage the impact of the Workshop.

As far as I can recall, the first presentation on teaching and learning that I gave was at the tenth annual meeting of the Society for Teaching and Learning in Higher Education (STLHE), which took place at McGill in 1990.[2] I gave a

---

[2]In fact, I appear to have already been helping to develop the developers. *The McGill Reporter* (May 24, 1990) stated: "Professor Myron Frankman of Economics was helping [Susan] Cowan and [Catherine] Gerols use e-mail to contact participants so that they could cut down on phone bills and save long waits for mail. Before he knew it, he'd been signed up to conduct a workshop on 'Expanding the Classroom with E-mail' (8)."

hands-on demonstration of McGill's telnet-based Course Information Facility, a precursor of web-based learning tools, which had been introduced only two or three months earlier by McGill's Multi-User System for Interactive Computing (MUSIC) Product Group. I must have prepared 40 transparencies, showing every relevant screen. As the first of the participants straggled in, I abandoned my meticulously prepared plan in favor of getting each person started on an exploration of what the facility provided. As my objective was to impress upon the participants how easy it was to use the facility, what better way to achieve that end than by giving the minimum number of pointers to the participants and letting them see for themselves? As I learned later, one McGill colleague from Education who attended the workshop adopted the use of the Course Information Facility in the following semester.

That experience taught me two lessons. Hands-on computer workshops should be structured to allow each person to proceed at his or her own pace, with special attention provided to those experiencing difficulties. Given the diverse aptitudes of computer users, lock-step instruction is a sure way to frustrate all participants with a pace that is inevitably too slow for some and too fast for others. The second lesson was that when the occasion warrants, the meticulously prepared script should be cast aside in favor of what the moment seems to suggest is best.

Throwing away the script may be the only approach that is consistent with the following words of bell hooks (1994):

> *Excitement* in higher education was viewed as potentially disruptive of the atmosphere of seriousness assumed to be essential to the learning process. To enter classroom settings in colleges and universities with the will to share the desire to encourage excitement was to transgress. Not only did it require movement beyond accepted boundaries, but excitement could not be generated without a full recognition of the fact that there could never be an absolute set agenda governing teaching practices. Agendas had to be flexible, had to allow for spontaneous shifts in direction. Students had to be seen in their particularity as individuals . . . and interacted with according to their needs. . . . Seeing the classroom always as a communal place enhances the likelihood of collective effort in creating and sustaining a learning community. (pp. 7–8)

Since my participation in the Workshop, I have had numerous occasions to function in my role as an Apprentice Developer. When I created a web page for my courses in September 1994, I gave several presentations of the page to diverse groups, including the Senate Committee on Computing. There have been a number of other presentations, principally on the role of information technology (IT) in learning, to workshops organized by the

Faculty of Arts[3] and the CUTL. Most recently, I gave a presentation in December 2001 to the WebCT Special Interest Group (SIG) of the use I made of WebCT in one of my courses. The title of that presentation—Students as Content Providers—illustrates my next point. It may be said that I function as an Apprentice Developer in my interactions with my classes where, in an active learning chain, I enable them to enable the learning of their classmates.[4]

The Context of Learning

Is there as well an art of learning? Those who have conversed with me about teaching and learning know that I persistently shift the focus from teaching to learning and to enabling learners. This paper is no exception, in that I shall emphatically privilege learning in discussing my own experience with the Workshop, my association with CUTL, my association with students in and out of the classroom, and my view of the future of learning. That I have found involvement with the CUTL so congenial over the years is attributable to the focus of the Centre, which has been principally on learning. When one approaches CUTL faculty developers, invariably the first question asked by them concerns the learning outcomes of the supplicant.

Whether one gives pride of place to teaching or learning, most of the academic work of undergraduates in North America takes place in a context where the fragmentation of learning into one-semester (or trimester) courses is the rarely questioned norm. Of necessity, my work and that of the CUTL, including the Workshop, resides within such a context. At McGill most instruction takes place in 13-week packages, with students expected to take five such units per semester. In the Faculty of Arts, it is entirely possible for a student's semester course load to be comprised of offerings each with a distinct technical vocabulary from five different disciplines. Even in a single field, such as Economics, much of the terminology in an undergraduate majors course in, say, International Economics will be distinct from that used in Econometrics.

Assignments in each course are set independently, with the only restriction at McGill relating to the use of in-class examinations during the final two weeks of classes each semester. The dates of midterm exams and assignment

---

[3]College of Arts.
[4]The following quote has appeared on each of my syllabi during the past decade: "The basic premise of . . . 'active learning' is to create a community of interest within the classroom in which students think of themselves as enabling each other's learning." Richard F. Elmore, in Christensen, Garvin, and Sweet (1991, xv).

submissions often coincide, which requires of students either exceptional organizational skills or the development of a loss-minimizing triage strategy. The
likely outcome for many students is that lessons will not be well learned and
assignments will not be fully developed. Were we to try to design a system
expressly intended to frustrate effective learning, it is doubtful that we could
succeed as well as the current system does.

Students are subject to variations in degree of control by the course
instructors. Control is the operative word. Common to our times, McGill
radically abandoned in loco parentis in most of its dealing with students but
firmly retains that approach with respect to learning, the area that is central
to its mission.

Linder (1970) has written about the harried leisure class. The professoriat
is surely on the front line of this harried segment of the population. Already in
the 1940s, Barzun (1944) spoke of the role of the sabbatical leave as allowing
professors to have their coronaries off campus. If the professoriat was over-
burdened then, imagine the quantum increase in stress levels nearly 60 years
later. As demands on one's time grow, devoting attention to networking related to teaching and learning is likely to be the first casualty. Devoting "too
much" attention to one's students is still unlikely to produce much academic
recognition and certainly would not be anywhere near sufficient to secure either tenure or promotion. It is sufficient that course evaluation scores lie
somewhere between 3.5 and 5.0 for our professorial duties to be considered
by our peers to have been generally well done.

We seem not to be questioning our pedagogical approaches and even to
be unsure of what questions should be asked. Inertia plays a potent role in
the maintenance of the status quo. While we insist that our research must be
cutting-edge, world-class quality, we make no demands that teaching should
reflect recent advances in our understanding of the learning process.

Focusing on learning is nothing new. There are countless approaches,
among them experiential learning, active learning, constructivism, cooperative
learning, and student-centered learning, that share a recentering of educational
practice away from the "sage on the stage." These approaches all represent
challenges to the reigning paradigm. However, as we learned from Kuhn
(1962), it is never sufficient to *merely* demonstrate convincingly the
bankruptcy of a reigning paradigm and/or the superiority of an alternative
worldview. It is not only ideas that must be swept aside but also the entire jug-
gernaut of default settings, rules, institutions, and physical structures that keep
a system firmly entrenched. Paradigm shift is no simple matter. Dominant dis-
courses are in our heads, embodied in our classroom architecture and in our
grading and record-keeping systems. Major institutions are structured around

testing and records transmission, such as the Educational Testing Service in Princeton, and processing centers, such as the Ontario Universities' Application Centre. Such reinforcing systemic relations are referred to by Illich (1973) as radical monopolies, far more unshakeable than single firms in an industry.

And yet epochal changes do occur and the educational system is, in fact, not a monolith. There are pockets of change, most particularly at the primary and secondary levels. Universities, however, are the most resistant to change. In February 2000 I did a survey of students in my capstone seminar in International Development Studies. Most of the students in the class were from the Faculty of Arts and were in the final year of their undergraduate programs. The following are two of the questions that I asked them:

1. To what extent, if any, did you experience student-centered learning, active learning, or some variation thereof prior to coming to McGill?

2. To what extent, if any, did you experience student-centered learning, active learning or some variation thereof at McGill?

I undertook the survey to provide myself with supporting evidence for a motion that, acting independently as an Apprentice Developer, I had submitted for the consideration of the Faculty of Arts, calling for the creation of a Committee for the Enhancement of Arts Education. The text of the motion follows:

> Faculty resolves that an ad hoc committee with equal faculty and student representation be established to consider options for enhancing the quality of the Arts education at McGill; this committee to consult the membership, including students, of the Faculty and to report its findings and recommendations to the Faculty.

I had already gotten some negative e-mail reactions from colleagues when the motion was circulated to the Arts electronic discussion list; most notably: "Forget it, we're stretched thin already." "Don't waste our time. We've already reformed our programs." "What more could we possibly do?" The "program reform" referred to consisted principally of giving students more freedom of choice by reducing the number of courses required for major and minor programs. To assure a broader exposure, students were required to complete a major and a minor in two different fields of study. The entire reform process gave no consideration to pedagogical issues beyond an abortive call for the creation of some team-taught courses.

The questions were sent to the students by e-mail and they were asked to respond within 24 hours. Of the 36 students who received the survey, 39% (14)

responded. The results strongly suggest that McGill is not meeting the expectations of many of its students and that we are out of step with the kind of approaches students have been exposed to prior to their arrival.

Here are some of the student responses to the survey: At least two mentioned student-centered interactive learning at the CEGEP level (Quebec's pre-university collegial two-year system). Several referred to extensive interactive learning at the primary level, the secondary level, and/or other universities. Four students referred to valuable experiential learning experiences, which included the McGill Panama field semester and a mandatory first-year Geography field weekend. Paradoxically, the latter field weekend, for which students received one credit (i.e., one-third of what is given for the normal one-semester course), fell partial victim to the Arts Curriculum Reform that standardized the total number of credits in a program. The field weekend is no longer required for students doing either the B.A. major concentration or joint honors in Geography. The Panama program was described by a joint honors student as "the best educational experiences of my life." That same student had the following to say of student-centered learning:

> It was the norm for me. I was in a public board of education . . . and was in the enhanced program from grade two onward. Almost all of my primary education was largely individualized, even though the classes were fifteen to twenty students. In high school, this continued, although the classes were slightly larger—twenty to twenty-five. In most cases, it meant that we all learned on a common theme, but did individual or small-team work, each unique. . . . Thus, coming to McGill and having lecture-format classes . . . was a shock, and to some extent still is repugnant to me.

This student noted of one of the departments in which he did his joint honors that "there has been absolutely no student-centered learning—the department seems to discourage it for the most part at the undergraduate level." Another student said that not only had her entire pre-university academic career been marked by student-centered interactive learning, but it had been prominent at CEGEP and in the year that she spent at another university prior to coming to McGill. She went on at some length about specific failings that she had perceived at McGill and concluded by saying: "I apologize if that's a little bitter, but I'm afraid you tapped a nerve." Another concluded in a similar vein: "We have perpetual conversations about our old expectations and present disappointments with the university system."

Another honors student who is currently pursuing his Ph.D. at a leading U.S. university expressed his overall satisfaction with his education at McGill, but added, "I have taken considerable advantage of the add/drop period to ensure that I take as many classes that suit my learning style as possible." He found fault in the "overemphasis on exams in the Arts at McGill. I, for one (and I have it on good information that I am not unique), forget nearly everything I have written on an exam within a few weeks. Yet, when I write an essay, I can, for several years, paraphrase my findings for anyone who cares to listen." I should add here as one of his professors that I remember well at least one of the joint papers he submitted to me in 1998–1999 and the joint seminar project (an interactive CD-ROM teaching unit for students aged 11 to 13) that he submitted in April 2000.

One student expressed doubts about the place of interactive learning at a university; others felt that large class sizes precluded any such initiatives. Yet another found the opportunity provided by small classes to be unrealized: "Even in my small classes (five and six people, for example) lectures continue. With only five to six people, I see a great forum for student-centered learning, but it never happens!"

At the time of the survey almost seven years had elapsed since my first Workshop. While I don't recall an identifying label being used to describe the methods we discussed in the Workshop, I think it safe to apply the active-learning label. The Workshop approach reflects noble but limited objectives. By now (June 2002), there have been ten annual Workshops and well over 200 faculty members who have had the experience, yet it would appear that a sizable majority of our over 17,000 full-time undergraduates would not have benefited from a change in pedagogy.

Veblen (1904) long ago spoke of "The Cultural Incidence of the Machine Process." Is our obsession with teaching, rather than learning, a consequence of the machine process with its emphasis on measurement and control? Today, we need to grasp the cultural incidence of information technology on all aspects of human interaction. Yet in some ways, we haven't even fully internalized the machine process. Many of our lectures still proceed as if the instructor had the only existing copy of the manuscript under consideration. Today's eager students could often access via the Internet the latest documentation of which the professor is not even aware.

As my professorial career, which is now in the second half of its fourth decade, has progressed, I have become increasingly convinced that we should center our concerns on learning, and design what we do in the university to promote learning rather than trying to perfect objective measures of course performance, then shaping our teaching to performance on tests. We have a means-ends confusion that is ill-suited to preparing leaders, preparing citizens, and fostering imagination and risk-taking. Indeed, one view holds it isn't a question of promoting learning, but of creating favorable environments for a natural inclination to find expression (Gopnik, Meltzoff, & Kuhl, 1999).

Our context has changed significantly, but our institutions are slow to respond. The information age carries with it a different logic and different imperatives than the age of the machine. Even those who didn't grasp the significance of the prescient message of Marshall McLuhan (1965), who viewed the medium as the message and spoke of a "global village," must by now recognize that the ubiquity of e-mail and the worldwide web has assuredly changed the social environment, and, with it, the learning environment.

The shift from a focus on teaching to a focus on learning represents a major paradigm shift, which requires changes in many of our conscious and subconscious default settings. The shift is not limited to the construction of a concept map or including small-group discussion in courses that are otherwise little changed and where the ultimate control, which rests with the instructor, is the determination of a grade.

Much lip service has been paid across North America to the 1998 Report of the Boyer Commission on Educating Undergraduates in the Research University, *Reinventing Undergraduate Education: A Blueprint for America's Research Universities*. As far as I am aware, there has been at McGill no campus-wide discussion of this potentially revolutionary document. To my mind, fully embracing the premises of the Boyer commission report could have major implications for the way in which the learning environment is organized. Imagine the erasing of boundaries between teachers and learners. Imagine as well the common search for understanding in which it is recognized that any member of the team may well have something of value to add to the collective venture, and that each can contribute something distinctive.

The emphasis of the Boyer commission report on inquiry-based learning can be regarded as resulting from advances in our understanding of how learning occurs combined with recognition of the vastly changed larger context in which learning takes place. While readers may be familiar with the Boyer commission report, they may not be aware of three influential reports that have been issued since its appearance that respond to the report and/or the larger contextual change for learning that we all share. These are the 1999 Report of the Committee on Undergraduate Science Education of the Center for Science, Mathematics, and Engineering Education of the U.S. National Research Council, *Transforming Undergraduate Education in Science, Mathematics, Engineering, and Technology*; the 2000 Report of University of California, Berkeley, Commission on Undergraduate Education; and the 2001 University of Michigan Report of the President's Commission on the Undergraduate Experience.

The report on undergraduate education in science, mathematics, engineering, and technology (SME&T) proposes to tackle the "two cultures" problem, not merely by requiring that all students take an SME&T course, but by recommending that these courses be redesigned to include topics both intellectually challenging and near the frontiers of inquiry, which would engage students in discussing problems they would find timely and important.

For students pursuing programs in SME&T inquiry-based learning, collaborative work between different categories of learners would become the standard:

> *All* programs in SME&T would be structured to allow as many undergraduate students as possible to engage in original, supervised research under the tutelage of a faculty or senior graduate student mentor. Undergraduates would become involved with as many phases of a research project as time permitted. These might include experimental design, searching the literature, performing the research using modern scientific instruments and techniques, analyzing and interpreting data, and preparing a report for publication or presentation at an institutional, regional, or national scientific meeting.

The sweeping implications of these recommendations to the U.S. National Research Council led the committee to stress that *"top officials in colleges and universities will need to play a special role*: they will need to exert strong leadership, to display a deep understanding of the issues, and to provide tangible support for the necessary changes to take hold."

The Berkeley commission, which was co-chaired by the university's Vice-Chancellor, clearly proclaimed the priority which it believes the formation of undergraduate students deserves:

> A large research university, especially one as distinguished as UC Berkeley, is particularly well positioned to emerge on the cutting edge of undergraduate education. We have the opportunity—even the obligation—to engage students in inquiry-based learning from the outset of their undergraduate careers. We have the obligation to provide an integrated liberal arts education that produces broadly literate future citizens. Our students deserve informed guidance at all stages of their education from both faculty and staff advisors. And as an institution we need to set as a priority the ongoing assessment of undergraduate education, so that we may address other imperatives as they arise.

Like the report on SME&T, the Berkeley report gives pride of place to inquiry-based learning, which is the first of its categories of recommendations: "1. Integrate inquiry-based learning into every phase of the undergraduate education." As the director of McGill's interdisciplinary undergraduate programs in International Development Studies, I applaud that priority and am especially pleased by several of the commission's specific recommendations, which I would be delighted to see implemented at McGill for all students:

- Ensure that students who have declared a major have access to good methodology courses and apprenticeships in their disciplines.
- Nurture and sustain programs on campus that provide mentored opportunities for students to synthesize classroom learning with outside experience in the community.
- Provide every student with a defining capstone experience in his or her major.
- Create intellectually integrated clusters that reach beyond the bounds of an individual course.

The University of Michigan's report traces achievements triggered by consideration of the undergraduate experience in 1989–1990, which anticipated some of the Boyer commission themes. Michigan established theme semesters as well as over 200 first-year seminars, which provide small-group experience to all of the entering students in the College of Literature, Science and the Arts. The university also created an Undergraduate Research Opportunity Program (UROP), which places more than a thousand undergraduates annually in faculty research projects for academic credit or work-study support. Among the points addressed in the 2001 report is the removal of barriers to interdisciplinary and intercollege study and collaboration. Nor are faculty motivation and reward neglected: The report recommends that resources be provided and practices nurtured "that renew the faculty commitment to undergraduate education and enhance student-faculty interaction."

These reports are a beacon of hope that inertia is being overcome and that university practices are responding to the changed context of learning. If institutions that are held in high esteem[5] are once again setting the pace, pressures for change elsewhere will become irresistible. The lesson of these examples is that a changing context is a reformer's most valuable ally. When the external environment sends signals that are palpably similar to one's own calls for change, possibilities become more propitious.

---

[5]See Stanford University's Campaign for Undergraduate Education, which is described as "the largest undergraduate campaign undertaken anywhere, ever." Available from Stanford University website: http://cue.stanford.edu/home.html/.

Conclusion

Ursula Franklin (1992) has spoken of the critical role of the earthworm in social change:

> Social change will come through seeds growing in well prepared soil—and it is we, like the earthworms, who prepare the soil. We also seed thoughts and knowledge and concern. We realize there are no guarantees as to what will come up. Yet we do know that without the seeds and the prepared soil nothing will grow at all. (p. 121)

The labors of McGill's Centre for University Teaching and Learning and its Apprentice Developers can be likened to that of the earthworm. The CUTL has patiently and persistently worked to prepare the ground for both immediate and long-term change at McGill. A culture of excellence in learning is not something that is created overnight. It is not the product of a targeted fundraising campaign nor of high-level reports, but rather of sustained efforts to change the attitudes and repertoires of individuals, and to change the operating rules of an institution and its countless semi-sovereign constituent parts. The CUTL's efforts have continued in an environment where effective support from the university administration, beset by tight budgets, has waxed and waned.

CUTL can point to both successes and potential in the quest to create a culture of excellence in learning at McGill. I shall limit myself here to what might be regarded as the tip of the iceberg. In the success category, CUTL has been active in working with at least three faculties that have embarked on major changes in their approach to learning: Law, Management, and Medicine. In the potential category, one must point to over 200 past Workshop participants who have instituted changes in their own practice and influenced others in their departments and faculties. While the Workshop participants are no doubt preparing the soil, they represent a significant potential whose goodwill could be tapped for increasing the pace of change at McGill.

A culture of excellence in learning is shaped slowly and in diverse ways. Change on a Faculty by Faculty basis is one component; consistent support from the top administration is another, as is the contagion of the daily examples of professors and students who are hooked on inquiry. By leveraging student initiative, enthusiasm, and curiosity through inquiry-based learning, the complementarities of "teaching" and research can be multiplied.

We may be closer to a change of culture at McGill than we recognize. The Workshop has prepared the ground and sowed the seeds. The moment may well be at hand for effectively networking the Apprentice Developers and their acolytes to bring in the harvest of liberated learning.

References

Banner, J., Jr., & Cannon, H. (1997). *The elements of teaching.* New Haven, CT: Yale University.

Barzun, J. (1944). *Teacher in America.* Boston: Little Brown.

Boyer Commission on Education (1998). *Reinventing undergraduate education: A blueprint for America's research universities.* Princeton, NJ: Carnegie Foundation for the Advancement of Teaching.

Christensen, C. Roland, Garvin, D., & Sweet, A. (Eds.). (1991). *Education for judgment: The artistry of discussion leadership.* Cambridge, MA: Harvard Business School.

Committee on Undergraduate Science Engineering, and Technology, Center for Science, Mathematics, and Engineering Education, National Research Council. (1999). *Transforming undergraduate education in science, mathematics, engineering, and technology.* Retrieved December 10, 2002, from the National Academic Press website: http://books.nap.edu/html/transund/index.html/.

Franklin, U. (1992). *The real world of technology.* CBC Massi Lecture Series (Rev. ed.). Toronto, Canada: Anansi.

Gopnik, A., Meltzoff, A., & Kuhl, P. (1999). *The scientist in the crib: Minds, brains, and how children learn.* New York: William Morrow.

Highet, G. (1950). *The art of teaching.* New York: Random House.

hooks, b. (1994). *Teaching to transgress: Education as the practice of freedom.* New York: Routledge.

Illich, I. (1973). *Tools for conviviality.* New York: Harper & Row.

Kuhn, T. (1962). *The structure of scientific revolutions.* Chicago, IL: University of Chicago.

Linder, S. (1970). *The harried leisure class.* New York: Columbia University.

McGee, R., & Caplow, T. (1965). *The academic marketplace.* Garden City, NY: Doubleday.

McLuhan, M. (1965). *Understanding media: The extensions of man.* New York: McGraw-Hill.

President's Commission on the Undergraduate Experience. (2001). *Assessing the undergraduate experience.* Retrieved July 23, 2003, from the University of Michigan website: www.umich.edu/pres/undergrad/commissionreport/.

Stanford University. The Campaign for Undergraduate Education. Retrieved December 10, 2002, from Stanford University website: http://cue.stanford.edu/flash4.html/

University of California, Berkeley. (2000, September). *Commission on Undergraduate Education.* Retrieved December 10, 2002, from the University of California at Berkeley site: http://learning.berkeley.edu/cue/index.html/

Veblen, T. (1904). *The theory of business enterprise.* New York: A. M. Kelley.

IO

THE CHALLENGE TO
UNLEARN TRADITIONAL
LANGUAGE

Richard (dik) Harris

The Course Design and Teaching Workshop is undoubtedly effective: Its alumni have gone on to apply what they learned in many diverse ways. However, although for some learning was quick, and implementation immediate, for others learning was slow—even painful—and took longer to incorporate into practice. Of the four alumni whose accounts are presented here, I am perhaps the one who most represents this latter group. And so, rather than speaking to the changes in my teaching practice, I chose to reflect on the process of my transformation, providing a counterpoint to the Workshop theme of the earlier chapters.

The Workshop of May 1994 was my first exposure to the Centre for University Teaching and Learning (CUTL) and its members. I had been back at McGill one year since a sabbatical leave, and, with batteries recharged, had persuaded my department to adopt—and let me teach—a new course that would introduce first-year physics majors to computers and computing in the context of their chosen discipline. What better reason for attending the Workshop?

Yet, it was not at all what I expected. My more than 20 years of experience as a physics instructor had not prepared me for the context, the conflict, and, yes, the challenge of that week. I was confident of my skills as a teacher, taking them for granted, I suppose, and so was anticipating an opportunity to discuss, perhaps, the implications of introducing a "skills" course into a traditional academic program or maybe to encounter others who had struggled with the same issues in other contexts. I did not expect to find my teaching "credentials" at center stage.

I found the starting point so unexpected, the discourse so alien to that of my own discipline, that merely staying engaged was a challenge. Yes, the presentations and the readings made sense—but in *their* own culture, *their* own tradition. Not only did I have to learn a new language, but I had to unlearn my own. That challenge preempted my energy for the week—and I never did "design" my new course.

Looking back, however, the week was the beginning of an adventure. A number of other serendipitous factors conspired to enrich the journey—not least my five years as a member of Quebec's education think-tank, Conseil supérieur de l'éducation—and to bring me where I am today. As I write this, I am on sabbatical leave once again, but this time exploring the world of faculty development, of educational research, and of cognitive science as a Royal Bank fellow in the CUTL itself.

How did I get here, and what are the lessons that I have to share? My personal challenge has been to unlearn the traditional language that in my discipline of physics is used to address the issues surrounding teaching. To unlearn was necessary for me as a prerequisite to reevaluating and reworking my commitment to teaching in terms of a commitment to the quality of my students' learning. And since helping others make explicit this link between teaching and learning is a large part of the challenge that faces CUTL, my experience provides some pointers for the successful completion of the task.

Language

So, part of my challenge has been to learn a new "language." What does this mean? In the literal context of a second language such as French, it is not only to become fluent with a new vocabulary but also to become comfortable with a new grammar and a new mode of expression. And in Introductory Physics, it is not so different. In my mind, the journey that I have traveled recently shares many of the same signposts as the physics journey traveled by my students. It will be interesting—and maybe instructive—to examine my challenge from this point of view.

At a superficial level, the difficulty that many students have with physics is the unfamiliar use of familiar vocabulary. For example, the distinctions between "speed" and "velocity" and between "position" and "displacement" are crucial for the development of kinematics. In teaching this material, I often used to make an analogy with learning a new language, but only recently have I come to see that, as described in Arons's (1990) classic text, the vocabulary as such is not the real difficulty. Rather, it is a pointer to a tightly organized set of concepts: the "grammar." Mastery of these concepts requires far more than the rote learning of vocabulary. In Arons's words:

> Since the words, to begin with, are metaphors, drawn from everyday speech, to which we give profoundly altered scientific meaning, only vaguely connected to the meaning in everyday speech, the students remain unaware of the alteration unless it is pointed to explicitly many times—not just once. Students must be made aware of the *process* of operational definition and must be made to tell the "stories" . . . in their own words. (p. 15)

Thus, for me, the CUTL Workshop was of itself insufficient because I heard the vocabulary for only the first time. After the Workshop was over, the ill-formed ideas were in my mind for a long time—perhaps gradually taking shape but not in a conscious way. I remember sporadic interactions with the CUTL member who had been my small-group leader, trying to make sense of the new language in the familiar but restricted context of teaching physics lecture courses and in the recurrent frustration of trying to redesign physics curriculum. The frustration arose not only because the same situations would constantly recur, but because I could find no way to articulate, let alone integrate, what was taking shape in my mind. I remember a sense of disconnection with the CUTL experience, even though, looking back, there must have been gradual "progress." Indeed, my participation in the activities of the Conseil supérieur, of which I had just become a member, must have aided the process since the extensive reading required of me often pertained to the same themes.

At that time I had not found my way to the physics education literature. I doubt that I had even read Arons, let alone the more recent physics education literature that expands on Arons's ideas. Had I done so, my emerging grasp of language might have improved more quickly. For example, Redish (1999) gives an interesting survey that takes a perspective "embedded in the general principles of learning theory that have been developed by cognitive scientists and education theorists." (p. 562) He introduces what he calls "scientific constructivism" to describe how students might construct science for themselves, building patterns of association to their existing knowledge. He points out the importance of recognizing this existing knowledge: Students never were the empty vessels sometimes imagined by their teachers, so the incompetent high-school science teacher (!) is *not* solely responsible for their difficulties with university physics. Indeed, he says, it would be better to speak of "preconceptions" (Arons, 1990) than the more usual and vaguely pejorative "misconceptions" since they arise from the language and grammar of every day.

Redish goes on to specify that students require guidance in their constructivist process and gives examples of how, explicitly, this can be done. In physics, perhaps the best-known examples come from McDermott's team (McDermott, Shaffer, & Group, 1998) at the University of Washington, which has developed a series of tutorials to supplement the traditional introductory physics course. Graduate student teaching assistants are trained to be Socratic resource persons as the students work through structured laboratory exercises and attempt to answer the questions that arise. The approach is thus founded on the idea that students must be guided to confront the ways in which their new physics knowledge is not congruent with their preconceptions. There is very substantial evidence (McDermott, 1991; McDermott & Redish, 1999) that after these tutorial sessions, students display measured learning outcomes that dramatically surpass those from more traditional environments.

All of this, of course, had parallels in the sputtering development of my own new language and has parallels also in the literature more familiar to "educational developers."[1] Much later, following the trail shown to me by my colleagues in the CUTL, I found, for example, an essay by Jerome Bruner (1966), who was one of the earliest cognitive scientists to study the problems of pedagogy. I read:

> To instruct someone . . . is not a matter of getting him to commit results to mind. Rather, it is to teach him to participate in the process that makes possible the establishment of knowledge. We teach a subject not to produce little living libraries . . . but rather to get a student to think . . . for himself. (p. 72)

Similarly, in the more recent literature, I came to appreciate that much of the thrust of Ramsden's (1992, 1993) writings centers around the distinction between "surface" and "deep" approaches to learning: the distinction between those who "intend only to complete the task requirements and who distort the nature of the task" (p. 46) and those "who intend to understand, and who maintain the structure of the task." (p. 46) He cites overwhelming evidence that the latter group succeed much better in their studies, and stresses, therefore, the importance—necessity, even—that teachers adopt approaches and provide environments where deep learning is enhanced.

Recent contributions by Entwistle and coworkers (Entwistle, Skinner, Entwistle, & Orr, 2000), for example, go so far as to relate such approaches to the essence of "good teaching."

---

[1]The term "educational developer," favored by the European school (Ramsden, 1993), for example, seems to me more apt than the more generic "faculty developer."

But the context of my challenge is more particular. Starting with my language and culture as a natural scientist, what were the particular impediments to my learning the new language at that first CUTL Workshop? What have been the impediments since that time? Has the existence of my own discipline-based culture played a significant role? How might I describe my experience in that first Workshop in a manner that transcends mere personal characteristics?[2] What about my learning experience since the Workshop?

Eventually, I found a structure for my answers in the literature. An early reference was the work of Schwab (1962), who uses the various (natural) sciences to illustrate how disciplines differ in what he calls their conceptual and syntactical structures. These structures are both included in what Shulman (1986) calls "content knowledge," but the distinction is crucial here: Learning to use the language of a new discipline requires both the vocabulary and the grammar. Exposure to new ideas may result in only the rote acquisition of vocabulary, but the learning of the vocabulary requires the acquisition of the rules of legitimate syntax. Were my difficulties with the Workshop a measure of my grammatical deficiencies?

Again, in the literature, I found some partial answers. Following in the footsteps of Schwab—although they do not reference him directly—Handal, Lauvås, and Lycke (1990) reflect upon the role played by academic "cultures" in university teaching and in faculty development. Their definition of "culture" is taken from Becher (1989, 1994), so that it includes both the culture and the structure, in the anthropological sense, of an academic "tribe." In Becher's terms, this culture is intimately related with the cognitive aspects of the disciplines: a clear parallel with Schwab (1962). However, what is interesting in Handal et al.'s (1990) article is not so much the analysis of how teaching is carried out in the natural sciences, but rather the observations of how and why natural scientists react to the message that they present as faculty developers.

Handal et al. observe that natural scientists "seem to be concerned with particular and restricted aspects of the theory and practice of university teaching,"(p. 320) such that they "tend to expect clear-cut answers regarding specific teaching tasks."(p. 320) And why?—because they themselves, as students, had not benefited much from university teaching and consequently had not developed an awareness of its potential. Many physicists, indeed myself included, would identify themselves with David Halliday, coauthor of a

---

[2]The complete typology has four categories: (1) hard pure, natural sciences; (2) soft pure, humanities and social sciences; (3) hard applied, science-based professions; (4) soft applied, social professions.

famous introductory textbook, who is cited by Redish (1999) as saying that "what he enjoyed most as a student was sitting down by himself alone in a quiet room with a physics text and going one-on-one with the authors of the book." (p. 564)

Are physicists, natural scientists, particular—singular—in this respect? The evidence suggests that we are. Braxton (1995) assembles a variety of evidence suggesting that compared with our colleagues in other disciplines, we are less susceptible to efforts to improve undergraduate education. Handal et al. (1990) associate our behavior with the dominant "rationality" of our disciplines, members of the "hard pure" cluster in the typology of Biglan (1973).[3] When this rationality—driven by research-based, manipulative, controlled action—does not prove effective as applied to teaching, they argue that we revert to using common, subjective knowledge about teaching, gathered from our own experience. Further, when confronted with an alternate rationality, and even when it is intellectually accepted, we find it difficult to think and act differently. Language again.

Reflecting on that analysis, it seems to me that the Workshop made a number of implicit assumptions that I did not grasp until much later and which were at variance with my own expectations. Not having previously thought about my teaching in a contextual, structured way—because my professional development as a physicist had not provided me with the language to do so—I was expecting a much more directive discourse. Since I had questions, in my own language, I was expecting answers—or pointers to where the "answers" might be.

Instead, I was offered a new language with which to refashion my questions. At the time, I had no awareness that there was a well-developed syntax for this language, and so I was not prepared to adopt it, let alone, in the short space of time available, begin to acquire fluency in it. Maybe it would have helped if the Workshop that week had made my task more explicit—in much the same way as the novice physics students, struggling with new concepts, need a scaffolding for their learning. But maybe not, for after all "The principal function of education—and higher education in particular—must be to help individuals to their own intellectual feet: to give them conceptual starting points and an awareness of what it means to learn and understand something *so that they can continue to read, study, and learn as need and opportunity arise, without perpetual formal instruction*" (Arons, 1990, p. 318; italics added).

---

[3]No comment.

And indeed for me, now, it seems that my understanding needed time to germinate, to give rise, eventually, to a distinct change in perspective. This is an idea that is also present in the literature. For example, Entwistle et al. (2000) observed such changes in their study of students taking a one-year post-graduate teacher training course. Using a combination of methods, including questionnaires and interviews, they explored these students' emerging views on "good teaching." Although their study is primarily concerned with the student teachers, they claim that their conclusions apply equally well to the university situation. They suggest that the initial impetus for a change in perspective on teaching and learning comes from reconsidering the nature of knowledge within the discipline in question. For student teachers, this "content knowledge" is likely less complete than for a university instructor, but nevertheless was likely formed within the same culture—and employing the same language. Many of the characteristics of untutored student teachers, after all, mirror those of their untutored university instructors (Grossman, 1989)—just as, conversely, the incomplete comprehension of teaching and learning by these instructors mirrors that of the student teachers!

Traditional . . .

But language—in the extended sense defined above—has a larger context, the traditional practice and context of the university. At a "research-intensive" university such as McGill, this larger context is confronted by the questions posed by the Boyer report (1998) and the recommendations contained within it. Can such an institution be both research-centered and student-centered? Yes— presumably—because it provides an environment where "the skills of analysis, evaluation, and synthesis will become the hallmarks of a good education, just as absorption of a body of knowledge once was" (Boyer, 1998, p. 11).

Just as the language of a discipline can be an impediment to learning about teaching and learning, so the traditional language and culture of an institution can have the same inhibiting effect. Barr and Tagg (1995) describe this situation in terms of the persistence of the "instruction paradigm" in our institutions. The paradigm represents a limited focus on instruction—teaching—to the exclusion of student learning, thereby confusing the means with the end purpose of the institution's existence. They argue that it seriously inhibits the improvement of student learning because within its limitations it is not possible to increase outputs—"more teaching"—without a corresponding increase in costs for scarce resources. In contrast, a "learning paradigm" permits, even facilitates, improvement by opening up a larger domain of possibilities. Guskin (1994) gives many illustrations of how this might be done.

Two illustrations from my own context at McGill will make the point more clearly. My own department—excellent though it is in terms of its research output—has never developed a way to systematically review our undergraduate curriculum. Over the years, the same issues are recurrent: the purpose of our majors program (as distinct from our honors program, which self-evidently leads to post-graduate work); the role of laboratory work in preparing students for life after graduation; the shortage of teaching personnel, which severely strains our ability to deliver our programs—a shortage that has become particularly acute in recent years. Successive department chairs have tried to address these issues, in isolation, by asking questions about courses and course content—the "instruction paradigm" in action—but the underlying issues have never gone away. Had we instead focused on student outcomes and student learning, the consequences could have been profound.

A similar situation appears at the Faculty[4] level, where there is acknowledgment that our freshman program overtaxes and maybe even discourages our students. There have been attempts, at least twice, to make structural changes—but without success. Since, like my department, the Faculty operates, by default, with the "instruction paradigm," thinking outside the box is seriously impeded, and a whole range of ideas never comes to be discussed.

McGill is not alone, of course. There is strong circumstantial evidence that very few of North America's top research universities have adopted the "learning paradigm," that very few have made teaching and learning what Shulman (1993) calls "community property." Although most, if not all, such institutions have placed a strong reference to teaching—and maybe student learning—in their mission statements, few can point to important initiatives that give teaching and learning a share of center stage. An ongoing comparative analysis of the yearly College Student Survey, administered by the Higher Education Research Institute at UCLA, provides some evidence in this respect: Over a ten-year period, students at only around 10% of the (American) institutions analyzed showed improved satisfaction with their learning outcomes (Astin, 1998).

McGill does not participate in the survey, but if it did, it would not be among the 10%, even though our mission statement says:

> The Mission of McGill University is *the advancement of learning through teaching, scholarship, and service to society: by offering to outstanding undergraduate and graduate students the best education available; by carrying out scholarly activities judged to be excellent when measured against the*

---

[4]College of Science.

highest international standards; and by providing service to society in those ways for which we are well suited by virtue of our academic strengths. (McGill University, n.d.)

Seldom during my 30 years as a McGill professor have I witnessed a commitment to "the best education" that matches in intensity our commitment to our excellent research. And I do not exclude myself from this inclusive and undoubtedly unfair overstatement—which I should now explain.

The explanation is offered in the language that I have so recently come to comprehend since the translation of "best education" brings now a quite different meaning. What is at issue is *not* good intentions, nor even the existence of excellent teaching—though one might ask how this excellence is properly defined (Sternberg & Horvath, 1995)—but rather the institutional culture, the tradition in which these are situated. Does our tradition truly support the "best education?" I suggest that we are overdue to intentionally ask the question, although, of course, others have both asked and answered it.

Shulman (1993), for one, has used the example of university-wide centers for teaching and learning to make his point. In most institutions, he writes, such centers are "where faculty—regardless of department—can go for assistance in improving their practice. That's a perfectly reasonable idea." But he goes on:

> Notice the message it conveys—that teaching is general, technical, and a matter of performance; that it's not part of the community that means so much to most faculty, the disciplinary, interdisciplinary, or professional community. It's something general you lay on top of what you *really* do as a scholar in a discipline. (p. 273)

With very few exceptions, though notable ones,[5] here at McGill, Shulman's cap fits. My own department has never examined its teaching and the learning of its students in a way that transcends the preoccupations of the discipline itself, and my Faculty has never succeeded in finessing the disciplinary preoccupations of the participating departments. In both these cases—and in other situations across the university—I now see that progress requires an institutional culture that is supportive of "teaching as community property," that is, a language that transcends disciplinary boundaries. I submit that teaching and learning this language—and unlearning the traditional language—is a prerequisite for sustainable institutional change.

---

[5]The Faculties of Medicine, Law, and Management have all undertaken comprehensive reviews during the last few years.

Unlearn

So, how can an institution unlearn its traditional language? Only when a significant number of its faculty themselves unlearn. The question—and its answer—are, to me, the way to understand what is required of this institution as it sets out to define the "best education" of its mission statement. This realization has perhaps been the single most important consequence of my sojourn at CUTL—although, again, its roots can probably be traced to the Workshop!

The use of the word "unlearn" I owe to my daughter Nansi, who showed me its symbolic value in the context of transforming beliefs and attitudes related to human rights. Later, I was intrigued to notice it used by Perry (1970) in his groundbreaking study of intellectual and ethical development among college students in the 1960s. He was describing the characteristics of development as the learning of the new coupled with the unlearning of the old—entirely consistent with the dictionary definition of "unlearn," which reads "discard from one's memory; rid oneself of (a habit, false information, etc.)" (Barber, 1998).

Thus, to unlearn about teaching, it would seem important to know what "habits" of university teaching are current, and why. An insightful article by Fox (1983) seems to be the earliest study of this question: He concludes that most beginning teachers at his institution[6] view the subject material as "a commodity to be transferred to the students' minds." A later study by Menges and Rando (1989) gave results that were more nuanced but were still consistent with this transmission paradigm. They studied the assumptions made about teaching by graduate teaching assistants—beginning teachers also—and found that their orientations could be grouped into three equally important categories: interest in transmitting content, focus on helping students process the content, and concern with student motivation. Anecdotally, this situation corresponds well with what I observe of my physics colleagues—both new and old—to the extent that I can gauge their assumptions from often casual conversation about teaching.

Somewhat similar conclusions were reached in the review by Kember (1997), which analyzes several qualitative studies of university teachers' conceptions of teaching, including the one by Fox (1983) cited above. Kember (1997) argues that all the studies distinguish at least two broad orientations, teacher-centered and student-centered, which he claims are arranged along a quasi-linear continuum. The former orientation represents a focus on the

---

[6]Then Trent Polytechnic, now Nottingham Trent University.

transmission of content, well defined in disciplinary terms, whereas the latter focuses on the development of students' understanding. The analysis also suggests evidence for a transitional conception of teaching that recognizes the value of teacher-student interaction.

Prosser and Trigwell (1999) take a similar view. Based on their own research and that of many others, they identify three broad categories of instructors' conceptions of teaching, which they term *limited, intermediate,* and *complete* (p. 144). The first of these corresponds to Fox's beginning teachers, and also—anecdotally, at least—encompasses the majority of instructors in most institutions. Certainly, this was the case for the 24 science instructors interviewed by Trigwell, Prosser, and Taylor (1994) and for the 26 instructors in the subsequent study by Martin, Prosser, Trigwell, Ramsden, and Benjamin (2000). The *intermediate* category corresponds to those who see the importance of their teaching for helping students acquire knowledge of interrelationships among concepts, whereas those in the *complete* category actively pursue strategies for provoking change in students' conceptions. If these categories, however simplistic, represent the reality of the traditional language of university faculty, then shifting from one category to another represents the "unlearning" that we seek.

How do the shifts occur? What is the nature of this unlearning? Entwistle and Walker (2000) support Perry's idea (1970) of a pivotal stage of development at which "the relation of learner to knowledge is radically transformed." (p. 337) They use the detailed narrative of Walker's development as a teacher and identify a radical transformation during a lengthy period of practical experience and reflection, which took him from his initial focus "on course content and on learning as the intake, retention and reproduction of this course content" to a position in which "the point was to enable students to relate to the edifice of disciplinary knowledge *and to the business of learning* differently than most of them normally seemed to" (p. 349) (italics added). The pivotal stage seems to have been a realization of the discrepancy between his (Walker's) command of concepts and connections and the inaccessibility of these same concepts and connections to his students.

Interestingly, Kember (1997) also maintains that a major perspective transformation—an "unlearning (!)"—is necessary for significant change to take place. For me, however, this seems an overstatement: Much more compelling is Mezirow's (1981) view that "there appear to be two paths to perspective transformation: one is a sudden insight . . . [t]he other is movement . . . that occurs by a series of transitions." My own progression along the continuum was more erratic, less dramatic than that experienced by

Paul Walker: I find it difficult to identify a single defining incident, a pivotal point.[7] Rather, I can identify with a continuum of many stages (Samuelowsicz & Bain, 2001) along which progress is often intermittent and slow. How, then, to accelerate the progression?

One of those to address this question is Ramsden (1992, 1993). In Part 3 of his book (1992), there is a chapter entitled "What does it take to improve teaching?"—precisely! In it, he writes:

> These goals of development in teaching may be summarized in terms of a shift from a simple way of understanding teaching to a complex, relativistic, and dynamic one. . . . These changes emulate those which higher education (instructors), especially those in professional subjects, desire to see in their undergraduate students, and it may be helpful to conceptualize the process of learning how to teach in similar terms. (p. 250)

Thus, just as it is important that "students must be guided to confront the ways in which their new (physics) knowledge is not congruent with their preconceptions" (p. 3), so it is also important that instructors must be guided to confront their preconceptions about teaching. In effect, this *is* what happened to me during that CUTL workshop, although I did not understand the message clearly until much later in time. Is the confrontation of misconceptions, therefore, one of the key functions of the Workshop? Certainly yes, but the process is really a collective, institutional responsibility—a true challenge to the nature of the institution—although there will necessarily be key players, such as a CUTL, and key events, such as its Workshop. There will also be many routes to be found, depending, certainly, on the individual instructors and their disciplinary cultures and languages. Just as students differ in their expectations of learning, as they adopt either "surface" or "deep" approaches, so we should expect the same variety in instructors' expectations and approaches.

Challenge

The challenge of the educational developer seems easy to state: to bring the institution to an active engagement with "the best education available" (McGill University, n.d.). The implication, of course, is that the present state of engagement is inadequate—and there lies the real challenge because the

---

[7]Even though I distinctly remember the morning, in the autumn of 1997, in the midst of lecturing to 400 students in a freshman physics class, when the pieces began to fall into place.

institution often does not share that view of itself. Rather, as at McGill, there is a perception that "we teach well," and that the tenure and promotion process *does* place a sufficient importance on teaching performance. There is limited appreciation that "We can teach—and teach 'well'—without having the students learn" (Ward & Bodner, 1993, p. 873) or that evaluating the quality of teaching and courses "is often viewed as a test of effectiveness—of materials, teaching methods, or whatnot—but [that] this is the least important aspect of it. The most important is to provide intelligence on how to improve these things" (Bruner, 1966, p. 165) (quoted by Ramsden, 1992, p. 240).

What, then, to do?

I am tempted to argue that the top-down approach of Quebec's powerful Ministry of Education points the way. Over the last several years, successive ministers of education have imposed new structures and new language on the pre-university education system. The CEGEP network,[8] which offers two-year pre-university programs and three-year professional programs to high school graduates, now must contend with programs couched in the language of "objectifs et standards," with untraceable (!) roots in the literature on cognitive development. A charitable observer would see links to the language of learning outcomes and to a more student-focused curriculum, and could argue that the ongoing debate in the colleges will have a positive effect on the quality of education. Similarly, the reform in Quebec's primary and secondary schools (K–12) should have had the same result: the "compétences" are again very close to "learning outcomes."

Of course, the negative outcomes of the Ministry's initiatives have been just as evident: teachers with a sense of impotence and frustration faced with a bureaucratic process having no roots in their own experience and expertise. The lesson is there to be learned by the universities: The process of institutional change, be it in a primary school or a college, requires both careful management and informed leadership. The Quebec Conseil supérieur de l'éducation document, *The Management of Change* (1995), makes this point in great detail. The Conseil relied heavily on Fullan's (1993) analysis of mechanisms for institutional change in the pre-university sector, assuming, implicitly, that many of the issues transcend the classification of institutions.

To quote, in my own translation:

> In the context of change, the quality of an organization consists in valuing and giving responsibility to human resources, and in a working environment that encourages communication, collaboration—with partners both inside

---

[8]CEGEPs, Collèges d'éducation générale et professionelle.

and outside the institution—and openness to innovative practices from elsewhere. . . . In such an environment, the institution lives and develops by the success of its student body and the satisfaction of its staff.

Ramsden (1998) would undoubtedly agree. His book addresses the attributes of those who, in the university setting, are called to lead: to lead, but also to manage change. Much of the literature that he quotes also comes from the pre-university sector, but he argues explicitly and persuasively that the management issues at a university are no different from their nature in other institutions. Indeed, he points out that the same issues are addressed in the corporate management literature, where the Taylorist "top-down" philosophy no longer enjoys the credibility it once had.

To engage the faculty in the process of change thus requires that they understand why change is necessary. It requires that they bring their powers of analysis and criticism to bear on a different set of issues: the purpose and effectiveness of their own teaching. What Ramsden—and the Conseil—do not address, however, is why they would choose to do so. What would their motivation be?

Most faculty have asked themselves questions, at one time or another, about a teaching experience. Precisely because the culture of their institution/department/unit does not encourage discussion of such matters, however, such questions often go unanswered. And a CUTL with its limited resources can never provide unaided the just-in-time consultation that would be appropriate, nor the continuing contact that might facilitate continuing reflection. The motivation is present but leads to an impasse.

The challenge, then, for an institution, or more particularly for those within an institution who care, is to provide an outreach that operates at the department/unit level. It seems necessary to be present at these levels not only to respond to questions but also to stimulate and maintain an ongoing dialogue that speaks the language of the disciplinary culture and which helps unlearning to take place. "Working to improve teaching and the recognition of discipline-based pedagogy and scholarship is easier from within a discipline because insiders know the language" (Jenkins, 1996, p. 60).

Different institutions will undoubtedly achieve this objective in their different ways—but at McGill, the affiliate program of the CUTL would seem a good beginning. This program, which formally recognizes the commitment to CUTL activities of some of us whose "home" is a traditional department, cannot provide the impetus for unlearning that my sabbatical has given me. Nevertheless, it facilitates continuing contact, and therefore an ongoing unlearning, with the individuals and, by extension, with the faculties from which they come.

However, the nature of the outreach activities is at least as important as the existence of the activities themselves. For example, all of the possible activities cited by Jenkins (1996) are valuable only insofar as they provide an initial context for instructors to deepen their understanding of teaching and learning. As he says, the skill of an "educational developer"—the focus of an outreach operation—lies in helping this process so that instructors "will build out into wider and more student-centered concerns." (p. 56) This learning process, of course, must be informed by the same literature that describes the learning of students: in Perry's (1970) language—borrowed from Piaget—there needs to be not only "assimilation" of new experiences, but "accommodation" of existing expectancies to take account of them. Or, in Ramsden's (1992) words: "If educational development is about changing [instructors'] understanding of teaching, then the methods used to help them to change should reflect the imperatives of . . . a way [of learning] compatible with the changes we wish to see them make" (p. 262).

Are those of us who must do the outreaching equal to the challenge?—the challenge to sustain the unlearning of traditional language throughout the diverse disciplinary domains that make up the university? I hope so.

References

Arons, A. (1990). *A guide to introductory physics teaching.* New York: Wiley.

Astin, A. W. (1998). The changing American college student: Thirty-year trends, 1966–1996. *The Review of Higher Education, 21*(2), 115–135.

Barber, K. (Ed.). (1998). *The Canadian Oxford dictionary.* Don Mills, Canada: Oxford University.

Barr, R. B., & Tagg, J. (1995). From teaching to learning: A new paradigm for undergraduate education. *Change, 27*(6), 13–25.

Becher, T. (1989). *Academic tribes and territories.* Milton Keynes, UK: Open University.

Becher, T. (1994). The significance of disciplinary differences. *Studies in Higher Education, 19,* 151–161.

Biglan, A. (1973). The characteristics of subject matter in different academic areas. *Journal of Applied Psychology, 57,* 195–203.

Boyer Commission on Education. (1998). *Reinventing undergraduate education: A blueprint for America's research universities.* Princeton, NJ: Carnegie Foundation for the Advancement of Teaching.

Braxton, J. (Ed.). (1995). *Disciplines with affinity for the improvement of undergraduate education* (Vol. 64). San-Francisco: Jossey-Bass.

Bruner, J. (1966). *Towards a theory of instruction.* Cambridge, MA: Harvard University.

Conseil Supérieur de l'Éducation (1995). *Vers la maîtrise du changement en education.* Quebec City: Ministere de l'Éducation du Quebec.

Entwistle, N., Skinner, D., Entwistle, D., & Orr, S. (2000). Conceptions and beliefs about "good teaching": An integration of contrasting research areas. *Higher Education Research and Development, 19*(1), 5–26.

Entwistle, N., & Walker, P. (2000). Strategic alertness and expanded awareness within sophisticated conceptions of teaching. *Instructional Science, 28,* 335–361.

Fox, D. (1983). Personal theories of teaching. *Studies in Higher Education, 8,* 151–163.

Fullan, M. (1993). *Change forces: Probing the depth of educational reform.* London: Falmer.

Grossman, P. (1989). Learning to teach without teacher education. *Teachers College Record, 91*(2), 191–208.

Guskin, A. (1994, September/October). Restructuring the role of faculty. *Change,* 16–25.

Handal, G., Lauvås, P., & Lycke, K. (1990). The concept of rationality in academic science teaching. *European Journal of Education, 25,* 319–332.

Jenkins, A. (1996). Discipline based educational development. *International Journal for Academic Development, 1,* 50–62.

Kember, D. (1997). A reconceptualization of the research into university academics' conceptions of teaching. *Learning and Instruction, 7*(3), 255–275.

Martin, E., Prosser, M., Trigwell, K., Ramsden, P., & Benjamin, J. (2000). What university teachers teach and how they teach it. *Instructional Science, 28,* 335–361.

McDermott, L. (1991). What we teach and what is learned—closing the gap. *American Journal of Physics, 59*(4), 301–315.

McDermott, L., & Redish, E. (1999). Physics education research. *American Journal of Physics, 67*(9), 755–767.

McDermott, L., Shaffer, P., & Group, P. E. (1998). *Tutorials in introductory physics.* Upper Saddle River, NJ: Prentice-Hall.

McGill University. (n.d.). *Mission Statement.* Retrieved December 10, 2002, from McGill University website: http://www.mcgill.ca/secretariat/mission/

Menges, R., & Rando, W. (1989). What are your assumptions? Improving instruction by examining theories. *College Teaching, 37,* 54–60.

Mezirow, J. (1981). A critical theory of adult learning and education. *Adult Education, 32*(1), 3–27.

Perry, W. G. (1970). *Forms of intellectual and ethical development in the college years: A scheme.* Troy, MO: Hold, Rinehart & Winston.

Prosser, M., & Trigwell, K. (1999). *Understanding learning and teaching.* Buckingham, UK: SHRE and Open University Press.

Ramsden, P. (1992). *Learning to teach in higher education.* London: Routledge.

Ramsden, P. (1993). Theories of learning and teaching and the practice of excellence in higher education. *Higher Education Research and Development, 12*(1), 87–98.

Ramsden, P. (1998). *Learning to lead in higher education.* New York: Routledge.

Redish, E. (1999). Building a science of teaching physics. *American Journal of Physics, 67*(7), 562–537.

Samuelowsicz, K., & Bain, J. (2001). Revisiting academics' beliefs about teaching and learning. *Higher Education, 41,* 299–325.

Schwab, J. (1962). The concept of the structure of a discipline. *The Educational Record, 43,* 197–205.

Shulman, L. (1986). Those who understand: Knowledge in teaching. *Educational Researcher, 15*(2), 4–14.

Shulman, L. (1993). Teaching as community property: Putting an end to pedagogical solitude. *Change* (November/December), 6–7.

Sternberg, R., & Horvath, J. (1995). A prototype view of expert teaching. *Educational Researcher, 24*(6), 9–17.

Trigwell, K., Prosser, M., & Taylor, P. (1994). Qualitative differences in approaches to teaching first year university science. *Higher Education, 27,* 75–84.

Ward, R., & Bodner, G. (1993). How lecture can undermine the motivation of our students. *Journal of Chemical Education, 70,* 198–199.

II

TEACHING BETWEEN
THE CRACKS

Richard Janda

One of the insights I gained from participating in the activities offered by the Centre for University Teaching and Learning was that opportunities for learning are not restricted to the classroom. In mapping the learning outcomes that I sought, I became interested in what didn't fit into the topography of a course but nevertheless stood out as significant for my teaching. After all, a great deal of what we do as teachers comes through informal contact with students. Even the fact that we are addressed as "Professors"—those who make a profession of a vocation—suggests that it is not simply the body of knowledge that we convey in the classroom that makes an impression on students. It is also how we conduct ourselves when they are testing their own convictions and seeking out their own vocations.

I like to say that as a law teacher, much of my professional life is lived vicariously, through the success of my students. When I reflect upon what it is that has thrilled me most about teaching recently, what I wouldn't trade for any other métier, a few informal one-on-one encounters, most of them by chance, come to mind. Each of them, I hope, will contribute in a small way to a student's future success. There are, of course, highs that come in the classroom when one senses that a new idea might be dawning in some minds. But the classroom is always exhibitionist in some degree. There, the teacher is in performance. Although the important part of that performance is happening out in the audience, audiences don't like having themselves put on display. It makes them squeamish. There is a mantra of "active learning" recited by teachers who seek to be good contemporary pedagogues and reject the old-fashioned passivity of the classroom. But the classroom sometimes looks like a small barnacle on the leviathan called "the entertainment industry." And so one feels the pressure to ensure that the character the teacher plays in the classroom is entertaining, at least for its quirks and foibles.

Which brings me back to living vicariously as a teacher—the very opposite of display. If there is pedagogy in helping others to succeed, it is not captured entirely in course concept maps and planned learning outcomes. It is contained in moments that present themselves spontaneously between student and teacher to share or draw out some lasting lesson. Occasionally, the interplay of these moments as mediated by the teacher—unbeknown to the student—serves to transfer learning between students. This essay seeks to recapture and present with the greatest possible fidelity three such recent moments. It is meant as a reflection on the informal dimension of teaching—teaching between the cracks, if you will. By putting this dimension of teaching on display in writing, I acknowledge a paradox. But think of it as a secret shared among teachers. In addressing informal learning, this piece is an attempt to map learning outcomes that are probably unmappable but nevertheless validated by the reflections prompted by my association with CUTL.

The Convert

Ernesto has always been intense. His eyes widen perceptibly when he speaks, and his gestures sweep. Some time ago he had worked out a variant of the "Tobin tax" that would ultimately put an end to currency, a proposal he described with enormous insistence.

One afternoon as I was coming back from picking up my mail, there he was, strolling down the hall in front of me. I hadn't seen him for some time and asked where he'd been. "I've had an amazing experience," he said, "one I never expected would happen to me. I have discovered the beauty and the truth of Islam." I wasn't quite sure what to say, but out came, "Well that is quite remarkable and wonderful, especially at this time. How did it happen?" A moment of hesitation fluttered across Ernesto's face, and his eyes glanced up and down. Then he poured out a torrent. He spoke of the perfection of the *Qu'ran*, a book that could never have been produced from the human imagination. There were well-reasoned details of argument concerning the synthetic quality of Islam, a religion that recognized and acknowledged prior revelations, but which absorbed, integrated, and reformed both Judaism and Christianity to produce a pure, unobstructed pathway to God. He felt, he said, a unity and completeness to his life that had always eluded him before. In the midst of this profession of faith, Ernesto expressed a concern. He allowed that he was surprised to discover that his newfound religion caused him to abandon some cherished former beliefs. "I thought I had enlightened views about the status of women and the morality of homosexuality. I now realize that I must have been mistaken in those views. But I am still trying to come to terms with this." The moment was rendered all the more poignant because standing just behind Ernesto, waiting patiently to speak to me, was Ernesto's friend Omar. Omar, whose family is Muslim, had introduced Ernesto to Islam, and Omar is gay.

"Can't it be argued that Islam, at its origins, aimed and helped to emancipate women?" I asked. Ernesto quickly agreed, noting that the Prophet spoke movingly of the duty to honor and to protect women. He argued, for example, that Islam is best understood as having restricted rather than allowed polygamy as compared with earlier practices, and that if the Prophet himself had more than one wife, it was because he was supporting women and children who otherwise would have been destitute.

"So, obviously, what we learn from the teachings of the Prophet depends upon some appreciation of historical context and on a wise interpretation of how those teachings apply to us," I allowed.

"Of course," Ernesto replied. "The *Qu'ran* is evidence of its own truth and authenticity, but a good Muslim must take that truth and apply it in his own life. This means that each Muslim must study the *Qu'ran,* the life of the Prophet and the teachings of wise scholars who have best understood these things."

"And is it not true that the Prophet himself urged the faithful to study the *Qu'ran* for themselves and to exercise their own reason and judgment?" I asked.

"This is a very important point that is often misunderstood in the West," Ernesto replied. "One of the great attractions of Islam is that it praises reason. I would say that it is the perfect marriage between reason and revelation."

"What, then, is the scope for personal judgment of a good Muslim when confronted with teachings that don't seem right? If I understood you properly, you said a moment ago that initially you found that the teachings on women and homosexuality didn't make sense to you."

"Well," Ernesto replied, "one must show humility. I don't claim to understand everything about Islam. I'm just learning. There are a lot of wiser and better people who have thought about the same questions and concluded that the teachings of Islam are what they are."

"But do you think that Islam would be diminished somehow in your eyes if its teachings on women and homosexuality corresponded to what you had believed before your conversion? Can't you be a good Muslim and believe in the equal treatment of women or in nondiscrimination against homosexuals?"

After a moment's hesitation, Ernesto answered. "As I said, I'm struggling with this. Part of me wants to say yes, but part of me believes that is just pride. Who am I to make these judgments? I'm simply grateful that my life has been given a meaning and purpose. I think I have to take everything that comes with that."

"I can see your conundrum," I replied after a moment's hesitation of my own. "Isn't it odd that even if the teachings of a great religion urge us to use our own judgment and reason, at the very point at which this matters, it feels wrong to do so? I suppose we don't trust ourselves. There is certainly something to be said for deference to those who've gone before us, like parents, teachers, and elders."

"Right, but obviously that can be taken too far," Ernesto replied. "For example, my parents haven't converted."

"I guess the point is that we should learn from those whom we recognize as having something to teach us about the question that consumes us. In your case, I guess you've come to the conclusion that the best teachers come from within Islam."

"But where else could they be?" Ernesto was quick to reply. "Surely a nonbeliever would have nothing to teach about matters of faith."

"Well, surely religions have something to teach even the nonbeliever—otherwise conversions would not be possible," I ventured with a hint of unease. "Can't this be reciprocal? Can't religions learn something from each other and even from nonbelievers?"

"Perhaps," said Ernesto, "But not in matters of faith. After all, the atheist might be learned in secular things and even the Devil can quote scripture. But the believer is not about to trade places with the unenlightened. I know that might sound arrogant, but it really isn't. Faith is open to everyone. It's like saying that I have nothing to learn about walking from a toddler. That isn't arrogant."

"But maybe you do have something to learn about walking from a toddler. Ask the toddler what walking is, whether it is hard, why the toddler would like to be able to walk better. I'll bet you can't remember those answers and sensations, and they certainly put walking in perspective, don't they? I have a friend who had to learn to walk all over again after an accident. He said he felt like a toddler without having the perspective of a toddler."

"Okay, fair enough." Ernesto allowed. "Maybe my example wasn't very good. Being a toddler is part of a process of learning how to walk. Being a nonbeliever is not part of a process of becoming a believer. They are two different states of mind, or of the soul, if you will. They just don't overlap. Maybe a better analogy is to the difference between a person with perfect pitch and a person without it. The person with perfect pitch isn't arrogant to conclude that she has nothing to learn about identifying notes from the person without perfect pitch."

"Maybe not about how she lives the experience of having perfect pitch, although even there she might learn something from comparing her experience with that of a person without perfect pitch. I have a colleague in Music who studies perfect pitch. Part of his methodology is to compare the experiences of those with and without perfect pitch so as to understand what characterizes the different capacities. The analogy to your situation might be as follows: One can learn from the experience of those outside Islam so as to shed light on why Islam might teach what it does about women and homosexuality. This might then put you in a better position to judge whether you should accept those teachings or not."

This met with silence and Ernesto's eyes darted as he thought of what to say. Finally, he blurted out, "I can't pick and choose among beliefs I find attractive or convenient. I'm either a Muslim or I'm not. *Islam* means submission to God, to God's will. It's not for me to decide what God's will is."

I felt the conversation trailing off, and Omar was pacing in the background, looking increasingly agitated. So I decided on a final volley. "I must say that I have always found this to be a problem about the great religions. When we submit to God, we are always in some measure submitting to the opinions of men. We submit to the opinions of great past teachers, great past interpreters, to Prophets who are not themselves God. Yet if revelations are to be believed, God himself adapts his word or re-articulates his meaning. Moses and Jesus are revered within Islam and yet the final revelation to Muhammad is understood to have superseded what they received. God came into history to those great Prophets in three separate revelations of what submission to God's will means. And if I recall properly, the *Qu'ran* teaches reverence for those who maintain a faith in the earlier revelations. Nonetheless, I think it is fair to say that from the perspective of Islam, Jews and Christians have tried to freeze as an eternal truth what emerged when God entered history at some specific moment to address a specific human context. I gather that from the perspective of a Muslim, Islam precedes Judaism and Christianity since the spoken book, the *Qu'ran,* is a perfect transcription of the created book of the universe, which precedes all religions. But it is also acknowledged that the revelation of the *Qu'ran* occurred at a specific point in time. Now, if I understand what you're saying, you are telling me that what God revealed to Muhammad through the intermediary of the Angel Gabriel some 1400 years ago, and subsequently has been interpreted and applied by billions of people, retains a constant and eternal truth. Why does faith prompt us to characterize God's revelations as eternal when they themselves emerge in a finite and time-bound setting? Why can't we see each of the revelations, even those outside the Judeo-Christian-Islamic tradition, as shedding some light on a relationship with God and revealing a dimension of God's truth? Why must we see each revelation as exclusive and total?"

Perhaps I invested too much feeling in the last remarks, so that Ernesto was taken somewhat aback. In a flustered sort of way, he replied, "But it would not be a perfect revelation if it were partial or confined in time. It is the very unity and completeness of the revelation that commends faith to it."

"You could believe in God's perfection and unity without having to believe that each of God's revelations to imperfect and incomplete human beings at specific points in time could become a complete and perfect pattern of life. I thought the *Qu'ran* itself acknowledges that it is not a complete code. You're studying law, after all, and you know that codes aren't complete, even when they fail to acknowledge this."

With a mixture of puzzlement and exasperation, Ernesto let out a question. "But what kind of belief in God could possibly leave to the believer the choice as to which beliefs should be retained?"

"Well, I can't pretend to know. But I can give you an example. I have always admired Gandhi's dictum that all religions are to be revered but none is to be taken as true. He would teach Islam, Judaism, Christianity, and Buddhism, all the while proclaiming himself to be Hindu. At the same time, in fighting against the idea of caste, he declared that Hindu teachings were wrong and should be replaced. So, there you have a remarkable figure whose very belief in God led him to reject some of the teaching of his religion."

"He was an amazing man," Ernesto replied.

"I think it would be sad if you couldn't retain your critical perspective on Islamic teachings at the same time as celebrating your newfound faith. There is no real contradiction between the two, is there?"

"I don't suppose there is," Ernesto replied, with a look of half relief that I found reassuring. Behind us, Omar was looking far less agitated as well.

The Outcast

I hadn't seen Saul for some time. At the beginning of the year, he had been a regular participant in my first-year law class. While the remarks he made were always interesting, they tended not to be brief. At first, the others in the class showed that they were a tad impressed by his self-assurance. But over time, I could sense pockets of impatience that spread throughout the class. For increasing numbers, impatience turned into hostility. Then, Saul stopped coming to class.

I ran into him outside the library a few weeks before the end of term. We exchanged greetings, and I told him I missed his interventions. He said he'd like to come by to speak to me in my office.

When he came later that week, I wasn't quite sure what to expect. As the conversation unfolded, it was ostensibly about garden-variety administrivia: exam format, readings, and the like. And then Saul said: "I don't want you to take my absence from class personally. I've had some complicated things happening in my life and I haven't been coming to any classes much." "That's too bad," I said. "I know you're a really smart guy and will undoubtedly pull through your exams. But this is a bit risky. You don't want your performance to suffer, especially given your obvious talent." "I know. But as I've told you, I've been spending a lot of time looking after my mother since her stroke, and her situation has been deteriorating of late."

The conversation could have ended there, but it felt to me as if Saul didn't want it to. So, I resumed: "You know, law school is a pretty unforgiving place in many ways. I hope you haven't felt browbeaten by your classmates." Saul hung his head. "To tell you the truth, it's been rough." "I have this theory," I continued. "I think that if we abolished all classes and all formal evaluation and simply said to an incoming class of law students: 'In three years you'll be eligible for the Bar; go to it,' we'd still end up with a bunch of proto-lawyers at the end. Most of legal education happens outside the classroom, in the way students handle and develop their own relationships. A part of it that really depresses me is the way pecking orders get established. When I think of all these smart people learning about how to elbow their way past each other, I sometimes believe I'm participating in a crime against humanity. Today we fight for the scarce supply of grades, tomorrow for the scarce supply of top-paying jobs, and farther off in the future for the scarce supply of blue-chip clients. In this kind of world, your success looks like my failure, your prominence like my subservience. Law school in a state of nature is only vaguely about justice."

It was with a flash of bitterness mixed with some depth of sadness that Saul finally replied, "I'm just interested in ideas. Maybe I get carried away sometimes. But people assume I'm trying to show off. They assume I have an agenda. And they think I'm wasting their time."

"There is a problem about getting labeled in this Faculty.[1] Labels are always unfair. They read: 'self-important know-it-all' or 'flake' or 'lightweight.' They tend to stick."

"That's why I decided to lie low; out of sight, out of mind."

---

[1] The College of Law.

(*I Think There's a Better Way*)

"There's probably a better way. You know, you have a lot of interesting and important things to say. They don't all have to come out at once, and they don't all have to come out in class. But they should come out in class sometimes. That should be a way of testing ideas. I sometimes get the rap that I allow discussion to meander off topic and don't control the agenda well in the classroom. For some people, however, any time any student speaks at length, the class is by definition off topic, since only the professor sets the exam and thus only what the professor has to say can be relevant. If I had my druthers, I'd say almost nothing and let people talk. The old-fashioned Socratic method of *The Paper Chase* fame had that virtue to it, although it was often an instrument of terror and control. But there is now a deep-seeded expectation among many students that the professor delivers content and that the members of the class receive it. Instead of running headlong into that, you can engage it at an angle, selectively."

"I'm afraid it may be too late. You talked about being labeled, and that's happened to me. I've been made to feel that my comments aren't welcome. Little things do it, not just nasty remarks—the way people pass you in the hall, the way they leave you out. I'm only consoled when I get back my marks and see that my professors think I'm not a turd—at least in what I write."

"Over time, I've seen people who get labeled and stay labeled, as well as people who manage to get rid of a label. You may decide, in fairness, that you don't give a shit about what other people think and that you're going to pursue your own studies in seclusion. That has some costs, as I'm sure you can imagine. You can also decide that you'll seek out a *modus vivendi* with your classmates, and draw on affinities and friendships with those who enjoy discussing with you. There are a lot of good and interesting people around the Faculty and it would be unfortunate to miss out on that—for them and for you. It's easier to wander in the desert when you're not alone."

"I've got some experience of going it alone, you know." Saul paused and gave me a searching look. "Can you imagine what it's like growing up as the only Jewish kid in a lower-class district of Sarnia?"

"Not exactly. I'll tell you the only experience I have. When I was going to the University of Toronto for undergrad, I had a friend who was taking a class on Jewish philosophy with me. Emil Falkenheim was the professor."

"You had Emil Falkenheim!" Saul interjected. "I used to read his stuff when I was in Israel."

"Yes. Took three of his classes. Anyway, my friend invited me to come to the Holy Blossom Temple for Yom Kippur because Professor Falkenheim was going to give a talk about the meaning of this holy day. On the way home afterward, I was musing about his words on the bus when I noticed some 12-year-old kids in Catholic school uniforms pointing at me and whispering. 'See him—he's a Jew. They're the ones my father talks about. They've got some strange ceremony today. They stop eating. Weird, eh?' I'm not Jewish, but I could feel the combination of fear and loathing those kids were expressing, and it was under my skin as I got off the bus. Just then, coming from the other direction, were some gangling high school students. 'Hey Jew Boy,' one of them called out. 'You think God can protect you from us?' I wasn't particularly afraid, but I did feel like the last thing I wanted to say was that I wasn't Jewish. When I finally got home, I decided to fast."

"We had crosses burned on our front lawn and feces smeared on the house. I had to learn that when you're rejected by those around you, you fend for yourself."

"That's certainly a formative experience. Others in your class have had parallel ones—I think of Meg Atkinson, for example, who grew up at Kahnawake.[2] As people get to know each other, they exchange these experiences. We're supposed to be teaching citizens at our Faculty, and if students can't learn to exchange ideas and experiences among themselves, something is wrong. Your situation is a failing of our Faculty. Wouldn't it be great for Muslim students to hear about the experience of a Jewish kid growing up in Sarnia, and for Jewish students to hear about what it's like to be a Muslim in Canada?"

"That's fine, but they've got to want to listen. This year is especially bad, and it's getting me down. Have you seen the debates in the student newspaper? They're taking on a religious dimension."

"Some of it is worrisome. But I think there are ways of contributing positively to discussion."

"Maybe, but I'm not too optimistic. Did you know that when a Saudi paper recently ran anti-Semitic trash, some people here thought it was funny?"

"You've got to take on that sort of thing. Look, let me come to the point. I get a lot from your ideas in class. It would be nice to see you again."

Next week, Saul wasn't in class. But he was there for the last two classes, and he did speak up.

---

[2]Kahnawake is a Mohawk reserve near Montreal.

The Pathfinder

When Saeed first came from Kuwait to pursue his Canadian doctoral studies in law, he set for himself an unusual task. Since he wanted to explore the relationship between Islamic law and international law, he thought he should first prove again to himself that the foundations of Islam were solid. To this end, he pursued a study of Judaism and Christianity, seeking to compare their internal logic against that of Islam. "This exercise of mine is entirely consistent with what the Prophet teaches," Saeed explained to me one summer afternoon on the terrace in front of the Faculty. "As Muslims, we are to show deep respect for other People of the Book, and we are also to use our own reason."

Saeed acknowledged an admiration for the idea of law developed within Judaism and his attraction to the idea of God's love within the Christian Gospels. But in the end, his enquiry confirmed to him the pre-eminence of Islam. "As great as Judaism is, its message is restricted to one people," he concluded. "Islam's message is universal." As for Christianity, he came to this pronouncement: "Muslims revere Jesus as a Prophet and the Virgin Mary as his mother. But with the greatest of respect, I must tell you that the idea that God had a son born of a woman seems to me to turn a great Prophet into a myth, and indeed to fall into polytheism. Islam acknowledges that Jesus and Mohammed were men, as were all the Prophets."

"How do you explain the origin of the errors in Christianity?" I asked.

"I suppose that unless there are rigorous methods of verification, when stories of a Prophet get told and retold, error and exaggeration can enter into the account. Perhaps for the teller of the story, there is not much of a leap between a virgin birth—which Muslims acknowledge—and the claim that a man is the son of God. Furthermore, since God is the origin of all, we are in a sense all God's children. But to claim the divinity of a Prophet is to break the commandment to worship only God. As for the story of the resurrection, Muslims acknowledge that Jesus was saved from his enemies and kept alive by God, but they do not accept the idea that Jesus died and came back to life."

"But if erroneous interpretations could enter into basic tenets of Christianity—and the idea of resurrection is central to Christianity—how does a Muslim ensure that the same kinds of errors do not enter into Islam? For example, the Prophet's Ascension into Heaven, or *Mir'aj,* if I understand properly, is only alluded to in the *Qu'ran.* Yet there is a whole complex tradition around it. How can one assure that this tradition is free of error?"

"It is essential to the discipline of Islam that there is an unbroken and carefully verified record of *Hadeeth,* which are narrations of the Prophet's life. As one becomes learned in Islam, one is able to give weight to authoritative accounts. The documentary record concerning the Prophet's life is excellent and quite complete, especially as regards the period of his mission. If I may say, I think that one of Islam's advances over its sister religions is that it introduces greater rigor into the preservation and verification of God's documentary record. This is very important for the jurist and for legal method."

"But help me to understand how a good Muslim jurist exercises judgment about what is authoritative and not authoritative. When there are disputes about matters of interpretation, how does the Muslim jurist proceed?"

Saeed paused and looked at me kindly. "This is a complex matter that requires an enormous amount of study. But to keep things brief, there is a science of historical criticism, or *Riwayat,* as well as a science of logical criticism, or *Dirayat.* A wise scholar is able to place *Hadeeth* and the various legal schools of thought into proper context and perspective through the application of *Riwayat* and *Dirayat.* The complete science of methodology concerning sources of law is called *Usul al Fiqh.*"

"And is the application of this science to a particular problem what is called *ijtihad,* or interpretation?" I asked.

"In a sense," Saeed replied, "although it has more elements. Obviously, *ijtihad* involves first and foremost the study of the *Qu'ran*—in its original Arabic form, I might add. The study of the Prophet's life, or *Sunnah,* is where *Hadeeth* enter in."

"Isn't there a famous dictum that the door to *ijtihad* is now closed and that the technique of the Muslim jurist is now *taqleed*—or following, imitating, what came before? Do you agree that this is the role of the Muslim jurist?"

"Not at all. Actually, I'm against this often-repeated notion. The question is, who can possibly close the door except God himself? God never ordained that Muslims should stop thinking."

"That makes sense since your doctoral project involves the relationship between Islamic law and international law. In other words, it seems to me that if one is going to give an Islamic interpretation to international treaties and instruments, this must involve an exercise of *ijtihad,* no?"

"It does to some extent," Saeed replied with a hint of diffidence.

"I suppose I would like to know to what extent it is an exercise of *ijtihad,* and to what degree any encounter between Islamic law and international law involves a process of mutual adaptation. In other words, I can imagine a narrow, and unconvincing, argument that any new institution introduced into Islamic law was itself a departure from Islamic law. Another way of putting this is that I think you could make a very important contribution in your doctoral work if you could clarify the ways in which Islamic law is flexible, and can adapt its institutional and doctrinal position to address contemporary realities."

"I agree with this and am grateful for your encouragement," Saeed replied.

"If there is any truth to the idea of closing of the door of *ijtihad*," I continued, "isn't it that scholars such as Averoes were said to have gone too far in elevating 'reason' above revelation? So, let me put a broader question to you, which I hope you won't find naive or disrespectful. Today, how far can an Islamic scholar go in elevating *ijtihad* as a matter of methodology without risking Averoes' fate?"

"May I elaborate upon this a little bit?" Saeed replied. "The law, or *Sharee'aa*, can be divided into three aspects: The first is *Aqeeda*, or the Creed; the second is *Ibadat*, or Acts of Worship; and the third is *Mo'amalat*, or Acts of Transaction or Socializing. Reasoning in connection with the first and second aspects differs from reasoning in connection with the third. God knows that the people He created are developing and indeed are going to develop things that the Prophet had never heard of. This is why, when it comes to the domain of *Mo'amalat*, the divine texts are very broad. Imam Shafi'i, in his valuable book *Al-Rislaa*, replied to the question of the permissibility of *Ikhtilaf*, or disagreement among the Islamic scholars roughly as follows, if I remember: 'On all matters concerning which God provided clear textual evidence in His Book or a *Sunnah* uttered by the Prophet's Tongue, disagreement among those to whom these texts are known is unlawful. As to matters that are liable to different interpretations or derived from analogy, so that he who interprets or applies analogy arrives at a decision different from that arrived at by another, I do not hold that disagreement of this kind is unlawful in the same way.' Thus, it is obvious that *Ikhtilaf* is a natural offspring of giving the lead to human reasoning in interpreting laws and rules. However, *Ikhtilaf* based on *Hawa* (opinions under the influence of passion and prejudice) is roundly condemned by Islam, and is referred to as *Zaygh*, or deviation from the righteous path. A major characteristic of opinions based on *Hawa* is the twisting of divine texts toward personal ends. *Hawa* is a sort of result-oriented decision making that is the bane of all proper juridical method. Permissible *Ikhtilaf*, on the other hand, is the outcome of the variation in the methodology of deduction and *Usul al Fiqh*. In particular, among true scholars there can be differences in the ranking and prevalence of sources other than *Qu'ran* and *Sunnah,* as well as natural and cultural variations in their intellectual capabilities."

"This makes sense to me. So most of what you plan to write about in your thesis, and indeed most of what it takes to align the frameworks of Islamic and international law, lies in the domain of *Mo'amalat*. Presumably because it offers greater scope for human reasoning, it would be possible to conduct a debate and discussion about *Mo'amalat* within Islam—perhaps leading to diverse approaches. Isn't the Prophet reported to have said that diversity among the people is God's bounty?"

"I'm not sure about the authenticity of that *Hadeeth*. But he admitted diversity in many other *Hadeeth*. Indeed, God admits it in the *Qur'an*."

"I understand there is another *Hadeeth* to the effect that 'my people cannot agree to error.' The interplay of the two ideas is important to clarify, I suppose."

"Exactly," Saeed replied. "You have made a long story very short."

"The term 'reason' is, of course, very slippery. Sometimes it is made out to be distinct from revelation. One need not accept this if one embraces the challenge of reasoning about new realities the Prophet could not have anticipated."

"Exactly," Saeed repeated.

"Well then, perhaps what is at stake is the following, to overstate it somewhat. It is critical to show that Islamic law remains a dynamic contributor to global, cosmopolitan law. I think this is equally important for the promotion of understanding on both sides of the dialogue—Islamic and non-Islamic. I do not mean to suggest that cosmopolitan law is in a sense hierarchically superior to Islamic law—we can assume the opposite is true."

"Yes," Saeed allowed. "But this requires a clarification of the term 'Islamic law.' That term may be correctly understood in various ways. It may refer to those laws that are derived from *Sharee'aa,* as opposed to those that have their roots in civil law systems, common law systems, or any other legal systems. It may also be understood as that group of laws, which are applied by Islamic states in accordance with *Sharee'aa*. Finally, Islamic law may refer to those laws that do not contradict with the rules and concepts of *Sharee'aa*—that is, an international convention can be seen as Islamic law provided that it does not contradict *Sharee'aa*. Thus, any laws, whether constitutional, civil, commercial, or otherwise may be considered Islamic so long as they do not conflict with *Sharee'aa,* which is itself a kind of ultimate inviolable constitution."

"Let me add that one can only imagine or construct global frameworks if these frameworks issue from each of the 'ultimate constitutions,' which must ground them," I ventured. "In other words, I think you go a step beyond arguing that as long as the global framework does not contradict *Sharee'aa* it is acceptable. I think you also want to show (unless I am mistaken) that international conventions can be interpreted and applied in an Islamic way."

"True," Saeed affirmed. "One of my aims will be to show that in these matters Islamic methodology can be applied by any interpreter, whether a Muslim or otherwise." "Yes," I affirmed in turn. "Ideally, one would want to show that Islamic methodology could and should inform all interpretation of international law."

"Yes," Saeed pursued. "Actually, what is confusing here is that we are using a term, 'Islamic law,' that can give rise to misunderstanding. It automatically connotes theology or even theocracy, which is not at all the appropriate connotation. The term 'Islamic' is used because Islam, as I and many others understand it, is a system of life."

"I think this is fine," I replied. "But in my opinion, one need not shrink from acknowledging the religious roots of Islamic law, which after all guides the beliefs and practices of 1.2 billion people."

"Of course," Saeed conceded. "But I worry that calling it 'Islamic law' labels it as foreign and illegitimate in the West. This label is now very difficult to remove. I should send you an article I found on the Internet the other day. It reproduced Patrick Henry's famous 'Liberty or Death' speech and simply suggested that the word 'American' be replaced by the word 'Palestinian' and the word 'British' by the word 'Israeli.' In this way, the author suggested, a foreign and unsympathetic conflict might be brought closer to home on this continent."

"Do send me that," I answered, "and I'll send you in return something I saw recently. It was an article in *Al Riyadh* from Saudi Arabia, translated into English. It described the Jewish festival of *Purim* and claimed that it involved consuming pastries baked with human blood. The editor later allowed that the article was not fit for publication."

"That was published in *Al Riyadh*?" Saeed asked incredulously. "You know, of course, that such nonsense comes from only a handful of people and can also be found directed against Arabs."

"Well, to counter such 'nonsense,' as you put it, I think it is urgent to show the linkages between international law and Islamic law, and to outline the positive contribution that Islamic law can, should, and must be allowed to make to the forging of international institutions. Do I overstate it?"

"Not at all," Saeed replied. "I'm sure I can do it. But I hope I can turn to you for guidance."

"I think the best role I can play is to act as a sounding board. Obviously, I can't tell you whether you are presenting an accurate picture of Islamic law. But I am excited about your project."

Saeed is still pursuing his project, which seems to gather importance with the passing of time.

Postscript by Barbara Mysko

Since Richard Janda was reluctant to identify what the conversations he depicted in fact explained about teaching, he asked me to read the paper and consider what it might offer to a student in this regard.

In reading "Teaching Between the Cracks" for the first time, I did encounter lessons to apply in my own life. These lessons relate to the dynamic relationship between reason and revelation in the pursuit of truth, the development of a sense and practice of tolerance, and the myriad opportunities for learning outside of the classroom. The themes leap out of the words exchanged in the conversations and emerge surreptitiously between the lines in the narrated gestures and other forms of unspoken communication. But these examples are not definitive—the themes in this piece mutate with each reading and with each individual reader.

In this way, "Teaching Between the Cracks" is about personal interpretation—personal interpretation of teaching style and individual approaches to learning. It challenges the reader to look past formal classroom teaching and reconsider the boundaries of the classroom. This might be like transformative learning, but it doesn't have to be.

This piece is about rethinking the teacher's marriage with pedagogy and structure, and about recognizing the limitless quality of learning. If one were to extract additional lessons about teaching from this piece, the lessons would tie into a notion of informal learning. They might relate to the indirect transfer of knowledge in networks of conversations and to the fluid nature of "curriculum" and the uncertain meaning of "fact." One might also derive a lesson from the structure of the piece itself. The storytelling format serves as a medium for communicating these ideas about informal learning and as a concrete example of an informal teaching tool.

However, as only one of many students reading this article, I can merely provide my individual interpretation of the characters' conversations. My snapshot of the conversations depicts three students struggling with the meaning of religious traditions as they pertain to their academic and personal lives. One student has discovered truth and beauty in a faith conversion, another student is dealing with the stress of being identified with a particular religious tradition, and a last student is seeking a path to tolerance through the Islamic tradition of reason and interpretation. Each student teaches the "teacher" something about faith while, unknowingly, exchanging lessons with each other.

The first student, Ernesto, is a recently converted Muslim who defends the purity and truth of the Islamic faith while hesitantly acknowledging the inconsistencies in the Islamic belief system. At the outset of the conversation, he defends Islamic views on women and homosexuality by describing the tradition's historical context. But as Ernesto pursues his line of reasoning, he starts to question his belief in the inherent equality of women and homosexuals, eventually arguing for total submission to the ultimate authority and will of God. What could have been a definitive statement on the ultimate truth of the Islamic faith turns into a deeper discussion about the role of questioning and reason in the practice of faith.

While Ernesto states that human beings must submit to the divine authority of God, he posits that they must also defer to the teachings of Muslim leaders (and not Christian or Jewish leaders, for example) on questions of spirituality. The teacher challenges Ernesto with the example of Gandhi, a renowned and respected Hindu who taught his followers about the belief systems of all of the great religions while promoting and instilling reverence for all these traditions. Ernesto concedes that he can still maintain his critical perspective while celebrating his newfound faith. While Ernesto has learned that there is a role for questioning in the practice of faith, the teacher has learned of one student's experience of joy in his faith conversion.

The lesson does not stop there. In the second conversation, the "outcast" character is presented as a student struggling with first-year law school. This student comes from a marginalized Jewish background and regularly encounters ostracism and alienation in his academic life. Whereas Ernesto discovers the beauty of the religious experience, Saul must contend with the harsh consequences of religious "identification." Furthermore, although Saul is inquisitive and intelligent, his unique learning style sets him apart from his classmates and results in backlash.

While Saul describes how he constructs psychological walls to protect against this backlash, the teacher suggests alternative ways of dealing with the difficult reality of first-year law school. The resulting exchange suggests that academic performance is inseparable from personal life and that teachers can play a role in breaking down these personal barriers. While such personal conversations are challenging and the role of the teacher is not entirely clear-cut, they are also all too familiar. They push the boundaries of traditional notions of classroom learning and fact-based curriculae.

The first and second conversations contrast the hopefulness of religious revelation with the harsh consequences of religious identification. This contrast reveals the personal aspect of faith, apart from its textbook interpretations. These experiences are combined with the third conversation to complete a journey from revelation to reason. In the third conversation, the student aims to demonstrate the positive contribution that Islamic law can make to the development of international law. Like Ernesto, Saeed defends the preeminence of Islam, but seeks to prove this preeminence through an academic comparison of the internal logic evident in Islam, Judaism, and Christianity. Through his exchange with the teacher, he reveals his deeper belief that no tradition is free of error and that Islam's greatest contribution is its admission of diversity and promotion of tolerance.

Finally, each of these characters creates his curriculum, applying the lessons learned through conversations to daily life. In this way, these conversations challenge the reader to rethink traditional notions of classroom learning, and provide lessons for the further construction of one's own life curriculum.

PART IV

FACULTY DEVELOPMENT
THE BROADER PICTURE

The first time we offered the Course Design and Teaching Workshop more than ten years ago, we, the members of the Centre for University Teaching and Learning (CUTL), were the only instructors. The following year, we invited a few of the previous year's participants to work with us as co-instructors. The result was a powerful learning experience for all and we have never turned back. The simple act of inviting others whose disciplinary affiliation is not "Education" to join us in our work as faculty developers has had innumerable spinoffs. The most salient is the creation of an extended network of professors in various faculties whom we can rely on and collaborate with to advance the scholarship of teaching. The activities that these individuals have undertaken go far beyond "designing a course" or "improving their own teaching." This reaffirms our belief that the Workshop promotes more than a few tips about teaching; that it inspires individuals to think about broader issues concerning teaching and learning. In Chapter 12, we elaborate on our own conceptual understanding of faculty development: what it entails, and ways in which it can be implemented and evaluated. In Chapter 13, we anchor this conceptual portrayal by presenting two case examples of our work in the Faculties of Management and Engineering.

One point of clarification: In these two chapters, as in the rest of the book, the term *Faculty* with a capital *F* is used to denote the unit made up of several departments or programs. In the American context, this would be referred to as *college* or *school*. Written with lower case *f*, *faculty*, used with or without the word *member*, refers to individual academics.

12

TOWARD A COMPREHENSIVE FRAMEWORK OF FACULTY DEVELOPMENT

Lynn McAlpine and Alenoush Saroyan

We have elaborated our philosophy and our thinking about teaching and teaching development through one particular activity, the Course Design and Teaching Workshop. However, the Workshop is only one of the many things we at the Centre for University Teaching and Learning (CUTL) do as faculty developers. It does not occur in isolation, nor can it be understood in isolation. It is situated within a broader conceptual framework within which we view faculty development in terms of interactions among individuals, departments, and faculties to support activities that improve teaching and learning in the university. The framework has emerged over time through our work as faculty developers and also from our personal responsibilities and experiences as academics engaged in research, teaching, and service.

Our goal in this chapter is to describe the broader picture of our work within the university context and in relation to the mandate of CUTL. The approach we take in working toward our mandate involves modeling and engaging others in a scholarly approach to teaching. We describe in some detail the principles or assumptions underlying our work and how these inform a range of different types of activities, of which the Workshop is one. We aim in this chapter to provide tangible and concrete ideas as to how we engage and support other academics in the scholarship of teaching and provide them with the resources to act as faculty developers themselves. Throughout the chapter, we highlight ways in which our approach is both similar to and distinct from other approaches to faculty development. The chapter ends by articulating our future vision for faculty development.

Interaction Patterns with Others

The Workshop is the one activity we do collectively, and we believe this has been instrumental in changing our thinking about faculty development. Each time we observe its impact in relation to our individual research and faculty development activities, we realize how essential an experience it has been and continues to be in our own professional development.

One of the most striking changes in our perspective that we largely attribute to the Workshop is a shift in how we view our role in working with others. In the past, our perspective was more that of *doing things for* others. We would, for instance, conduct activities such as a program evaluation, or develop and conduct an alumni survey for the university. Our current approach is better characterized as seeking to *work with* those who come to us with a specific request. Instead of conducting a program evaluation by ourselves, we now offer to assist the individual or unit requesting that service to be the lead in designing and carrying out the evaluation. We have found this to be advantageous in two ways: It engenders ownership and it leads to the development of local expertise and empowerment. In effect, we have redefined our role as *the resource,* the support network, and the advocate for others who are engaged in teaching development.

This shift from doing things for others to working with others is evident in the history of the Workshop. In the first year, the members of CUTL were the only facilitators of the Workshop. Nonetheless, we realized that collaborative interaction among colleagues helps individuals make greater sense of some of the issues they are confronted with personally. Moreover, participants are often more successful in clarifying peer concerns and answering questions in very meaningful ways. We also found that several participants developed an interest in teaching development and wanted further contact with us. This led us, for the following year, to invite some of these individuals, albeit in a somewhat random fashion, to act as co-instructors in the small groups of the Workshop. Our invitations gradually became more intentional, and we starting asking potential co-instructors to make a bigger time commitment and to attend planning, briefing, and debriefing meetings linked to the Workshop.

Another sign of the change in our perspective was that we initially occupied center stage in the large-group sessions of the Workshop. We simply did all the presentations. Now, we ensure that previous participants share this role of instructing with us.

Finally, we have developed and adopted a vision of distributed leadership both conceptually and in our practice. Our partners in this process are other professors and our graduate students. Over time, we have been increasingly intentional in using the Workshop as a learning opportunity for both these groups. We have involved them as both participant observers and active members of the team. We find their feedback to Workshop participants and to us invaluable. One of the specific consequences of sharing the responsibility of delivering the Workshop with co-instructors from various disciplines is that we have been "forced" through a relatively lengthy engagement to negotiate a shared language and shared view of activities. We believe this has helped us to use less "technical" language, and more varied examples. We have consistently found that the co-instructors add a powerful element to our learning as well as that of the participants. In turn, the co-instructors report that this particular teaching experience is personally fulfilling and revives in them an excitement about teaching that they welcome. The feeling of helping others develop pedagogical expertise is particularly intriguing as they have rarely thought of themselves as anything but a subject expert. Extended interaction with these enthusiastic partners over time has made it possible to develop a network of "faculty developers," one which is continuously evolving. Our goal is to create a community of individuals from across disciplines who can talk about teaching with each other, share experiences, and help one another in making the learning experience of our students a memorable one.

The shift in perspective from doing things for others to doing things with others is manifest in other aspects of our work as well. For example, the CUTL has created the position of Affiliate Member with the approval of the McGill Senate. Individuals who have taken part in the Workshop, participated as co-instructors in past workshops, and engaged in teaching and policy development activities in their departments, faculties, and across the university for a period of five years are eligible for this appointment. The work of these individuals, whether done in collaboration with us or independently, is included in CUTL's annual report and documents our belief that all academics in the university share leadership responsibility for teaching development. The varied disciplinary affiliations, voices, and perspectives of the Affiliates have been particularly powerful in helping us adopt a language that other professors will understand with ease. Equally important is the presence of the Affiliates when we communicate concerns and ideas to the senior administration. Their input in helping us prepare CUTL documents that are to be used in the university is particularly significant. Finally, their contribution toward planning and implementing CUTL activities, whether in response to a request (e.g., curriculum review) or a new initiative (e.g., teaching portfolio workshop) has added depth and relevance to what we do.

Our Thinking on the Nature of Teaching

Another powerful impact of the Workshop on our perspective has been a shift from teaching development activities with a strong focus on teaching skills to activities that will help faculty make explicit their thinking about teaching. We have come to understand that when professors work toward such clarity, it inevitably leads to discussions about student learning. How is this evident in the Workshop? The course design process enables participants to lay out their thinking about teaching and learning, to critique it, and to get feedback from others. Participants become collectively engaged, sometimes for the first time, in in-depth and intellectually stimulating discussions about teaching and learning, experiencing what has been termed "the scholarship of teaching" (Weston & McAlpine, 2001). This involves making knowledge explicit, public, and available for critique and evaluation.

One of the mechanisms contributing to this shift in our thinking has been the debriefings we do after each day of the Workshop. These sessions are a significant learning and development tool for us, one made more powerful by the presence of the co-instructors. Debriefings influence subsequent iterations of the Workshop, but more important, they enable us to continuously examine the assumptions underlying our own thinking and the way they influence our actions.

Focus on Multiple Levels of Interaction: Professors, Chairs, Deans, and Committees

The Workshop is an environment in which individuals talk in depth about the factors that influence their teaching. On Thursday of the Workshop, for instance, all the concerns and issues relating to the evaluation of teaching emerge. This provides a window for all of us to consider the variation of the teaching experience across the university. It makes apparent how departmental and Faculty[1] expectations influence the nature of teaching for each professor and the nature of learning for students. Those involved in the Workshop become aware of the inconsistent expectations of such issues as the number of courses taught by professors, the different purposes of introductory courses, and the availability and varied work contexts of teaching assistants.

Variations in experience emphasize the difficulty for individuals, particularly those new to the university, to undertake changes in teaching if the cultural ethos of the department or Faculty is in conflict with the proposed

---

[1]College or school.

change. For example, a professor might be convinced of the validity of using criterion-referenced assessment, but the affiliated department may espouse norm-referenced assessment. This has made us increasingly aware that sustaining teaching improvement as an ongoing process and preoccupation is possible only if it emerges as a systemic process. In order to support individual efforts to enhance teaching and learning, we need to work at all levels of the system, including with individual professors and instructors, with departments and faculties, and with the university at large.

It is for this reason that in the Workshop we try to connect with a range of university resources through the brown-bag lunch sessions. We invite administrators representing other university units that support teaching and learning to lead these sessions. Individuals have included the Director of the Office for Student Disabilities, whose office is responsible for ensuring that students with disabilities are recognized and have access to the systems they need to participate successfully in the life of the university. It has also included the Associate Dean, Graduate Studies, to inform participants of their responsibilities in relation to graduate supervision. As well, we consistently invite an instructional designer from the Instructional Communications Centre, the university unit responsible for supporting professors' and students' use of web-based learning, to talk about ways in which this unit can provide help.

In our activities other than the Workshop, we also directly draw on individuals from across the university to provide their perspectives. Experienced chairs provide their expertise in a workshop on the role of the teaching portfolio in tenure and promotion. We seek the active involvement of chairs and deans in undertaking curriculum projects. We provide information to them about the appropriate use of student course ratings. We seek to be members of Faculty level and university committees that address teaching and learning issues. We require that deans review and provide matching funds for a competitive teaching and learning innovation fund that the CUTL administers. Overall, what we try to do is take into account all levels of the institution in thinking through our programming and deciding how best we can engage others as partners in advancing our mission.

Interactions with One Another

The Workshop was, until the writing of this book, the only activity that brought us all together to work jointly on the same project. Now, we see the value of these interactions in supporting our own growth in understanding teaching and learning. The briefings and debriefings are essential as they provide us the opportunity to realize the value of our similarities and differences, to negotiate meaning, and to find out where and how we agree or disagree. The Workshop provides us with the opportunity to see each other teach, which gives us a sense of one another's practice. Perhaps as a consequence, we have developed a shared or more consistent way of working with professors. Most important, the Workshop provides the opportunity to test new ideas collectively; the abstract or hypothetical is made real, and critiqued, and implementation is evaluated.

The experience with the Workshop has also broadened the scope of our research. We are all engaged in independent research programs, but our work in the Workshop has, in effect, been a sort of laboratory school where we can try out, identify, and determine issues that need to be investigated. This has resulted in joint publications by CUTL members about the Workshop at McGill (Saroyan, Amundsen, & Cao, 1997) and as a component of a project funded by the Canadian International Development Agency in Indonesia (McAlpine & Winer, 2002). It has also led to joint publications with Affiliate Members about how working together has changed our understanding of teaching and learning (Amundsen, Saroyan, & Frankman, 1996; McAlpine & Harris, 1999, 2002). Also arising from these experiences are publications or presentations with professors with whom we have worked in other activities (Meterissian, Tremblay, Seely, Weston, & Morgan, 2001; Nasmith & McAlpine, 1995; Saroyan, Harris, & Cooperstock, 2000; Saroyan & Snell, 1997).

In short, the Workshop has helped us to continue to learn and grow together, and it has strongly influenced our present vision and practice of teaching development throughout the university.

We now turn to the broader picture of faculty development at McGill University.

The Broader Picture

Our overall goal for teaching development is to support individual and institutional efforts to enhance teaching and learning. The vision underlying this goal is to engage others in a scholarly approach to teaching. Thus, we have worked to elaborate a framework that depicts a continuum of growth toward the scholarship of teaching (Weston & McAlpine, 2001).

The University Where We Work

McGill University in Montreal, Canada, is a research-intensive university, traditionally seen as an academic enterprise that emphasizes scholarship and research. There are about 1300 full-time academics distributed among 12 faculties and a Centre for Continuing Education. Professors are expected to contribute nationally and internationally to disciplinary scholarship by applying for and receiving grants, conducting discipline-appropriate research, and publishing widely in peer-reviewed journals.

While McGill expects professors to be active researchers and contributors to their scholarly communities, the university also places a strong emphasis on quality instruction at the undergraduate level (degree programs in 17 academic fields) and graduate level (studies in close to 60 disciplines). Professors are expected to value and model excellence in teaching just as they do in research. Teaching and graduate supervision is evaluated, and in the recent past professors have been refused tenure or other awards because their teaching was not of the expected quality. There is considerable pressure, even beyond tenure, to maintain strong research and teaching dossiers.

The Role of CUTL in the University

The Centre for University Teaching and Learning (CUTL), created over 30 years ago, is the oldest center of its kind in Canada. It supports the enhancement of teaching and learning across the university, and although in the past it reported to the Vice President, Academic, it has recently begun to report to the Vice Provost, Information and Systems Technology.

CUTL has a three-fold mandate: to provide teaching development through a range of activities, to support the development of university policies that enhance teaching and learning, and to conduct research that contributes to our understanding of teaching and learning in higher education. This mandate involves a range of activities, including membership on committees dealing with issues of teaching and learning, individual and departmental consultations, workshops, extended curriculum projects, grant writing, conducting research, and publishing.

The strategy by which we hope to accomplish our faculty development work in the university is premised on our belief that leadership for teaching and learning is the responsibility of all faculty members. We are working toward developing a distributed network, a web of individuals across the university who are knowledgeable about teaching and committed to supporting their colleagues in undertaking activities that will enhance teaching and learning. With limited funding resources, it is only through a strong network of interested partners that we can hope to enhance our understanding of teaching and learning and effect change in both policy and practice.

The network presently includes "formal" Members of CUTL, Affiliate and Adjunct Members who hold formal appointments, a large group of other professors who are regularly invited to collaborate with CUTL, and more than

15 graduate students enrolled in the Department of Educational and Coun-selling Psychology who receive supervision for master's and doctoral research by CUTL members. As noted earlier, Affiliate Members are individuals who have consistently contributed to the enhancement of university teaching and learning, and their accomplishments are included in the CUTL annual report. The Adjuncts contribute their expertise, again on a voluntary basis. These in-dividuals work in other settings and wish to support the work of CUTL.

The distributed network also includes those who regularly support the work of CUTL in workshops and committees and who may become future Affiliates. For instance, a growing number of professors have acted as co-instructors in the Workshop. Other professors have participated in and won a competition to be appointed for one year as a Faculty Associate with the goal of carrying out teaching development activities in their unit. Some have been active members of the committee that adjudicates the Teaching and Learning Improvement Fund, or regularly present at workshops or have won teaching improvement awards and become models and mentors for their colleagues. Thus, although we are small in formal numbers, we are large in terms of indi-viduals who are intent on enhancing teaching and learning and are willing to share their knowledge and enthusiasm with their colleagues. Almost all mem-bers of this network are alumni of our Course Design and Teaching Workshop.

It is critical to provide ongoing support to all these individuals so that they can, over time, assume leadership roles in their respective units. They have a profound understanding of the teaching and learning context in their discipline and their own faculties and departments. They know the kinds of expertise that we can provide, and they feel comfortable calling on us. We now see ourselves as the nucleus of a spider web, with a view to develop-ing and supporting a distributed leadership among our colleagues across the university. As our connections with various units strengthen and as our infor-mal membership grows, the whole enterprise of teaching development becomes more of a sustainable reality. In Chapter 13, we provide two exam-ples that show how such networks can be created in a bottom-up or top-down approach.

An extended distributed network is, of course, a way of leveraging the limited funding resources we have, but it more importantly incorporates a collegial vision of the place of teaching in the university. The process of nego-tiating this exchange of ideas and the making of decisions also develops a community that can learn to use a common language to talk effectively about an essential academic role: teaching. In this model, the specific contribution of the CUTL core membership is to offer empirically based ideas that may be useful in informing teaching and learning decisions. This perspective may be different from that held by other faculty developers, but we believe the nature of our interactions with other professors is similar to what other faculty developers do. Gullat and Weaver (1997), for example, have identified desired characteristics of faculty development that appear to encompass those defined by many others (e.g., Brawner, Felder, Brent, Allen, & Miller, 1999; Cuban, 1992; Marincovich, 1998), and they include the ability to

- address what faculty need to learn and provide rationales.
- make the process meaningful and relevant.
- attempt to solve authentic problems.
- organize activities around collaborative problem-solving.
- facilitate an ongoing process.
- encourage systematic evaluation of professor efforts.
- provide opportunities to develop a theoretical understanding of pedagogy.
- recognize impediments and facilitators of the change process.

We, too, support these values, but our view of faculty development is broader, and in the following we highlight those aspects that we believe are distinct.

We situate ourselves and our relationships with others within a view of teaching as a scholarly activity (Boyer, 1990). This is, for us, a critical focus. Scholarly activity arises because groups of scholars band together (physically or virtually) to discuss issues of mutual concern in their area of learning or inquiry. Shulman (1993) has described the nature of our membership in these groupings as "communities of conversation, communities of evaluation" (p. 6). Shulman has contrasted this community life of the researcher with the pedagogical isolation we experience when we close the classroom door. He suggests that if we want teaching to be highly valued, then "we must change the status of teaching from private to community property" (p. 6).

The CUTL Mandate and the Scholarship of Teaching

There are different ways of creating communities of conversation related to teaching. We believe we are able to model and develop these within each aspect of the CUTL mandate: the support and development of policy, the development of teaching and learning, and research into the teaching and learning process in higher education.

Policy Support and Development

A main venue by which we address this responsibility is membership on various committees at different levels of the institution. Our role in these committees is to provide expert advice. We bring empirical findings from the literature to the attention of others in order to inform and influence decision making. We also support policy development by informing administrators on an individual, more informal basis of trends and changes occurring elsewhere. An example of this would be our involvement in a recent review of university policy on course ratings. CUTL members on this committee over a two-year period provided other members with relevant research as well as the documents related to prior work on student course ratings. The result of this exercise was a new policy on student course ratings that was passed by the Senate. In the meantime, members of CUTL summarized the research on administrative use of course ratings and provided this document to all chairs and deans so they could be better informed both in their ongoing decision making and in considering the revised policy in the Senate.

Our view is that the creation of teaching policies requires public discourse and some public scrutiny of practices. The policies themselves may also imprint and ultimately be entrenched in the ethos of the institution. For instance, there is a policy in place to provide students with access to the results of course ratings (which are administered for all courses), and there is present talk of making these more accessible through the web. More recently, the new policy on graduate student supervision is beginning to make people aware of an aspect of their teaching that may have not received much attention in the past.

Teaching Development

We also sustain a range of activities to support teaching and learning development. Some work is focused on particular individuals who contact CUTL for information or wish to work with the teaching improvement counselor on some particular aspect of their teaching. Other work involves groups of professors. This may involve workshops or other kinds of interventions, such as curriculum review projects. We welcome these activities as they are often more powerful than topical workshops in developing a sense of community among members of a program area or department. In our experience, the intellectual and social coming-together of faculty is the basis for effective program and curriculum development. The CUTL has also developed and administers a teaching improvement fund. Proposals submitted by individuals or groups of professors are reviewed by a committee of peers. Reports on the impact of funds on learning are submitted at the end of the grant period, and many award winners publicly disseminate the results of their work (McAlpine & Gandell, 2003).

Research into Higher Education Teaching and Learning

Our research focus is often cited as a way in which the CUTL is different from other centers. Through our programmatic research, we study phenomena related to teaching and learning. This research frequently involves us in lengthy discussions over extended periods of time with professors in our university and elsewhere. Through these interactions, many professors have become active researchers of their own practices by exploring their teaching in ways of which they had not previously thought; for instance, by meeting in symposia with other professors participating in the same research (e.g., McAlpine & Weston, 2002). We also actively seek to engage in classroom research, both among ourselves and quite intentionally with other professors in the university. We model the potential of conducting and reporting classroom action research through this process. The latter may involve helping professors find disciplinary venues for reporting their efforts (Banji, Gottesman, Finkelstein, & Winer, 2002; Winer & Cooperstock, 2002). We model and engage others in evidence-based teaching through programmatic and classroom research. Participants become increasingly aware that decisions about teaching can be based on the assessment of empirical data.

We fulfill each of the three aspects of the CUTL mandate, and we work toward a vision of a community of scholars across the university by adopting and modeling a scholarly approach. This results in a distributed network of individuals, knowledgeable about and committed to teaching. It is a network that is able to support respective colleagues in their own faculties and across the university in undertaking change that will enhance teaching and learning. We increasingly and happily find ourselves the nucleus of the web, with our role shifting toward the support of their efforts.

Assumptions About Teaching and Faculty Development

Collectively, as members of CUTL, we share four assumptions in furthering teaching development in the university. (These have also been briefly described in Chapter 2.) The first is the need to recognize and find ways to balance or maintain a positive tension among a multitude of factors in the university that impact our work. The second is the need to think systemically. The third is the need to think and act programmatically. The fourth is the need to evaluate the impact of our work. We elaborate on these four assumptions in the following.

Maintaining a Positive Tension

The university environment is one in which there are many competing, and not infrequently, opposing factors. Our goal is to appreciate the value of these factors and to attempt to maintain a positive tension among them so that the fullest advantage is taken of each of their benefits. Here are some examples of these tensions:

- *Proactive versus responsive activities.* Our activities can be characterized as being proactive or responsive. Proactive activities are those that we intentionally plan and initiate because they are congruent with our beliefs and our mandate. They promote new ideas and make CUTL visible. These activities are most easily seen in, for instance, our active membership on committees, our coordination of the teaching improvement fund, and the distribution of a schedule of planned activities, including a list of workshops and projects. In this type of work, we are like many other centers (e.g., Menges & Weimer, 1996; Travis, 1996). At the same time, we believe strongly in being responsive to need—that is, being ready and able to provide the support necessary for individuals and units actively engaged in resolving some instructional issue. This creates a constant tension between planning and initiating a range of teaching and policy development activities, and yet banking time and energy to address expressed needs as they arise. The latter is important since we always explore the potential to extend these initial one-time interactions into more extended and more powerful faculty development initiatives.

- *Generic versus discipline-based activities.* Again, we believe both are required. The goal is to maintain an appropriate balance of both kinds of activities (Weston & McAlpine, 1999). Generic activities bring together individuals from across disciplines who are interested in teaching and seek like-minded people. The advantage of generic activities is that they lend themselves to multidisciplinary participation and thus to multidisciplinary perspectives. The culture of each Faculty, however, influences what is important to those within it (Becher, 1989), the nature of the teaching and learning tasks, and the resources that professors can access for teaching. It is imperative to also work within faculties and departments if we wish to enhance teaching and learning, and wish to create groups of like-minded people who can support each other. The advantage of discipline-based activities is that they promote the explicit discussion of pedagogical content knowledge (Shulman, 1986). One example of the implementation of this discipline-based approach is the arrangement we have negotiated with our Faculty of Engineering[2] to provide on-site support for faculty-initiated activities. CUTL receives funds in exchange for the CUTL member who works on site. An arrangement of this nature with Engineering is described in Chapter 13.

- *Teaching development versus policy development.* Our mandate and the perception of our work is that both teaching and policy development are essential. This may be somewhat different from other approaches in which the focus is almost exclusively on teaching development (e.g., Travis, 1996). Policy development requires creating a consensus across large numbers of people. It may involve long-term, labor-intensive preparatory work and may ultimately prove unsuccessful. Yet we see it as critical in creating a positive culture for teaching and learning. Teaching development has less power than policy development to change the institution as a whole, but more potential to change the specific teaching and learning environment of students. Thus, we see these two aspects, teaching and policy development, as going hand-in-hand in synergy. For instance, McGill now has a policy requiring the submission of a teaching portfolio for tenure as well as promotion. CUTL was actively involved in helping the Vice President, Academic to develop the policy, which was subsequently approved by the Senate. We have provided support for this policy in a variety of ways since it was approved. We have worked with chairs to help them define criteria for interpreting and assessing teaching portfolios in their own departments. We have offered workshops for tenure committees and professors to inform them of guidelines to follow in the development and evaluation of portfolios. We have offered annual workshops on creating and maintaining teaching portfolios in order to inform tenure committees and professors of the nature of portfolios. We have also worked with individuals to develop their portfolios and in some cases to improve their teaching so that they can meet the teaching requirements of the university.

- *We as experts versus others as experts.* Our expertise is based on our academic training and research, and it is very much influenced by the cultural community (Becher, 1989) in which we work as researchers and

---

[2]College of Engineering.

teachers. Other academics bring their expertise based on their own academic cultures. We need to invest the time to thoroughly explore these diverse knowledge domains and integrate them with our own to address the concerns of professors and departments wanting to enhance student learning (McAlpine & Harris, 1999; Harris, in this book). The process makes explicit to the faculty developer the context-specific nature of the teaching and learning tasks, and to the professor the potential of general pedagogical knowledge to inform particular teaching issues.

- *Programmatic research versus action-based classroom research.* One of our academic responsibilities is to engage in systematic research, conceived programmatically, so that it has the greatest potential to inform the field, in our case, of higher education. We are at the same time practitioners who wish to learn from our own work. We therefore engage in what McKeachie (2002) has called classroom research. We define this as the systematic and rigorous analysis of our own teaching practices in order to develop better practices. We are more fortunate than many other professors in that our programmatic research on teaching and learning in higher education is quite easily linked to our own practices of teaching and faculty development. We still must deal with balancing both programmatic research and classroom research. We must model the possibility to other professors of viewing one's own teaching as a basis for research while still maintaining the disciplinary "research agenda." Here, we also gratefully acknowledge the continued funding support that we have received from the Canadian Social Sciences and Humanities Research Council and Quebec's funding councils.

Thinking Systemically

We believe that we need to think systemically while maintaining a balance among competing tensions. Change in one part of a system implies change elsewhere in the system, and administrative structures and policies are frequently more powerful mechanisms for change than the efforts of individuals. Thinking in terms of the entire system—in this case, the university—requires working concurrently at multiple levels using multiple approaches. We need to approach teaching development from the perspective of supporting those who wish to engage in enhancing institutional as well as personal teaching practices. We try to think strategically, recognizing that it takes time for individual commitment to change, for links to forge, and for a community to form.

Faculty development programs at many universities focus at the level of the individual, whether the professor or the graduate student. This is indeed important since it is the individual professor or teaching assistant who is on the "front line" in terms of student learning. This level of action is very apparent in our proactive activities (as evidenced in the published schedule of CUTL events), yet we view it as insufficient to reach our broader objectives. When individuals work within organizational structures and without the appropriate institutional supports, their individual efforts may have little effect. Change is required at the institutional level as well (e.g., Biggs, 2001). Thus, we attempt to integrate our work with individuals with our work within departments, faculties, and the university. Much of the work we do at the individual level focuses on teaching development whereas work at the departmental level usually combines teaching and policy development. Work at the Faculty[3] and university levels tends to target policy development. The following listing of some of our activities reflects our efforts to work systemically at all levels of the university:

Individuals
- Develop courses
- Interpret and respond to course evaluations
- Analyze teaching delivery (e.g., video analysis)
- Assess student learning
- Integrate technology in teaching

Departments
- Review curricula
- Develop TA training programs
- Develop programs
- Support non-classroom-based teaching (e.g., clinical supervision)
- Pilot innovative courses

Faculties
- Help develop policy to evaluate teaching
- Support programs to integrate new faculty
- Provide advice to survey alumni
- Offer expertise sitting on teaching and learning committees
- Provide background material to administrators

---

[3]College level.

University-wide

- Provide advice to both formal and ad hoc committees that are developing policies related to teaching
- Keep the university informed about trends and new ideas

As well, we endeavor to create links between our university and other institutions in a number of ways. For instance, we build teaching development links between McGill and other institutional teaching centers, we invite discipline-specific scholars for talks on teaching and learning, often in partnership with various faculties, and we are now participating in an international faculty development initiative. Most recently, we have entered a multilateral agreement with two other Canadian universities and four European universities to develop an international graduate program in faculty development.

Thinking and Acting Programmatically and Incrementally

This approach reaffirms our belief that we are engaged in a comprehensive "curriculum" of faculty development, one in which over time and with appropriate support, others will be able to assume leadership for faculty development and discipline-based collegial activities.

Such sustained efforts to improve the culture of teaching and learning require a conviction to use every opportunity to initiate contact and not be put off by the slow process of incremental change. An initial contact, whether with a professor or an administrator, related to a very specific need can evolve into something that has a much broader impact on the department or the Faculty.[4] Time and again, we have found that the first response to a voiced need turns into an opportunity that leads to a collaborative long-term relationship aimed at improving teaching and learning. It is often possible to see, through subsequent interactions, the broader needs of the program or department from the vantage point of individual needs. Thus, we rarely see ourselves as providers of a service that terminates "at the end of the day." Rather, we see ourselves as the nurturers of relationships, and we put every effort into making each one sustainable so it will be fruitful to the individual in the short term and will benefit the larger university community in the longer term.

Our desire to think systemically and programmatically and the reality that change is a slow and incremental process require that we communicate regularly with each other to maintain a shared focus and integrated approach

---

[4]College.

to our programs. CUTL core members meet every three to four weeks to update each other, plan proactive initiatives, review ongoing and newly initiated faculty development activities, and consider appropriate plans of action in response to recent events and requests. We also incorporate in our meetings opportunities to discuss the underlying thinking that drives our faculty development activities. This book was written through meetings of this kind.

Members and Affiliates meet a couple of times each term to decide on broad goals and strategies for CUTL. Affiliates are particularly important members of CUTL because they inject an "outsider" perspective into our deliberations. They operate "on the front," so to speak, and can direct our ideas in ways that will be most effective. There are other activities that bring together, for instance, winners of the Teaching Improvement Fund and alumni of the Course Design and Teaching Workshop. There are also less formal interactions with deans and chairs to find out their needs and keep them informed of the nature of our involvement in their faculties. All these activities are carefully planned to forge links among individuals, groups, and CUTL members. Finally, we hold annual retreats (one with only core members and one with Affiliates) to review the previous year and make plans for the coming year.

We proceed by thinking incrementally and systemically, by acting programmatically, and by maintaining a positive tension among competing factors. Our goal is to find ways to link the many different activities in which we individually engage to leverage the impact of our work. We constantly remind ourselves to hold our goal and our vision before us, and look for ways to use individual starting points as opportunities for expanding our network. Growth often occurs by building on the opportunities that emerge.

Measuring the Impact of Our Work

Establishing the impact of faculty development work is not an easy task. It is an ongoing challenge for us, one that we believe we share with all other teaching development centers. Our work is, in effect, human resource development. We are not organizationally integrated into the ongoing life of the institution, a characteristic we share with other human resource development units. The work of students and professors continues regardless of whether there is a faculty or teaching development unit. The quality of the teaching and learning may not be optimal, but as long as students continue to apply, register, and complete courses and programs, the system is functional. What need does a teaching development center serve?

Our view is that the mission of the university is to provide high-quality learning for students. The experience students have of learning is influenced by their courses, their programs, and their faculties. These, in turn, are strongly influenced by the policies and practices related to teaching and learning that create Faculty and departmental cultures. Our work and mandate are fundamental in that they are intended to enhance courses, programs, and policies. Thus, we have a responsibility to collect the evidence that supports our case, formatively for ourselves and summatively for administrative purposes.

The Weimer and Firing Lenze (1994) categorization was designed specifically for assessing the effects of teaching development interventions in higher education. It proposed five levels of assessment:

1. Teacher attitude through self-report
2. Teacher knowledge from tests or observations
3. Teacher skill from observation
4. Student attitude from self-report
5. Student learning from tests or observations

Similarly, Kirkpatrick (1982) proposed four levels of impact for human resource development in a business setting. The progression, in contrast to Weimer and Firing Lenze (1994), moves beyond the level of individual learning and includes, as a last level, the extent to which there is institutional benefit or change as a result of individual efforts at change.

We have relied on these frameworks in the past for assessing impact—for instance, collecting teacher feedback on attitude and learning after workshops, and gathering data on teacher skills, student attitude, and learning in individual consultations. However, as our understanding of teaching development has changed, we have realized that the underlying principles of these schemes are not consistent with our present notion of teaching development. The reader will recall that one shift in our perspective has been from doing things for others to helping others do the work themselves. Another shift has been from activities with a strong focus on teaching skills to activities that help others make explicit the thinking underlying teaching. As we have learned that we are not really engaged in teaching but rather in supporting and facilitating student learning, our view of the assessment of teaching development has necessarily become equally sophisticated (Saroyan & Amundsen, 2001).

We find that the Weimer and Firing Lenze (1994) scheme, designed to track more traditional kinds of interventions such as workshops and consultations, is no longer adequate to track the impact of the broad range of activities that we include in our teaching development work. For instance, CUTL was actively involved in developing the policy requiring a teaching portfolio for tenure and promotion. How do we document this impact? It cannot be through assessing professors' actions or students' attitude since the places where the impact of this work is most evident is in the decisions in departmental and Faculty tenure and promotion committees. Moreover, we alone were not the developers and initiators of the policy. In other words, as soon as we move from formal short-term interventions with individual professors to long-term interactions with groups of professors and from affect and learning to actual changes in policies and institutional practices, we need a different way of thinking about assessing impact.

The fourth level in the Kirkpatrick (1982) scheme is somewhat useful here, at least conceptually, in that it focuses on the extent to which there is institutional benefit or change as a result of individual efforts at change. This appears to afford a more systemic analysis of impact and thus is useful in relation to our view of faculty development. Establishing cause and effect in examining systemic change can be particularly difficult, however, since profound changes in teaching often coincide with other institutional changes. First, as already stated, we are not working in isolation; many individuals are contributing to efforts at enhancing teaching and learning. Second, other variables beyond our knowledge and control will influence the assessment and make it difficult to understand the influence of our own interventions. Third, as soon as we move further from any event, the task of documenting impact becomes increasingly complex, time-consuming, difficult, and potentially expensive. For instance, it would be interesting to know the impact of distributing a brief summary of research on administrative use of course ratings to chairs. We know it has had some impact because of follow-up phone calls to our unit. However, identifying a way to document the impact of this kind of intervention seems next to impossible.

We have struggled, though not to a satisfactory conclusion, to find ways of tracking these more distant but important levels of impact, particularly in relation to how our policy development activities affect the context in which professors teach and students learn. Over the past couple of years, we have generated a number of criteria that are long-term indicators. We hope these will become the foundation of a relational database. The database will allow us to see the links among different activities and outcomes over time. This database links first-level impact (e.g., satisfaction, repeat participation in CUTL activities) with more profound evidence of effectiveness (e.g., changing teaching practice, demonstrating leadership in a department, disseminating experiences at conferences). Our intention with the database is to trace how our work and the work of Affiliates influences the institutional climate in terms of both policies and practices over time. For instance, how many students are affected by a change in policy in a department and what is the nature of the impact? What happens to pre-tenure professors at risk who initiate contact with us and later apply for tenure and are successful? What is the impact on professors and students of a new program we help a department to create?

We believe that anecdotal evidence can be equally important. The database includes information about events beyond our more formal planned faculty development activities. For instance, that a full professor from our Faculty of Science chose to spend his sabbatical leave at CUTL and had the agreement of the Dean of Science sends a powerful message about our work. Nevertheless, finding ways to balance reports of quantitative impact with evidence of this kind is a constant struggle.

In our attempt to find ways of tracking distant but important levels of impact, we have found a recent article by Biggs (2001) to be useful in addressing the issues with which we are grappling. He proposes that one of the fundamental problems facing teaching development centers is that the focus of work is most often on the individual. He suggests that the focus of teaching development should be on teaching within the entire institution. He suggests that the ideal situation would be one in which

1. CUTL, like the institution, has a clear espoused theory of teaching and learning, and does not focus on teaching tips, or a more recent tendency, on technology.
2. CUTL is involved in creating a learning environment throughout the institution, and all central decisions bearing on teaching and learning involve the experts in teaching and learning.
3. CUTL has a formal relationship with each teaching department since actual decisions about programs are made here.

Biggs notes three definitions of quality that are relevant to this discussion. The first is quality as value for money or public accountability. Criteria associated with this kind of quality are the number of Ph.D.s on staff or more graduates for fewer dollars. This notion of quality is the one with which most professors, administrators, and the public are familiar, and it is often used when making summative comparative judgments retrospectively. The second definition of quality is illustrated by the question, "Are our programs producing the results we want in terms of student learning?" A third definition characterizes quality as transformative. Criteria for this dimension could include the transforming of students' perceptions of how they apply their knowledge to world problems or changes in professors' conceptions of their roles as teachers.

We believe that the institution must also hold an espoused theory of teaching and learning, and must have built-in mechanisms for continual review and improvement if quality is to be defined in this way. Laurillard (2002) has compared this needed institutional conversation to the professor's internal conversation, which allows one to learn from experience. In other words, the institution needs to engage in a series of internal conversations (within a department, within a Faculty) in which teaching and learning practices are made explicit, examined, and assessed. Only by continually reflecting on university practices can one learn the extent to which the espoused theory is being implemented successfully and the factors that are inhibiting success. In other words, one can look for places where alignment among the elements of espoused theory and institutional policies and practices breaks down and seek institutional mechanisms for change.

The challenge for us is, on the one hand, to ensure that the institution develops and articulates a view of teaching and learning and, on the other hand, to develop ways to assess our work within the context of the institutional framework. If we compare activities of CUTL against the criteria proposed by Biggs (2001), we fare not too badly. We have a clearly espoused theory of teaching and learning, and we do not focus on teaching tips or technology. CUTL is attempting and succeeding to some extent in creating a learning environment throughout the institution. CUTL does not have a formal relationship with each teaching department in the university, but we are working to this end (two examples are provided in the next chapter). Finally, we have an initial system in place to document some of these efforts.

Clearly, we still have work to do. The institution as a whole does not have a vision or espoused theory of teaching and learning. We are currently working with a Senate subcommittee to try to make this happen. More important, central decisions bearing on teaching and learning only rarely involve CUTL. This leads us to the final part of this chapter in which we describe our long-term vision.

Our Vision

Teaching for the advancement of learning is the first mission of our university, as it is likely to be the case for most others. We (CUTL members) have thought about the meaning of this statement and have put ourselves through an exercise to elaborate it in concrete terms. What follows is the outcome of this thinking, much of which has been done in the context of a series of discussions with our senior administration.

In our view, the university should "define a clear vision of teaching and learning, and articulate ways to implement the vision. . . . Included in the vision would be an approach to undergraduate education that would make McGill distinct, a view on the uses of new technologies that would optimize varied learning opportunities, as well as creative responses to issues such as large classes" (CUTL External Review Document, 2001). This is the only way we could hope to assess the alignment that Biggs (2001) proposes among espoused theory and institutional policies and practices that support and enhance student learning.

Such a vision would, we hope, include an increased flexibility in how the institutional structure for learning is perceived. For instance, learning might not be driven in terms of a three-credit course equivalent to 39 hours of "contact" time. Rather, contact time with professors could vary depending on the learning outcomes desired; instructional decisions might focus on structured "out-of-class" learning time among cohorts of students who support and sustain each other. Our understanding of "teacher" would also change and might include undergraduates as peer teachers, graduates as junior teacher-scholars, and professors working in teaching teams with graduate and undergraduate students.

Some of the ideas of the 1998 Report of the Boyer Commission on Educating Undergraduates in the Research University (The Boyer Commission, 1998) might also become part of our vision. Research-based learning might become the standard with an inquiry-based freshman year and a multidisciplinary focus.

The university would, consistent with our vision, provide financial incentives to faculties and departments to create teaching development positions in their units. These would be filled with individuals from the departments who wished to dedicate a percentage of their time to teaching development. The university could provide financial incentives for major curriculum reviews that assessed program outcomes with respect to student learning. A measure of success would be the extent to which each course in the program contributed toward specified program outcomes.

Our role as a teaching development center would increasingly become that of an advocate for a variety of activities initiated at various levels, all with the purpose of enhancing student learning. A measure of success could be our ability to support and engage others in assuming leadership roles in advancing teaching and learning. It would be possible to measure the extent to which individual professors participated and contributed to the development of policies and practices intended to enhance teaching and learning. Similarly, it would be possible to determine the extent to which professors engaged in researching their own teaching and were successful in this regard (Weston & McAlpine, 2001).

Finally, we would imagine that valuing teaching and learning would be manifest in the creation of a senior administrative position such as Vice President, Teaching and Learning. In this scenario, CUTL and all other units mandated to support teaching and learning would report to this office.

In terms of CUTL itself, we envision its future as a unit driven by concern with effective teaching and learning throughout the institution. This would require formal structures that would support the involvement of everyone who wanted to contribute to this goal. It would also require linking students and professors as well as technical units and library resources in teams with faculty developers. As such, activities would be undertaken by learning teams composed of several stakeholders, including

- a faculty developer, the team leader, with expertise on teaching and learning in higher education

- a professor or professors with the subject-matter expertise that is the focus of the project or workshop since teaching and learning tasks vary by discipline

- a student or students from the relevant discipline to participate in planning and to provide feedback—particularly insightful information could be provided on the impact of new technologies on learning

- a project technical consultant to oversee and coordinate development of materials (e.g., web sites, online, and hard copy materials)

- a librarian or library technician to help define appropriate resources, verify reliability, and ensure student and professor access in the library or online

The university would provide funds for professors and students to participate in these teams as well as funds for faculties and professors to have partial or full-time cross-appointments on a rotating basis (e.g., three years) to work within CUTL, furthering teaching development activities in their departments or faculties.

Faculties would show leadership in promoting learning by applying for competitive awards to create a climate in which teaching is recognized and rewarded. Award winners would receive university funds to, for instance, develop and implement policy for the appropriate assessment of teaching effectiveness, or develop an explicit description of the knowledge and skills expected of a graduate.

There would be an experimental teaching space, a large, flexible open area, with movable walls to create break-out rooms equipped with the latest technology. Our experience has been that professors often feel limited in exploring innovative practices because of the physical environment in which they give their courses. Such a space would enable them to loose their imaginations. A competitive process would be used each term to decide which courses would be taught in the space. The space would be constructed to enable easy observation and data collection of teaching and learning to better understand the impact of the innovative practices. Documenting appropriate instructional uses of technology as well as the use of information resources, and evaluating these "experiments" would be an essential aspect of the research done here.

Our overall goal would be to continue building a community of scholars engaged in teaching development and to support a distributed leadership as it evolved and grew. Our ultimate hope would still be that the answer to the question, "Who is responsible for teaching development in the university?" is, "All of us in the university are responsible for the development of teaching and learning regardless of our subject-matter expertise, our academic experience, or our administrative role."

References

Amundsen, C., Saroyan, A., & Frankman, M. (1996). Changing methods and metaphors: A case study of growth in university teaching. *Journal of Excellence in Faculty Teaching, 7*(3), 3–42.

Becher, T. (1989). The significance of disciplinary differences. *Studies in Higher Education, 19*(2), 151–161.

Bhanji, F., Gottesman, R., Finkelstein, A., & Winer, L. R. (2002, July). *"Too exhausted to learn!" An innovative Web-based situated learning environment for pediatric critical care medicine*. The 10th Ottawa Conference on Medical Education, Ottawa, Canada.

Biggs, J. (2001). The reflective institution: Assuring and enhancing the quality of teaching and learning. *Higher Education, 42,* 221–238.

Boyer Commission on Educating Undergraduates. (1998). *Reinventing undergraduate education: A blueprint for American's research universities*. Princeton, NJ: Carnegie Foundation for the Advancement of Teaching.

Boyer, E. L. (1990). *Scholarship reconsidered: Priorities of the professoriate*. Princeton, NJ: Carnegie Foundation for the Advancement of Teaching.

Brawner, C., Felder, R., Brent, R., Allen, R., & Miller, T. (1999). *1997–98 faculty survey of teaching practices and perceptions of institutional attitudes toward teaching*. Southeastern University and Colleges Coalition for Engineering Education. Retrieved January 31, 2003, from: http://www.succeednow.org/search/seepaper.asp?paperid=474/

Cuban, L. (1992). Managing dilemmas while building professional communities. *Educational Researcher, 21*(1), 4–11.

CUTL. External Review Document (2001). *Brief to Search Committee for the Principal,* Montréal, Canada:McGill University.

Gullat, D., & Weaver, S. (1997, October). *Use of faculty development activities to improve the effectiveness of U.S. institutions of higher education.* Paper presented at the Annual meeting of the Professional and Organizational Development Network in Higher Education, Hines City, FL.

Kirkpatrick, D. (1982). *How to improve performance through appraisal and coaching.* New York: Amacom.

Laurillard, D. (2002). *Reinventing university teaching* (2nd ed.). London: Routledge Falmer.

Marincovich, M. (1998). *Ending the disconnection between the student evaluation of teaching and the improvement of teaching: A faculty developer's plea.* Palo Alto, CA: Stanford University, National Center for Postsecondary Improvement.

McAlpine, L., & Gandell, T. (2003). Teaching improvement grants: Their potential to promote a scholarly approach to teaching. *Journal of Further and Higher Education, 27*(2), 187–194.

McAlpine, L., & Harris, R. (1999). Lessons learned. Faculty developer and engineer working as faculty development colleagues. *International Journal of Academic Development, 4*(1), 11–17.

McAlpine, L., & Harris, R. (2002). Evaluating teaching effectiveness and teaching improvement: A language for institutional policies and development practices. *International Journal of Academic Development, 7*(1), 7–17.

McAlpine, L., & Weston, C. (2002, July). *Reflection on teaching. Using an empirical model to analyze, improve and learn about your own practice.* Paper presented at the Higher Education Research and Development Society of Australia, Perth.

McAlpine, L., & Winer, L. (2002). Sustainable faculty development: An Indonesian case study. *Innovations in Education and Teaching International, 39*(3), 205–216.

McKeachie, W. (2002). *Teaching tips* (11th ed.). Boston, MA: Houghton Mifflin.

Menges, R., & Weimer, M. (1996). *Teaching on solid ground. Using scholarship to improve practice.* San Francisco, CA: Jossey-Bass.

Meterissian, S., Tremblay, F., Seely, A., Weston, C., & Morgan, G. (2001). Problem based learning for the teaching of surgical oncology to second year medical students: A pilot study. *Annals of the Royal Faculty, 34*(8), 501–504.

Nasmith, L., & McAlpine, L. (1995). Teaching by case discussion: A framework for teaching clinical decision-making. *Medical Teacher, 17*(4), 419–430.

Saroyan, A., & Amundsen, C. (2001). Evaluating university teaching: Time to take stock. *Assessment and Evaluation in Higher Education, 26*(4), 337–349.

Saroyan, A., Amundsen, C., & Cao, L. (1997). Incorporating theories of teacher growth and adult education in a faculty development program. *To Improve the Academy, 16*, 93–115.

Saroyan, A., Harris, R., & Cooperstock, J. (2000, October). *Applying pedagogical principles to teaching and learning with technology.* Paper presented at the multicultural perspectives on the use of technology in education, Montréal, Canada.

Saroyan, A., & Snell, L. (1997). Variations in lecturing style. *Higher Education, 33*, 85–104.

Shulman, L. (1993). Teaching as community property: Putting an end to pedagogical solitude. *Change* (November/December.), 6–7.

Shulman, L. S. (1986). Those who understand: Knowledge growth in teaching. *Educational Researcher, 15*(2), 4–14.

Travis, J. (1996). *Models for improving college teaching: A faculty resource.* Washington, DC, George Washington University, Graduate School of Education and Human Development: ERIC Clearinghouse on Higher Education.

Weimer, M., & Firing Lenze, L. (1994). Instructional interventions: A review of the literature on efforts to improve instruction. In K. Feldman & M. Paulsen (Eds.), *Teaching and learning in the college classroom* (pp. 653–682). Needham Heights, MA: Simon & Schuster Custom Publishing.

Weston, C., & McAlpine, L. (1999). Toward an integrated approach to instructional consultation. In C. Knapper & S. Piccinin (Eds.), *New Directions in Teaching and Learning, Vol. 79, Using consultants to improve teaching* (pp. 85–95). San Francisco: Jossey-Bass.

Weston, C., & McAlpine, L. (2001). Integrating the scholarship of teaching into disciplines. In C. Kreber (Ed.), *New Directions in Teaching and Learning, Vol. 86, Scholarship revisited: Perspectives on the scholarship of teaching* (pp. 89–97). San Francisco: Jossey-Bass.

Winer, L., & Cooperstock, J. (2002). The "Intelligent Classroom": Changing teaching and learning with an evolving technological environment. *Computers and Education, 38,* 253–266.

13

DEVELOPMENT ACTIVITIES

CASE DESCRIPTIONS FROM MANAGEMENT AND ENGINEERING

Lynn McAlpine, Alenoush Saroyan, and Laura Winer

We described in Chapter 12 the four assumptions of faculty development underlying our work at the Centre for University Teaching and Learning (CUTL), the ways these influence the range of activities in which we engage, and our vision for the future. The first assumption involves maintaining a positive tension among the various competing, and not infrequently opposing, demands of our work. These include a balance between proactive and responsive activities, between generic and discipline-based activities, between an emphasis on teaching practice and policy development, between us as experts and others as experts, and between programmatic research and classroom or action research. The second assumption supports the need to think systemically, recognizing that change in any one part of the university system implies change elsewhere in the system; moreover, that administrative structures and policies are frequently more powerful mechanisms for changes in teaching and learning than the efforts of individuals. The third assumption is to act programmatically. This refers to the need to constantly envisage and find ways to link discrete faculty development activities to generate greater impact. The fourth and last assumption requires evaluating the impact of our work in ways that are meaningful to us and to others in the university community. In this chapter, we provide extensive descriptions of two recent faculty development cases that exemplify the enactment of these assumptions.

We describe each case in some detail and then specify how each demonstrates the four underlying assumptions. The cases exhibit contrasting starting points. The first case, the Faculty of Management,[1] demonstrates how a

---

[1]College of Management.

small initiative by two professors resulted in change that is now embraced by an entire Faculty. CUTL's role in this case was initially responsive. In contrast, in the second case concerning the Faculty of Engineering,[2] our initial role was proactive. The faculty development activities that evolved in this Faculty began with a CUTL initiative to encourage deans to financially support and thus direct teaching development in their own faculties.

We offer these two cases not as templates of what should occur, but rather as instances of what has occurred. We believe that readers may find in these accounts opportunities we have missed or see other equally valuable contributions that a teaching development center might have offered and we did not.

Case One: Management

Year One

In the winter semester of 2000, two professors from Management contacted the CUTL member responsible for the competitive Royal Bank Teaching and Learning Improvement Fund to explore the feasibility of developing their idea as a proposal. They were both members of a pedagogy committee (one was the chair) that sought to understand how to achieve and maintain teaching excellence in the Faculty. They had few resources to support their work. Their project proposal involved creating a "snapshot" of teaching and learning in the Faculty. Specifically, they wanted to document and analyze the current teaching practices in the Faculty, as well as generate alternative practices by looking for best practices elsewhere. The data collection and analysis plan included interviews with professors, students, administrators, and alumni, and a review of course materials and course ratings. They also wanted to identify places where teaching issues were contested, and where divergent opinions and teaching practices were creating problems. The intent was to understand the actual teaching practices of the faculty. Finally, they wanted to conduct a review of the pertinent teaching literature. Their overall goal was to create a profile of teaching excellence toward which they could strive. The human resources proposed for the project, subsequently the Pedagogy Excellence Project (PEP), were nine graduate students who would receive credit for their work and would carry out the project under the guidance of the two professors who initiated the project.

The PEP proposal was vetted and approved by the dean of the Faculty as he had to agree to provide matching funds in the event the proposal was

---

[2]College of Engineering.

selected. Once internally approved, it was submitted and subsequently reviewed favorably by the adjudication committee of the Royal Bank Teaching and Learning Improvement Fund, composed of eight professors drawn from across the university. The funds for PEP were awarded in March 2000. The abstract of this project along with other successful proposals was published by CUTL before the projects began.[3] By this time, the two individuals who had written the PEP proposal had spent extensive time discussing issues around teaching. The dean had had to review the proposal and had committed the Faculty to provide matching funds; eight colleagues from across the university had evaluated the activity and others in the university had been informed about it. This scholarly pattern of making teaching knowledge explicit, making it public, and evaluating it continued throughout the project.

The Royal Bank Teaching and Learning Improvement Fund requires that a CUTL member be attached as a consultant to every project that it funds. Activities of the consultant have included meeting with award winners and the dean and associate deans, keeping in touch via e-mail and phone calls, conducting literature searches, participating in various related committees, facilitating workshops, and interviewing and analyzing data. In the particular case of PEP, the CUTL consultant began meeting with the two professors in the summer of 2000. Her first suggestion was that it might be useful for one of them to take the Course Design and Teaching Workshop. One agreed to do so. Concurrently, the two faculty members and the CUTL consultant began to map out concrete strategies for implementing PEP, including these:

1. Working with the nine graduate students to help them understand their roles

2. Engaging others in the Faculty in decision making related to the project

3. Informing the entire Faculty of the project

4. Collecting and analyzing data

5. Preparing a report to disseminate findings in the Faculty

Each of these tasks is described in the following.

The first task of the CUTL consultant, after consulting with the award winners, was to search the literature and provide articles and other information related to teaching and learning in the university, more specifically, in management education. These were used to provide a structure for a series of

---

[3]The process of peer review and publication of the teaching grants submissions has been purposely developed to treat teaching as a scholarly activity (Boyer, 1990).

seminars with the graduate students (one of which was facilitated by the CUTL member) in the first six weeks of the autumn term (2000). The goal was to provide the students with a coherent framework for the work they were to carry out.

A Faculty[4] steering committee was created by the award winners to guide the decision-making process of the project. It met regularly for the duration of the project. Nine professors, including two associate deans, two students (from the PEP team), and the project initiators served on the committee. The dean (who was new and from outside the university) also attended the committee meetings from time to time. He thus became informed about the project and the role CUTL was playing, as did the associate dean.

The next step was to inform others in the Faculty about the initiative. A web site was created, presentations were made to the Faculty council, and students were solicited for comments by student associations regarding the project. Within a couple of months, everyone in the Faculty was aware of PEP and invited to provide input.

A major role of the CUTL consultant was to provide expertise and support in the classroom research aspect of PEP. The CUTL consultant and a graduate student associated with CUTL provided help in designing the study, determining the sample to be surveyed, reviewing the questions to be asked, actually interviewing individuals when confidentiality was necessary, and analyzing some of the data. By the end of the data collection, a sizable proportion of the entire Management faculty had been interviewed and every student who wished to participate had been surveyed. The following winter term, the team work was devoted to data analysis and the preparation of the report and its review by the steering committee.

The final report was presented to the Faculty Council of the Faculty at the end of the academic year (2000–2001). It was approved and PEP was sent to the Faculty's Academic Council for action. What had begun as an idea between two professors had become a year-long Faculty engagement in which many issues about teaching and learning in the Faculty had been made explicit and public, and evaluated in different contexts. Faculty members and students had engaged in countless discussions about teaching, and this might never have happened without PEP. What emerged was an awareness of the nature of the changes that were collectively desired. PEP had achieved its stated goal, which was to document the state of teaching and learning in the Faculty, provide an arena in which to discuss and contest relevant issues, and create an agenda for change. Issues that emerged concerned the differing

---

[4]Committee at the college level.

expectations of tenured, tenure-track, lecturer, undergraduate, and graduate students about the allocation of teaching resources, the coherence of programs, the focus on grades by undergraduate students, and the impact of having a teaching staff who are largely part-time lecturers.

CUTL was concerned, as always, with the longer-term impact of the project. For instance, what sustained activities could result that would enhance teaching and learning practices and policies in Management? The initial project had, in fact, acted as a stimulus for generating other activities in the Faculty. Tangible outcomes have been numerous. In terms of the two professors who initiated the project, they have presented their work at a university seminar and are writing a paper for publication in a management education journal. As well, a joint paper with the CUTL consultant has been presented at a national conference (McAlpine, Maguire, & Lee, June 2002). Involvement in the project was found to be such a powerful learning experience for the nine graduate students that a second smaller Pedagogy Excellence Project (PEP) course was offered in the autumn so that a new set of students could follow up on some of the recommendations that came out of the project. At various workshops and committee meetings, reference continues to be made to the role of the project in initiating different aspects of the Faculty's self-study.

Year Two

At the end of the first year of the project, CUTL was asked to continue working in the Faculty of Management on a new project called Enhancing Educational Excellence (E3), which emerged from a recommendation in the final report of PEP. The specific goal of E3, as expressed by the dean, was to articulate ways in which

1. class time could be more focused on student-student and student-teacher interaction rather than lecturing.
2. out-of-class time would be better structured to support student learning.

This was easily restated as an overall teaching development goal: to enable participants in the project to engage in principle-based course design and evidence-based practice in which student feedback could help drive decisions. This project was conceived by the Faculty as an ongoing activity. Each stage is described in the following as Wave One, Two, or Three. The intention was that increasing numbers of people would become involved with each wave.

- *Wave One:* The first wave began after consultations among the dean, the associate dean responsible for the project, and the CUTL consultant assigned to the project. A major concern on the part of CUTL was whether there were sufficient faculty members to undertake the project. This was negotiated, showing a Faculty commitment to the project, and a coordinator was hired by the Faculty to work 28 hours per week on the project—whose role has been essential to the effective implementation of the project. She reports to the associate dean and is responsible for sustaining communication among those involved and also for carrying out the many tasks related to the project.

A task force on teaching was created in the academic year 2001–2002. One of the first tasks set for the committee by the chair (an associate dean who had sat on the PEP steering committee) was to elaborate program objectives for each program area (we return to how this emerged as an issue later).

Wave One began with a series of four Course Design and Teaching Workshops given by CUTL during the summer of 2001 and attended by the dean, ten professors, and three students (representatives of student societies), a library representative, and a technical consultant. The content of these four half-day workshops was very similar to the Workshop described in this book. The evaluation component was emphasized more, so that considerable time was spent on evidence-based practice and on ways in which formative feedback could be collected from students about the implementation of Wave One. It was also decided that all the new courses involved in Wave One would use "quality circles," where student ambassadors would meet regularly with the professor to provide feedback from students on what is working well and what could be improved (Angelo & Cross, 1993).

The course design elements produced by those who participated in the workshop series (e.g., concept maps and learning outcomes) were posted on a web site and were accessible to all workshop participants. Some of the participating professors had been actively involved in aspects of the PEP project, but others were new to the project. One of these professors approached the CUTL consultant during the Workshops about doing a master's degree in Education, and with the consultant's help was able to begin in the autumn. Her interest in teaching and learning led her to have a major role in Wave Two of this project.

Five new courses, which had been designed in the Workshop series, were implemented in the autumn of 2001. The dean visited all of the new courses to talk to the students, and the Faculty newsletter reported on the project. One of the professors (a teaching award winner in the Faculty) discussed the Workshop in an interview for the Faculty newsletter, and how as a result of attending he had changed his teaching. The student's society was also actively engaged in informing students about the project. Thus, the number of people in the Faculty engaged in discussing teaching and learning continued to grow.

The concept of quality circles was again implemented in the five new courses of Wave One to track needed changes. The CUTL coordinator hired by the Faculty visited and observed each class and reported to each professor what she saw. A midterm check-in workshop was held at the end of September to discuss needs and next steps. Professors who were teaching the five new courses reported that this was taking a lot of time, but they were having "fun." Their major concerns centered around assessment methods and whether these were well enough aligned with course learning outcomes to be an accurate assessment of student learning. To collectively address this issue, a Workshop was held. The CUTL coordinator examined alignment among the course design elements in the five new courses as a basis for discussion and action in the Workshop.

The students were generally happy with the new courses, but they had specific concerns that were expressed through the quality circles and other formative assessment methods. A meeting of all quality-circle ambassadors was held to look for themes or issues that emerged across the five new courses. The responses of the ambassadors were very positive, and they were able to provide very concrete suggestions for improvement. A summary of these findings was distributed to all involved and was used in planning Wave Two.

- *Wave Two:* The goal of the dean for Wave Two was to offer the series of four half-day Workshops to a new cohort of professors and thus expand the number of courses to be studied. The CUTL goal, as always, was to continue to create a distributed network and at the same time to ensure sustainability of the project within the Faculty once support was removed. So, one aspect of the discussions between the dean and CUTL was the importance of drawing on one or two professors who had participated in Wave One to be co-instructors in the new series of Workshops, thus creating sustainability through building local expertise. Consequently, the associate dean (chair of the task force) and the professor who had started the master's degree in Education, led the second series of Workshops. The CUTL coordinator's role in this phase included planning and debriefing, as well as providing necessary resource material and being present at the Workshops. This approach was similar to the one used in Indonesia by CUTL members as part of a project funded by the Canadian International Development Agency (McAlpine & Winer, 2002).

One of the many powerful ideas that emerged from these Workshops was the importance of applying the same systematic approach used in course design to program development. The associate dean on the PEP steering committee acted on this idea. He was named the chair of a task force on teaching and learning in the Faculty, and he set as the first agenda item for the committee an elaboration of program objectives for each program area.

A meeting of all quality-circle ambassadors was held to look for themes or issues that fell across the five courses. Responses of the ambassadors were very positive, and they were able to provide concrete suggestions for improvement. A summary of these findings was distributed to all involved and was used in planning Wave Three.

- *Wave Three:* This wave began in winter 2002 with an offering of the Course Design and Teaching Workshop to a third group of faculty, facilitated by the "in-house experts." The CUTL consultant's role in this iteration was to provide input as requested. During the same period, another proposal was submitted to the Royal Bank Teaching and Learning Improvement Fund to assess the impact on teaching and learning of the changes that had occurred during Wave One and Wave Two. This proposal was awarded, and thus the work of the CUTL consultant continues. In 2002-2003, this role has been to support the development and implementation of a formative and summative assessment scheme.

An interesting spinoff of Wave Three came as a result of continued questioning by Workshop participants of the Faculty guidelines on assessment. The dean proposed exploring a pass/fail/exception approach to grading. Workshop participants had become increasingly aware that the Faculty grading policy was not congruent with the design of the new courses. Currently, marks fall on a curve within 12 percentage points of each other, whereas the approach supported by the project is that learning outcomes drive the assessment and that grading should be criterion referenced. In other words, most students should be able to achieve the required learning. The grading policy has not yet changed, partially because of student concern about having a competitive GPA. However, the very fact that a change was discussed is clear evidence that professors have begun to examine their "taken-for-granted" practices and are particularly concerned if they find them incompatible with their changed thinking.

Summer 2002 was the end of Year Two and Wave Three. Twenty-five percent of faculty members had by that time participated in the Workshop and redesigned at least one of their courses.

Year Three

The contract for the coordinator hired by the Faculty for the project was renewed on a full-time basis, and she will continue to provide ongoing support in the academic year 2002–2003. The project web site has been expanded to include resource materials for professors. The project group has submitted a proposal to present the findings of the project at a discipline-specific conference.

The most evident changes to date include a consistent format used for course outlines/syllabi, the inclusion of learning outcomes and concept maps on the course syllabus, a plan to ensure more student-student interaction in classes, assessment methods that align with learning outcomes, and quality circles. Evidence of impact on student learning has already been reported (Smith, 2002) and another proposal for a teaching development project is being prepared for submission.

The description of the Faculty of Management case shows how an idea initiated by just two professors grew and expanded to the extent that it involved all of the Faculty. It is interesting to note that prior to the beginning of PEP, this particular Faculty had had minimal contact with CUTL. It provides a good example of the value of providing nonplanned responsive support (both financial and human) to those who are interested in raising the quality of teaching and learning in their own units.

We now consider the Faculty of Management in terms of the four assumptions underlying our approach as discussed in Chapter 12.

Convergence of the Management Project with CUTL Assumptions

Maintaining a Positive Balance Among Tensions

The two-year series of activities in the Faculty of Management models a strong discipline-based approach. We were responsive to a specific need (i.e., a request for advice by two professors). We were also proactive by, for instance, proposing that the Faculty make a commitment to hiring a faculty development individual on a long-term basis.

The primary focus of the project was on the development of specific courses, but some of the design aspects of these courses led to the development of expectations across the Faculty. The format used for course outlines/ syllabi, the inclusion of learning outcomes and concept maps on the course syllabus, and the stated plans for more student-student interaction in classes, for instance, are now expected of all courses in the Faculty. Quality circles, as used in the project courses, appear to be becoming institutionalized since professors and students have found them very productive.

We were very conscious throughout the project of developing a shared language and finding ways to ensure that concepts about teaching and learning were integrated into management discourse. This led to considerable discussions about the use of terms—for instance, reference to "client," not to "learner." We discussed the use of "learning points," not "learning outcomes" since that was a terminology with which some were already familiar. We focused on "leveraging" and "value-added" activities, not activities that "enhance learning."

Thinking Systemically

Our activities engaged us in working toward institutional as well as personal change. It meant thinking strategically, recognizing that it takes time to develop a nucleus of professors within a department or Faculty who can take leadership for teaching development. We and the other project leaders involved as many individuals as possible in the change process. This meant ensuring that a range of committees (with student membership) engaged in decisions, that the student societies were directly involved in the process, and that there were regular meetings with the dean. It is hard to imagine that any professor or student in the Faculty has not been involved over the last two years at some point in discussions about teaching and learning. The hiring and later the reappointment of the coordinator and the role played by the "in-house experts" show how a systemic commitment to teaching improvement made this project sustainable at the Faculty level.

Acting Programmatically

We envisaged our work as growing incrementally and involving a range of different kinds of activities over extended periods of time—activities such as workshops, committee meetings, interviews, and literature reviews. It also involved a vision and a long-term goal for whatever activities we engaged in. For instance, this could consist of seeking to have a coordinator of teaching development, encouraging others to carry out their initiative of applying the ideas in the E3 project to a reassessment of program goals.

Evaluating Impact

Both projects (PEP and E3) were clearly incorporated aspects of action research. Data were systematically collected and analyzed so individuals had formative feedback on the kinds of changes they were undertaking.

In the case of PEP, these data included interviews with students, academics, and others involved in supporting teaching and learning. Documents (e.g., course ratings, course outlines, Faculty policies) were analyzed as well. These provided the basis for multiple conversations among the stakeholders in the Faculty about the meaning of teaching and learning, as well as successive interpretations and reinterpretations. For instance, the PEP team would do an initial interpretation of data and take that for review to the steering committee, which in turn would add its interpretation.

Summative assessment of impact is evident in the stimulus that PEP created for teaching development in the Faculty. The recommended task force was charged with "proposing and implementing pedagogical and curriculum redesign in all delivery programs in line with the Faculty's new strategic initiatives and vision. . . . In the matter of pedagogy, it will assist the Faculty to implement recommendations of the Pedagogical Excellence Project."

The expertise of PEP leaders was recognized in that one of them was asked to sit on the "Bachelor of Commerce Curriculum Redesign Task Force." His task was not to represent his area (which had its own representative) but to ensure that recommendations from PEP were incorporated as fully as possible into this task force's work.

The standard course evaluations were adapted to include additional questions specific to the project as summative feedback. Quality circles were clearly another way in which impact was assessed. All data were used to propose further changes, and quality circles have continued to be used.

Individuals expressed an interest in documenting not only the effectiveness of the project approach in terms of actual learning but also in comparison with other approaches. One professor documented differences in learning between the "new" approach and the previous one, and reported them within the Faculty and at a conference (Smith, 2002). He did this on his own initiative, and in doing so he has clearly begun the process of modeling a scholarly approach to teaching. The CUTL coordinator has encouraged him to publish the results of his study.

The desire to document impact was also evident in successive proposals submitted for additional funding. These proposals involved a systematic collection of pre- and post-workshop data, including a comparison of student and teacher perceptions of learning goals and assessment methods. We find it intriguing that a Faculty that had very little contact with the CUTL prior to these projects could have turned around with one motivating contact and project. This is an example of the value of interventions that are not planned by CUTL, but to which CUTL is responsive. It further justifies the way in which we plan and implement our activities. The project also clearly demonstrates the shared leadership necessary for teaching development, and the importance of institutional commitment as represented in financial as well as in human resources. The CUTL could not have made these projects happen; they emerged from local concerns.

Case Two: Faculty of Engineering

The case of the Faculty of Engineering represents a top-down approach to development. Several years ago, the CUTL proposed to the deans the idea of contracting the time of a CUTL member to work in the Faculty on issues related to internal teaching and policy initiatives (McAlpine, Weston, Donald, & Gandell, 1998). The dean of Engineering was intrigued by this proposal, and we are now in the fourth year of what has turned out to be a very fruitful collaboration. In exchange for funds, a CUTL member spends time in the Faculty carrying out Faculty-initiated teaching development activities. These funds can in turn be used to finance other CUTL activities. The initial agreement was for a one-year appointment, specifically aimed at supporting the teaching development of new professors anticipating the tenure and promotion process. The dean then renewed the contract for three successive years, the second and third year based on the success of the model—and despite budget cuts.

The CUTL representative reports directly to the dean of Engineering. This is key to raising the importance given to teaching in the Faculty, as well as having a spokesperson for teaching and learning who is clearly untainted by any departmental politics. Over the years, activities have included facilitating workshops, preparing teaching- and learning-related papers and reports, engaging the dean and associate deans in related issues, conducting literature searches for issues of concern, participating in various committees, and providing consultations to individual faculty members.

Year One

The year began with a meeting between the newly appointed dean and the newly appointed CUTL consultant. A certain amount of discussion was required to come to a mutual understanding of expectations. It was agreed that the CUTL consultant would work primarily with nontenured faculty, not just new hires, in whatever way would be appropriate to support the development of their teaching. A secondary activity was to sit on the Faculty Committee on Teaching and Learning (COTLEF), which had experienced mixed success over the previous years. A professor who had worked extensively with CUTL and who also was the chair of COTLEF (Ralph Harris, author of Chapter 9), was identified as the main resource person for introducing the CUTL person to the Faculty.

The initial project proposed by the CUTL consultant and accepted by COTLEF and the dean was a workshop called Workshop on Improving

Teaching in Engineering (WITE). It was again a modified version of the Workshop described in this book. Summative evaluation feedback from the professors attending the Workshop reflected a general move from seeing courses as a list of topics to a more systemic, concept-based approach. They were very positive about the opportunity to take the Workshop with their engineering colleagues. The common language, background, and concerns as well as shared teaching challenges and related content all contributed to the positive nature of the experience for them.

The workshop was a success, but by January it became clear that the more reactive approach taken by the CUTL consultant was not enough; only minimal requests for support were forthcoming. The CUTL consultant decided to seek out the departmental chairs and ask them to identify the key issues involved in the improvement of teaching and learning in the Faculty. A more proactive plan was consequently established for the second year.

The main accomplishment of the first year was for the CUTL consultant to gain recognition and credibility with the faculty members. This occurred in a range of ways and included the consultant's being a member of COTLEF and providing advice that was perceived as useful, consulting with the chairs about their perception of needs, and listening carefully and responding credibly to the small number of requests that did occur.

Year Two

The Faculty of Engineering was in a growth phase in terms of both human and physical resources. There had been a significant number of new hires in the last several years. The Faculty was also now in the throes of planning a new building, with a primary mandate to provide teaching space as opposed to research space. The dean asked the CUTL consultant for advice in creating physical spaces that would enhance teaching and learning. The CUTL consultant responded by organizing the visit of an administrator from another Canadian engineering Faculty that had undergone an even larger design project. The resulting session on the "architecture of learning" was targeted at the dean and associate deans as well as the department chairs. A report was also prepared for the dean, assessing the instructional pluses and minuses of MC13, the showpiece high-tech teaching environment planned by the faculty for the new building. A description of the teaching environment as well as the results of the evaluation project can be found in Winer and Cooperstock (2002).

Policy issues became more important in Year Two. The Associate Dean, Academic asked the CUTL consultant to assist in the redesign of the course rating form for the Faculty. The dean requested a document summarizing the research about the use of course evaluations in Engineering faculties. Little information specific to Engineering was found, but a more general document was prepared by CUTL and distributed to deans and chairs in all faculties. It outlined the research relating to how to interpret results for administrative purposes as well as a companion document for professors about how to interpret ratings to improve their own teaching.

Over time, more and more Engineering professors began to recognize the role of pedagogical expertise in advancing their personal dossiers along the tenure and promotion path, and increasing numbers sought individual consultations and expressed an interest in the Course Design and Teaching Workshop. The format of the Workshop was changed in Year Two in response to feedback. Participants in Year One indicated that they liked being together as an Engineering group but found doing the Workshop during the term to be difficult. So, in Year Two, it was arranged that one of the small groups in the annual CUTL Workshop would be reserved for Engineering Faculty, with the group leader being the CUTL Engineering person and the co-instructor being an Engineering professor, an alumnus of the Workshop.

In Year Two there was also a new chair of COTLEF, who devoted significant efforts to improving communication about teaching and learning across the Faculty. The first attempt was a newsletter, which was later transformed into part of the Faculty web site, with a link to CUTL web resources. COTLEF decided that the web site was more congruent with existing modes of communication in the Faculty and would better disseminate information about teaching.

At the end of Year Two, teaching and learning concerns in the Faculty were being explicitly addressed and made public and accessible to others. These are all hallmarks of treating teaching as a scholarly activity (Boyer, 1990). Leadership for teaching within the Faculty was emerging, being supported, and being recognized.

Year Three

In Year Three, there was again a new chair of COTLEF, as the previous year's chair had become an associate dean. This committee became a real focal point for development as it had been originally intended. Training of teaching assistants, an expressed desire by the chairs in Year One, became a priority for COTLEF as the new chair was willing to lead this initiative. It was decided to design a Workshop for teaching assistants (TAs) to be delivered by the chair of COTLEF, four TAs, the CUTL consultant, and a CUTL Affiliate Member, with participation of the Associate Dean of Student Affairs. This was successful enough that a second Workshop was immediately scheduled for the winter semester. COTLEF recommended to the dean, *as a companion action,* the creation of a Faculty TA award to acknowledge outstanding contributions by up to three TAs. The first awards were given at the following June convocation.

The CUTL consultant was invited for the first time to the orientation for new faculty offered in September. She was also asked to meet with representatives of the Canadian Engineering Accreditation Board to discuss Faculty initiatives with respect to teaching and learning, specifically addressing questions that Faculty administrators felt less prepared to answer. The CUTL consultant was also involved in more centralized planning, making it possible to initiate links between university-wide activities and Faculty needs. The Faculty of Engineering provided the kickoff speaker for a new university-wide CUTL initiative (a Visiting Lecture Series on Teaching and Learning in the Disciplines), for example. COTLEF took responsibility for many aspects of this event, including arranging planning meetings, contacts with the speaker, and a dinner for a small group from Engineering and the speaker to discuss issues on a more intimate basis than afforded by the larger speaker session.

The CUTL consultant was instrumental in setting up a more formal selection process in the Faculty of Engineering for the Royal Bank Teaching and Learning Fund awards. In previous years, the dean received the applications at the last minute and had to decide, on his own, whether to support projects with matching funds. A subcommittee of COTLEF was set up to review the proposals and suggest modifications to applicants, and even helped negotiate external financial support for one project that had potential interest to other university units. The proposals that went forward had thus been subject to a more rigorous review process. The hope was that this would not only result in a higher success rate for applications but also would afford greater impact from those projects that were subsequently funded.

The Faculty of Engineering case illustrates how, over a long incubation period, ownership in teaching and learning became invested in the Faculty. We turn to considering this case in light of our underlying assumptions.

Convergence of Faculty of Engineering Teaching Activities with CUTL Assumptions

Maintaining a Positive Balance Among the Tensions

The three-plus-year initiative in the Faculty of Engineering again models a strong discipline-based approach. The dean and the chairs had constructed the agenda for teaching development and had wanted to draw on Engineering-based research. When possible, the CUTL consultant did this, while at the same time drawing on the general instructional literature when appropriate.

The activities undertaken were both responsive (e.g., the TA workshop) and proactive (e.g., the WITE workshop). The primary focus was on teaching development, but there was also, for example, the revision of the required course ratings form, the creation of the Faculty TA award, and the establishment of the Royal Bank Teaching and Learning Improvement Fund adjudication committee. All of these have become established policies in the Faculty.

Thinking Systemically

Our activities engaged us in working from the perspective of institutional as well as personal change. It meant thinking strategically, working closely with the dean, the chairs, and individual professors, and recognizing that it takes time to develop a nucleus of individuals who feel knowledgeable and prepared to take leadership for teaching development. Efforts were made to engage as many people as possible in activities. For instance, design and delivery of the TA workshop involved six individuals from within the Faculty. CUTL supported COTLEF in taking an active leadership role, which was its original mandate.

Acting Programmatically

This project, like the one in the Faculty of Management, has required that CUTL envisage teaching development work as incremental growth over an extended period of time. It also involved a vision and a long-term goal. For instance, the CUTL consultant sought out and supported teaching leadership within the Faculty knowing that the concerns of the Faculty were perceived as discipline-specific. This was evidenced by the fact that those within the Faculty often sought out information about teaching and learning with Engineering faculties elsewhere before looking within the university.

Evaluating Impact

Evaluating the success of such an initiative relies on the interpretation of many different indicators, the first of which is simply its continuation. The dean has repeatedly committed funds from a budget that is subject to numerous claims. This is a tangible demonstration of the conviction that value is being received for money and is probably the single piece of evidence with the loudest voice. Another extremely encouraging indicator of the success of this initiative is that activities are continuing despite the change in the CUTL consultant—this initiative is clearly not dependent on the particular individual involved but has become self-sustaining. The structural change in establishing an internal review process for the Royal Bank Teaching Improvement Awards has resulted in an increased number of applications from Engineering and an increased funding rate. The TA workshops are continuing; the TA Award was received favorably by all departments and is now part of the standard award structure within the Faculty. The new chair of the Engineering Computing Committee, who happens to be an alumnus and recent co-instructor of the Workshop, has put teaching and learning issues on that committee's agenda. And finally, the current Royal Bank Faculty Associate is from the Faculty of Engineering. Any one of these facts individually would be exciting, but taken together they paint a picture of a Faculty engaged in taking ownership of and demonstrating real and sustained interest in teaching and learning issues.

In maintaining a positive tension among competing factors, thinking systemically, acting programmatically, and evaluating the impact of our efforts, the goal has been to find ways to link the many different activities related to teaching and learning taking place in the Faculty of Engineering. We believe finding ways to link these activities is essential in creating a network of leaders who will together create policies and practices that recognize and reward teaching and enhance student learning.

We hope these two cases have provided a flavor of what is involved in our approach to teaching development. We constantly remind ourselves that individual and collective initiatives like these are occurring every day in the university. We see our work as seeking out and recognizing these occurrences, so that through our support local teaching development leadership can be nurtured and grow.

References

Angelo, T. A., & Cross, K. P. (1993). *Classroom assessment techniques* (2nd ed.). San Francisco: Jossey-Bass.

Boyer, E. L. (1990). *Scholarship reconsidered: Priorities of the professoriate.* Princeton, NJ: Carnegie Foundation for the Advancement of Teaching.

McAlpine, L., Maguire, S., & Lee, M. D. (2002, June). *Pedagogy excellence project: A professor-student team approach to faculty development.* Paper presented at the Society for Teaching and Learning in Higher Education, Hamilton, Canada.

McAlpine, L., Weston, C., Donald, J., & Gandell, T. (1998). *Decentralizing faculty development at McGill: Increasing faculty-CUTL partnerships.* Montreal: McGill University.

McAlpine, L., & Winer, L. (2002). Sustainable faculty development: An Indonesian case study. *Innovations in Education and Teaching International, 39*(3), 205–216.

Smith, B. (2002). *Innovative outcome assessment in statistics education.* Paper presented at the Joint Mathematics Meetings, San Diego, CA.

Winer, L., & Cooperstock, J. (2002). The "Intelligent Classroom": Changing teaching and learning with an evolving technological environment. *Computers and Education, 38,* 253–266.

NEEDS ASSESSMENT

Course Design and Teaching Workshop

Name: _____ Academic Title: _____

Department: _____ E-mail: _____

---

1. Please provide a paragraph describing the course you have chosen to focus on during the Workshop. (If you have chosen an existing course, the calendar description is fine, provided you feel it is accurate and representative of what the course will be.)

2. Is this course ☐ elective or ☐ required?

3. Approximately how many students are expected to enroll in the course?

   If you are revising an existing course:

4. Have you taught this course before? _____ If yes, how many times?
   _____

5. Please describe your learners in the context of this course in whatever terms that are important to you and your teaching.

6. Please describe the instructional setting (e.g., large class, seminar, clinical teaching).

7. In order of importance, list what you expect students to take away from this course.

8. What teaching strategies have you used or are you planning to use in this course? Why these strategies?

9. How do you plan to evaluate student learning in this course?

10. On a scale of 1 to 10, where 1 is low and 10 is high, how would you rate your knowledge about teaching and your knowledge of the subject matter of this course?

    Teaching: _____   *Subject matter:* _____

11. How many years of university teaching experience do you have?
    McGill? _____
    Other postsecondary institution(s)? _____

12. What types of courses have you taught?

   ☐ Large lecture courses (80+ students)   ☐ Labs

   ☐ Small seminar courses   ☐ Other (specify)

   ☐ Tutorials

                                  _____

13. Which teaching methods have you used that you feel have been both effective (E) for the students and comfortable (C) for you:

   E   **C**

   ☐   ☐   Lecturing

   ☐   ☐   Small group discussion

   ☐   ☐   Large group discussion

   ☐   ☐   Computer assisted instruction

   ☐   ☐   Laboratory demonstration

   ☐   ☐   One-to-one tutorial

   ☐   ☐   Collaborative learning

   ☐   ☐   Other (specify) _____

14. What do you see as the main purpose of university teaching?

15. From your perspective, what are the top three responsibilities of a university professor and a university student?

Professor

(1) _____

(2) _____

(3) _____

Student

(1) _____

(2) _____

(3) _____

16. In your opinion, what characterizes good teaching in general? If you think this is different from good teaching in your field, please elaborate.

17. For you, what are the potential obstacles to good teaching?

18. What would you consider as a rewarding teaching experience? (You can write about a personal experience, student/peer feedback, etc.)

19. What would you consider an unpleasant teaching experience?

20. Describe any concerns you have related to teaching (e.g., speaking in front of a large group, deciding what to include in your course, etc.).

21. Generally speaking, how successful are you in implementing your instructional plans and ideas?

22. During the time you have been teaching, have you made changes in the way you teach or in the type of teaching materials you use? If so, what has prompted you to make the change(s)?

23. What do you expect to get out of this Workshop?

Please return the completed form electronically no later than _____.
If you prefer to send a hard copy, please send it through internal mail to CUTL, 3700 McTavish, Room 544E.

READING LIST[1]

1. Content

Novak, J. D. (1998). Meaningful learning for empowerment. *In Learning, creating, and using knowledge: Concept maps as facilitative tools in schools and corporations* **(pp. 19–34). Mahwah, NJ: Erlbaum.**
Donald J. G. (1983). Knowledge structures: Methods of exploring course content. *Journal of Higher Education, 54*(1), 31–41.
Jonassen, D., Beissner, K., & Yacci, M. (1993). *Structural knowledge: Techniques for representing, conveying and acquiring structural knowledge* (pp. 155–163). Hillsdale, NJ: Erlbaum.

2. Outcome

LaSere Erickson, B., & Weltner-Strommer, D. (1991). Knowing, understanding and thinking: The goals of freshman instruction. *In Teaching college freshmen* **(pp. 65–80) San Francisco: Jossey-Bass.**
Entwistle, N. (1998). Approaches to learning and forms of understanding. In B. Dart & Boulton-Lewis, G. (Eds.), *Teaching and learning in higher education* (pp. 72–101). Melbourne: ACER.

3. Strategy

Chickering, A., & Ehrmann, S. (1996 & 2003). *Implementing the seven principles: Technology as lever.* http://www.tltgroup.org/programs/seven.htm
Felder, R., & Brent, R. (1996). Navigating the bumpy road to student-centered instruction. *College Teaching, 44*(2), 43–47.
Graham, C., Cagiltay, K., Lim, B-R., Craner, J., & Duffy, T. (2001). *Seven principles of effective teaching: A practical lens for evaluating online courses.* http://ts.mivu.org/default.asp?show=article&id=839
Gijselaers, W. H., (1996). Connecting problem-based practices with educational theory. In *New Directions for Teaching and Learning* (Vol. 68, pp. 13–21). San Francisco: Jossey-Bass.

---

[1]**Boldface** references are required. The others are additional suggestions.

LaSere Erickson, B., & Weltner-Strommer, D. (1991). Encouraging student involvement in the classroom. In *Teaching college freshmen* (pp. 106–121) San Francisco: Jossey-Bass.

Saroyan, A. (2000). The lecturer: Working with large groups. In J. Bess (Ed.), *Teaching alone, teaching together: Transforming the structure of teams for teaching* (pp. 87–107). San Francisco: Jossey-Bass.

Woodberry, R. D., & Aldrich, H. E. (2000, July). Planning and running effective classroom-based exercises. *Teaching Sociology, 28,* 241–248.

4. Assessment

Ramsden, P. (1992). Assessing for understanding. *Learning to teach in higher education* (pp. 181–213). New York: Routledge.

Angelo, T. A., & Cross, K. P. (1993). What is classroom assessment? *Classroom assessment techniques: A handbook for college teachers* (pp. 3–11). San Francisco: Jossey-Bass.

McKeachie, W. J. (1999). What to do about cheating. *Teaching tips* (11th ed., pp. 97–102). Boston: Houghton Mifflin.

Shepard, L. A. (2000). The role of assessment in a learning culture. *Educational Researcher, 29*(7), 4–14.

Walvoord, B., & Johnson Anderson, V. (1998). Establishing criteria and standards for grading. *Effective grading. A tool for learning and assessment* (pp. 65–92). San Francisco: Jossey-Bass.

Walvoord, B., & Johnson Anderson, V. (1998). Managing the grading process. *Effective grading. A tool for learning and assessment* (pp. 9–16). San Francisco: Jossey-Bass.

5. Next Steps

Weimer, M-E. (2002). Responding to resistance. *Learner-centered teaching: Five key changes to practice* (pp. 149–166). San Francisco: Jossey-Bass.

Shulman, L. (1993). Teaching as community property. *Change, 25*(6) 3–4.

Toohey, S. (1999). Beliefs, values and ideologies in course design. *Designing courses for higher education* (pp. 44–70). Buckingham: SRHE and Open University Press.

GIVING AND RECEIVING CONSTRUCTIVE CRITICISM

Giving Constructive Criticism[1]

1. *Make the criticism relevant and appropriate to the context.* Address the performance/task at hand. For example, if the person is practicing one skill, don't criticize the lack of another.

2. *Criticize the performance, not the person.*

3. *Describe the situation carefully and accurately first.* Before offering critical judgement, discuss specific observable details. Whenever possible, phrase comments to distinguish between objective observation and subjective evaluation.

4. *Offer both negative and positive criticism whenever possible.* Although we talk often about positive reinforcement, criticism tends to be negative. Strive to maintain a balance between positive and negative comments. Always give the positive comments first. However, do not praise insincerely.

5. *Be specific: unambiguous and concrete.* Offer your criticism in unambiguous adjectives and concrete nouns. Avoid emotion-laden words, what semanticist S. I. Hayakawa (1978) calls "snarl" words and "purr" words. For example, what does it mean if someone says that your vocabulary was "colourful?" The receiver may correctly think that this is a compliment, but may think that you mean that you like words with lots of syllables. They heard the "purr," but did not get the message clearly. Use quotes and give examples of what you are referring to.

6. *Give ideas for how to improve.* Suggest alternatives, share ideas, indicate that you really do want to help the person.

7. *Concentrate on one or two of the main points.* Do not overload—it is demoralizing.

---

[1]These guidelines come largely from Verderber & Verderber (1983) in Leptak, J. (1989). Giving and receiving constructive criticism. *Lifelong Learning 12*(5), 25–26 (with adaptations and additions).

8. *Be direct.* Do not be so intent on not offending the receiver that your message becomes lost.

9. *Do not offer feedback on aspects of a performance that simply cannot be improved.* For example, I found it difficult to understand because of your accent.

10. *Give feedback only when there are indications that the receiver is ready to listen.* If not ready, the receiver will be apt not to hear it or to misinterpret it.

11. *Do not demand a change.* The concept of feedback should not be confused with asking a person to change. The receiver retains the right to decide whether to change or not.

12. *Giving feedback should not become "one-upmanship."* The receiver can go away feeling as though he is not as good as the giver, or may see herself as having been given a lecture from the lofty pinnacle of an imaginary state of perfection.

13. *The motivation must be to help, not to hurt.*

Receiving Constructive Criticism[2]

Few people enjoy evaluating the work of others. Some of us doubt our competence to judge others. Other critics recoil in anticipation of defensiveness or anger from recipients. There are even ethical concerns about the use of power and the damaging effects of exclusively negative criticism. But because most of us know that we are not perfect we do, deep down, want to know how to improve. To foster the interactive exchange necessary for constructive criticism, use the following guidelines when seeking feedback.

1. *Be sincerely receptive to an honest response.* Do not ask, "What do you think?" if you really mean, "Tell me what a great job I did." Once the potential critic understands your quest for praise, you will have difficulty getting insightful criticism when you really want it.

2. *Avoid contradiction between what you communicate verbally and nonverbally.* Ask for criticism with your arms crossed and a mean glare in your eye, and people will respond to your threatening body language instead of your request for guidance. The tone of your voice might also make your solicitation sound more like a dare than a genuine need.

---

[2]Prepared by Maureen Lucas, McGill University, October 1996.

3. *React positively, not defensively.* Critics need positive reinforcement, too. Reactions such as, "Thanks for the input—I hadn't seen it that way." or "What led you to that conclusion?" encourage your respondent to continue.

4. *Specify the type of criticism that you want.* Help the giver provide useful reactions by asking for feedback about specific things. General questions about ideas or feelings lead to general answers with little value. When you ask people if they like your work, the probable response is, "It was okay," which gives little direction for improvement. Guide your critic with questions about specific details, such as, "Did my introduction get your attention? Does my thesis state the point clearly enough?"

5. *Remember that almost any criticism can be helpful.* Instead of treating negative feedback as a derision of your personal character, think of it as revealing new information. You can benefit from knowing how others perceive your work or how it affects them, even if you do not agree with them.

6. *Confirm your understanding of the criticism.* To avoid misunderstanding, you should interpret, question, or paraphrase what you think you heard or read. When a critic says, "Perhaps you should completely rethink this argument," you might respond, "So you think I need more supporting evidence?" If the critic actually meant something else such as a complete change of topic, you will hear about it, and then you understand each other.

7. *Share your reaction to the feedback.* Knowing what was and was not helpful assists the giver in improving his skills at giving useful feedback. If he is uncertain about your reactions, he may be less apt to risk sharing in the future.

MICROTEACHING
FEEDBACK SHEET

Name of Instructor: _____

Name of Participant: _____

If you like, use the following points to provide feedback. If possible, provide feedback in terms of what was effective or not in accomplishing the goals of the session.

Organization

Pacing

Voice projection, eye contact, gestures

Use of materials (overhead projector, blackboard, etc.)

Interaction with us (the class)

MICROTEACHING FOLLOW-UP FORM

Day: _____

After viewing your videotape, please comment on the following. Some of the things you might think about while viewing your videotape are: organization, voice projection, eye contact, the way you answer or ask questions, and the use of materials (e.g., overhead projector, handouts, blackboard).

What was the purpose of this session?

Please describe what you thought was effective about your session in terms of reaching your goals. Why?

Please describe what you thought was *ineffective* in your presentation in terms of reaching your goals. Why?

What comments or suggestions from others did you find most helpful or interesting?

What might you consider trying to change and how might you go about it?

INDEX

A

Active learning, 17, 79, 117, 136, 158–61
See also Teaching and learning
strategies
Adjunct members of CUTL, 213–14, 223
See also Faculty development
Affiliate members of CUTL, 209, 214, 223
See also Faculty development
Amundsen, C., 118
Analysis of course content, 34–35
See also Concept mapping
Assumptions about teaching
disciplinary differences, 72, 173–74, 210
examining one's assumptions, 17,
74–77, 119–21, 127
teaching norms, 20, 23, 25, 75, 159,
176, 178–79, 210–11
See also Microteaching
Assumptions about teaching development
nature of university teaching and
learning, 17–20
professors as pedagogues, 15–17,
133–34, 153–54
university context, 20–21, 159–60
See also Faculty development

B

Barr, R. B., 175
Baxter Magolda, M., 57, 60
Beliefs
professor, 23, 105
student, 58
Biggs, J., 226
Boyer, E. L., 16, 17, 72, 163, 175

C

Case examples
Engineering (Faculty of), 219, 244–49
Management (Faculty of), 234–44
Centra, J., 21, 116
Centre for University Teaching and
Learning (CUTL). *See* Faculty
development, mandate of CUTL
Clark, R., 78
Committee on Teaching and Learning
in Engineering Faculty (COTLEF),
141, 244–47, 248
Community for teaching, 21, 209,
214–16, 230
Concept mapping
analysis of course content, 35–38
in course design process, 34–35
examples, 40–45, 154–55
mapping software, 48
related to learning outcomes, 67, 138
steps to construct, 38–50
stories, 138–39, 154
use with students, 37–38, 88
Context of the university, 78, 159–60,
162–66, 177, 181, 227
Control of learning, 159, 162
Course design process
checks and balances, 50, 67, 82
coherence and alignment, 33, 50, 67,
71, 82–83, 90, 97–98, 102,
106–7
graphic representation of, 33–34
instructional design, 6
to stimulate discussion of teaching,
145, 210
stories, 135

ABOUT THE EDITORS
AND CONTRIBUTORS

CHERYL AMUNDSEN is associate professor in the Faculty of Education at Simon Fraser University in Vancouver, British Columbia. Before coming to Simon Fraser University in 1988, she was a faculty member at McGill University for ten years, jointly appointed to the Centre for University Teaching and Learning (CUTL) and the Department of Educational Psychology. Her current research interests are in teaching development in higher education and the meaningful integration of learning technologies. This includes how university professors develop pedagogical knowledge in relationship to their subject matter, how they come to understand teaching, how they make instructional decisions (including the integration of various technology applications), and the effects of these aspects on student attitude and learning.

SUSAN COWAN is the Teaching Improvement Counsellor at the McGill Centre for University Teaching and Learning (professional staff). She is primarily engaged in assisting individual McGill faculty members as they analyze, develop, and improve their teaching skills and approaches in the context of their discipline and teaching/learning goals. Susan also works with departments and Faculties to help develop procedures and instruments for assessing and improving courses and teaching. She collaborates with other Centre members on various projects aimed at promoting and rewarding teaching excellence, such as encouraging nominations for national teaching awards and coordinating and facilitating teaching workshops and special events. She also participates on McGill University committees and work groups to establish guidelines for such teaching policies as those related to course and teaching evaluation and the use of teaching portfolios.

JANET DONALD is professor in the Department of Educational and Counselling Psychology at McGill University and the former director of the Centre for University Teaching and Learning. Her research focuses on the quality of post-secondary learning and teaching, particularly on fostering higher-order learning. She also investigates disciplinary differences in knowledge acquisition and methods of inquiry in higher education. Her most recent book is *Learning* *to Think: Disciplinary Perspectives* (2002), in which she consolidates twenty-five years of research on student learning in academic disciplines. In a previous book, *Improving the Environment for Learning: Academic Leaders Talk About What Works* (1997), she discusses optimal practices for improving student learning. In her articles and chapters, she examines disciplinary differences in knowledge validation, the role of higher-education centers in improving the academy, the evaluation of undergraduate education, and professors' and students' conceptualizations of learning. Donald won the Distinguished Researcher Award from the Canadian Society for the Study of Higher Education in 1994, its Distinguished Member Award in 1998, and the McKeachie Career Award from the American Educational Research Association in 2000. She was elected a Fellow of the Royal Society of Canada in 2001.

MYRON FRANKMAN, although an economist by training and academic appointment, is a committed interdisciplinarian. This commitment is reflected in his association since 1967 with McGill's Centre for Developing Area Studies and in his role in the creation and direction of McGill's undergraduate program in International Development Studies, which now enrolls more than 700 students. He is committed as well to active learning and has long been associated with McGill's Centre for University Teaching and Learning, at which he holds an appointment as a Faculty Associate. Frankman has devoted his career to questions of world order and global equity and has recently completed a soon-to-be-published manuscript on World Democratic Federalism.

TERRY GANDELL is assistant professor at the Centre for University Teaching and Learning and Associate Member in the Department of Educational and Counselling Psychology at McGill University. Terry is interested in enhancing teaching and learning in higher education, as well as in special education. Her current interests are in the evaluation of teaching and learning and the use of technology in higher education. This is an extension of her past research in which she investigated the use of telecommunications to deliver literacy instruction to adults with severe disabilities. Terry has been providing pedagogical consultation in different Faculties, most recently in the Faculty of Engineering. As coordinator of the Royal Bank Teaching & Learning Improvement Fund, Terry has overseen the adjudication and implementation of over ninety teaching initiatives in the past eight years. She has published on the impact of these projects as a scholarly approach to faculty development, as well as on the impact of the use of technology on professors' instructional choices.

DIK HARRIS has been a professor in the Physics Department at McGill for more than thirty years. He has always been interested in the challenges of teaching and curriculum development, but he found his greatest challenge in the Course Design and Teaching Workshop of 1994. Since that time he has become more involved with the activities of the CUTL, culminating in a sabbatical year (2001) spent at the Centre. He is currently the director of the Tomlinson University Science Teaching Project in McGill's Faculty of Science.

RALPH HARRIS is professor of Engineering in the Department of Mining, Metals and Materials and has been at McGill since 1981. His research interests span the spectrum from steel recycling to lithium manufacture and recycling. He is a named inventor with seven separate patents, three of which are licensed to industry and one of which formed the basis for a startup company to supply lithium metal to Quebec's half-billion dollar lithium metal polymer battery industry. Since the early 1990s, Harris has actively participated in improving teaching and learning in McGill's Faculty of Engineering, notably founding The Committee on Teaching and Learning in Engineering Faculty (COTLEF). Until recently, he was cross-appointed to the McGill Center for University Teaching and Learning. Harris has published his findings on the nature of faculty development, in particular on the synergy between pedagogical experts and subject matter experts, and the transformation that derives from reflection on the nature of learning.

RICHARD JANDA is associate professor at the Faculty of Law of McGill University. He was a clerk to Justices Le Dain and Cory at the Supreme Court of Canada and a Director of the Centre for the Study of Regulated Industries at McGill. He is currently the Fulbright Visiting Chair in Canadian Studies at Michigan State University.

LYNN MCALPINE is professor of Education and presently the Director of CUTL. She is actively involved in faculty development, both within and beyond McGill University. Of particular note is her co-editorship of the *International Journal for Academic Development*. While her research interests are varied, she generally addresses the relationship between teacher thinking and teacher action and its impact on student experience of learning.

ALENOUSH SAROYAN is associate professor of educational psychology and member of the Centre for University Teaching and Learning at McGill University. Her current research focuses on the process of pedagogical development of university professors, academic leadership and its impact on departmental outcomes, and issues and processes related to the reform of higher-education systems in developing countries. This research informs her teaching and her practice as a faculty developer and as a consultant to international organizations, such as the World Bank and the European Commission. She is actively involved in professional organizations, including the Canadian Society for the Study of Higher Education and the American Educational Research Association.

CYNTHIA WESTON is professor in the Department of Educational and Counselling Psychology and a member of the Centre for University Teaching and Learning at McGill. Her work focuses on teaching and learning in higher education. She has been teaching in the area of instructional design, assessment of student learning, and teaching and learning in higher education for over twenty years at McGill. Her current research, funded by the Social Sciences and Humanities Research Council of Canada, focuses on two areas. The first explores professors' use of reflection as a mechanism for improving teaching and constructing knowledge about teaching. Weston's research team has built a model of reflection and is now investigating the impact of professor reflection on student experience of learning. Weston's second area of research is an exploration into the characteristics of online learning and how faculty members can be helped to effectively integrate technology in higher education. Some of her current faculty-development projects focus on enhancing teaching and assessment in surgical contexts and developing teaching portfolios as part of tenure and promotion dossiers.

LAURA R. WINER spent three years at CUTL as assistant professor and is currently Senior Educational Technologist in the Office of the Deputy Provost and CIO at McGill University. She has extensive experience in academic faculty development at McGill and internationally. In addition to her teaching at McGill University, the Université de Montréal, and Concordia University, she has private-industry experience in analyzing, designing, developing, and delivering human performance technology projects. Her research into various aspects of educational and training applications of information and communications technology has received support from the Social Sciences and Humanities Research Council, the *Fonds québécois de la recherche sur la société et la culture,* and the TeleLearning Network of Centres of Excellence. She has published and presented numerous times on a variety of topics related to educational innovation, focusing on integrating information and communications technology into teaching and learning.